EXPLORING TEACHERS IN FICTION AND FILM

"Timely and well-informed, this valuable contribution to teacher education offers engaged, thoughtful and capably written commentary on the use of film with teachers. The idea central to this text, that prospective teachers should examine the central and not-so-mainstream cultural assumptions around teachers and teaching, is needed within the field of teacher education."

Dan Liston, University of Colorado at Boulder, USA

"I love this project! This is an amazing collection of authors and topics, and the book both goes beyond and expands current work around examining portrayals of teachers in popular film and media to actually focus on how that process of bringing critical analyses of films into teacher education programs would/could look."

Jennifer Sandlin, Arizona State University, USA

"Thoughtful and interesting, this strong volume in a burgeoning field meets a need for a book that is both about current film and fiction AND applies it for preservice and in-service teachers. Not only can students learn from fiction and film, they can, as the authors point out, resist stereotypic characterizations of teachers and schools, and point to a more vibrant and authentic educational discussion so vital to our democracy."

AG Rud, Washington State University, USA

This book about teachers as characters in popular media examines what can be learned from fictional teachers for the purposes of educating real teachers. Its aim is twofold: to examine the constructed figure of the teacher in film, television and text and to apply that examination in the context of teacher education. By exploring the teacher construct, readers are able to consider how popular fiction and film have influenced society's understandings and views of classroom teachers.

Organized around four main themes—Identifying With the Teacher Image; Constructing the Teacher With Content; Imaging the Teacher as Savior; The Teacher Construct as Commentary—the chapters examine the complicated mixture of fact, stereotype and misrepresentation that creates the image of the teacher in the public eye today. This examination, in turn, allows teacher educators to use popular culture as curriculum. Using the fictional teacher as a text, preservice—and practicing—teachers can examine positive and negative (and often misleading) representations of teachers in order to develop as teachers themselves.

Melanie Shoffner is Associate Professor of English Education, Purdue University, USA.

EXPLORING TEACHERS IN FICTION AND FILM

Saviors, Scapegoats and Schoolmarms

Edited by
Melanie Shoffner

Routledge
Taylor & Francis Group

NEW YORK AND LONDON

First published 2016
by Routledge
711 Third Avenue, New York, NY 10017

and by Routledge
2 Park Square, Milton Park, Abingdon, Oxon, OX14 4RN

Routledge is an imprint of the Taylor & Francis Group, an informa business

© 2016 Taylor & Francis

Library of Congress Cataloging-in-Publication Data
A catalog record for this book has been requested

ISBN: 978-1-138-94440-4 (hbk)
ISBN: 978-1-138-94441-1 (pbk)
ISBN: 978-1-315-67194-9 (ebk)

Typeset in Bembo
by Apex CoVantage, LLC

Printed and bound in the United States of America by Publishers Graphics, LLC on sustainably sourced paper.

*This work is dedicated to those doing the real work of
education in a world that prefers the fantasy.*

*In my own slice of reality, I dedicate this work to the former
teachers at Nathanael Greene Elementary School and
Southeast Guilford High School who gave me the
foundation I needed to be the academic I am.*

In particular, I owe a great deal to the following women:

*Cathy Brown Hiatt,
who helped me spell "convertible" in the 1st grade
without a hint of laughter;*

*Joyce Kilborn Key,
who supplied me with books I still own during 5th grade;*

and

*Angela Johnson,
who made me write my 10th grade research paper
on Faulkner's* The Sound and The Fury *despite
furious and tearful opposition.*

I hope I have made you proud.

CONTENTS

FOREWORD

We all have intimate familiarity with schools. Memories of school—of friends, of teachers, of achievement, of failure—have a powerful hold on us. Schools are emotionally compelling social institutions. As such, they have become ubiquitous in our popular culture. Television loves the school—whether it's the frivolity of *Saved by the Bell* or the deadly seriousness of *The Wire*. Literature exploits the drama of school in popular novels such as the *Harry Potter* series. And then there is Hollywood. Hollywood loves a good story about school because *we* love a good story about school, and we have for generations. From *Blackboard Jungle* and *Rebel Without a Cause* to *McFarland, USA* and *Easy A*, the school is fertile ground for dramatic stories that capture our collective attention.

The countless television shows, books and films about school are rich and meaningful artifacts that shed light on how our culture understands education— how we understand students, teachers, learning, achievement, failure and inequality. Embedded in the story of the school is the character of the teacher—the much maligned, much cherished or much ignored teacher. Sometimes the teacher is the focus of the story. Sometimes the teacher is at the margin of the story. Sometimes the teacher is the hero. Sometimes the teacher is the villain. But you can't tell a story about school without saying something about the teacher. Real-life teachers can't watch or read a story about school without learning something about how the culture makes sense of their job. And preservice teachers can't watch or read popular cultural representations of teaching without wondering what the heck they are getting themselves into.

I've long been fascinated by representations of education in popular culture. I've analyzed over 200 films about high school and found that the types of stories Hollywood tells depend on the social class of the student being represented (Bulman, 2015). Briefly, if the students in the film are poor, then the teacher is the hero at the center of the story. The point of this sort of film is for students to achieve academic success. If the students in the film are middle-class, however, the teacher is often at the periphery of the story; the hero is always a student. The point of these films is not academic success but for students to find their true selves. I use theories of American individualism to make the case that these differences reveal a class-based assumption in our culture, that poor kids need to listen to their teachers and pull themselves up by their bootstraps while middle-class kids are free to ignore their teachers and explore their identities.

I am not the only scholar to take an interest in representations of students and teachers in popular culture. Over the past 15 years, Mary Dalton, Jim Trier, Tim Shary and many others have focused academic attention on these cultural images. This unique field of study is delightfully multidisciplinary. Scholars in the fields of education, sociology, English, film studies and communication have contributed to this subfield. We each bring to the research our own disciplinary perspective and unique research questions. What has fueled this relatively recent interest in studying representations of schooling? Perhaps it's because many of us came of age in the 1980s, the golden era of the high school film (with 1985's *The Breakfast Club* the epitome of them all). But I also think the blossoming of academic interest in this area is due to the persistence of these images in the popular imagination, generation after generation. Clearly, these stories about students and teachers must be culturally powerful and meaningful. Each generation has its own batch of films, television shows and books that depict teaching and learning. And each generation sees, more or less, similar representations. After all, Mr. Dadier in 1955's *Blackboard Jungle* is not that different from Ms. Johnson in *Dangerous Minds* (1995) or Coach White in *McFarland, USA* (2015).

What are teachers and preservice teachers to make of these popular images? Why should the scholars in this volume spend any time researching the images of teachers in films, television and novels? The reason is that pop cultural products are not simply frivolous entertainment. The popularity of these books, television shows and movies tells us that they have struck a cultural nerve. We consume this popular culture because it resonates with us at some level in our collective psyche. Therefore, we can study them to learn something about our culture.

As I argue in *Hollywood Goes to High School*, however, these stories are fantasies, modern day folktales. These are the stories we tell ourselves about who we *think* we are or who we *wish* we were as a people—they are *not* a mirror of who we actually are. The representations of teachers in popular culture are exaggerated and unrealistic. Nevertheless, there are lessons embedded in these depictions that can be instructive to teachers. To access these lessons, teachers need to view these popular images with a critical eye. Otherwise, to take literally the salvation that Ms. Johnson offers her students in *Dangerous Minds* is to perilously set one up for bitter disappointment as an actual teacher. Reality is never so neat and clean. Similarly, to accept the image of the bumbling fools who teach Ferris Bueller is to question one's own effectiveness as a teacher in the classroom.

I believe that these contrasting images of the teacher uncover a cultural confusion about how we understand teachers and education in American society. On the one hand, we recognize teachers as competent professionals who serve important social needs—they help to socialize our children and prepare them for adulthood. We want to believe they know what they are doing and that they can succeed fabulously. On the other hand, we believe teachers are poorly trained, out of touch and ill-equipped to meet the complex needs of our children. We have fears that there is a crisis in education and that the teacher is to blame.

I imagine that real-life teachers feel both pride and shame when they see their professional image in the popular culture. Teachers, above all, know that these representations have cultural weight. These images have an effect on social perceptions of education and the teaching profession. But the images of teachers in film and fiction send messages about their profession that don't always hold up under scrutiny. It's up to teachers (and books like this!) to help the rest of us consume popular culture with a critical lens so that we separate reality from fantasy and learn something in the process.

Robert C. Bulman
Professor, Sociology
Saint Mary's College of California
Author of *Hollywood Goes to High School: Cinema,*
Schools and American Culture (2015, 2nd ed.)

ACKNOWLEDGMENTS

I have been fortunate to work with a number of clear-sighted and supportive people during the creation of this book. I am indebted to Routledge editor Naomi Silverman for her incisive input and good humor during each stage of the book's development. I thank Dan Liston, AG Rud and Jennifer Sandlin, who, as reviewers of the early manuscript, offered thoughtful feedback to shape the finished book. My thanks also go to the contributing authors; it was a pleasure to collaborate with the interested and invested people whose work makes up this book. Lastly, I am grateful to my doctoral student, Chea Parton, for her attention to the necessary editorial details that bring a project such as this to completion—no grad student ever responded so cheerfully to so many late-night queries on proper APA citation.

PREFACE

It's strange to think about your teachers as being people.

—Stephen Chboksy

Exploring Teachers in Fiction and Film: Saviors, Scapegoats and Schoolmarms is a book about teachers—not the teachers in the school down the road but the teachers in the movie theater across town. Teachers are recurring characters in the films we watch, the books we read, the comics we scan, the shows we record. They entertain us, they inspire us, they anger us—and they teach us. More importantly, they teach the very people intending to emulate or contradict their grand gestures and petty practices.

Exploring Teachers in Fiction and Film: Saviors, Scapegoats and Schoolmarms is also a book for teachers, both those in the process of becoming and those involved in that process. Students entering teacher education programs have seen the movies and read the books; consciously or not, they have been influenced by the teachers in these texts. In working with these preservice teachers to prepare them professionally, pedagogically and personally for their future career, teacher educators must address the potential impact of these fictional portrayals on their development as teachers.

This book examines what we learn from fictional teachers for the purposes of educating real teachers. In exploring the teacher images constructed in fiction and film, the authors in this edited collection consider how popular texts have influenced our understandings of and beliefs about the classroom teacher. They then turn their perceptive eye toward teacher education, considering how teacher educators can use the teachers found in popular culture as curriculum. As preservice teachers explore the fictional teacher as a text, they have the opportunity to learn from these positive and negative—and frequently misleading—representations of teachers they encounter on a daily basis.

I open the book with an introduction to fictional teachers and factual teacher education. In this chapter, I offer some perspective on the ubiquity of the teacher in popular culture, the potential impact of fictional representations on those who wish to teach and the counternarrative found in the real work of teachers today. Encouraging teacher educators to leverage these fictional teachers in support of preservice teachers' professional development, the chapter concludes with an overview of the four sections to follow.

Part I, "Identifying With the Teacher Image," consists of six chapters, with each exploring the ways in which examination of the fictional teacher image can engage preservice teachers in development of their teacher identity. Part II, "Constructing the Teacher With Content," turns to the development of teacher identity in specific subject areas; these five chapters focus on the ways in which preservice teachers can learn from fictional representations of English, mathematics, physical education and elementary teachers. The four chapters of Part III, "Imaging the Teacher as Savior," examine both the common image of the teacher savior and how this construction of the heroic teacher shapes preservice teachers' expectations and understandings of teaching. The book concludes with Part IV, "The Teacher Construct as Commentary." These four chapters address the need for preservice teachers to engage with teacher films that (mis)represent current issues in education: the politicization of reading, the negative portrayal of teachers, teacher accountability and survival of the profession.

The authors of the chapters in each section focus on the ways in which works of fiction and film (help to) explore, critique and/or resist specific images of the teacher. Using a variety of texts—popular movies, television shows, short stories, young adult novels, children's storybooks—the authors examine the complicated mixture of fact, stereotype and misrepresentation creating the image of the teacher in the public eye today before applying their examination of the fictional teacher to teacher education. Preservice teachers' understanding of education is often informed, reinforced and reified through the films they watch and the books they read. By analyzing the portrayal of fictional teachers from various perspectives, the authors are able to consider the development of real teachers, positing ways in which teacher educators can appropriate the teacher construct for meaningful analysis and discussion.

This book is a wide-ranging, in-depth exploration of the popular texts that construct and critique the teacher image, with each chapter connecting and applying its focused analysis to teacher education, generally, or content area teacher education, specifically. Rather than offering one point of view on the teacher construct, this book brings together a diverse collection of authors and teacher educators to examine the fictional teacher and provide differing approaches to, analyses of and implications for teacher education.

The ubiquity of teachers in popular culture, as well as daily life, all too often allows us—whether society, generally, or preservice teachers, specifically—to assume we know who teachers are, what they do and why they do it. The fervor with which those assumptions all too often result in mistaken beliefs, negative rhetoric and uninformed policies is the impetus for this book. If an unexamined life is not worth living, as Socrates explained, then an unexamined teacher is not worth emulating. My hope is that teacher educators and preservice teachers can use this book to examine the teacher representations all around them in order to better understand and enter a profession that is truly worth living.

INTRODUCTION

Melanie Shoffner

Teaching is, after all, a form of show business.

—Steve Martin

Nothing Is Sacred in Springfield

I remember when Bart Simpson arrived on the cultural scene. Aside from the t-shirts and catchphrases, there was my mother's displeasure when she found me watching such an irreverently rude show (we were more of an Andy Griffith and Laura Ingalls household). While my initial interest likely developed from pushing the buttons of societal outrage, I continued to watch Bart and his entourage because of the incisively intelligent humor.

Over the last 26 years, *The Simpsons* (Groening & Brooks, 1989–2015) has turned its satirical eye toward every topic imaginable, from relationships to religion, from family to fame, from culture to community—even Walt Whitman ("Leaves of grass, my ass!" being a personal favorite). I find it most "penetrating and scathingly funny" (Kantor, Kantor, Kantor, Eaton & Kantor, 2001, p. 186), however, when it turns to education. Why? Because

> Matt Groening and the show's writers have brilliantly captured the commonplaces and clichés of school life, as well as the pretensions and short-comings of teachers, and attack them all with precision and gusto . . . the show offers few solutions to educational problems or proposals for change. Its genius lies instead in exaggerating the situations and dilemmas that we all face as teachers and as citizens. The rewards are in the critical insights we gain and the laughter at our all-too-human foibles.
>
> *(Kantor et al., 2001, pp. 199–200)*

Within those exaggerations and dilemmas exists my favorite character, Edna Krabappel, Bart's long-suffering 4th grade teacher. Through Mrs. Krabappel, *The Simpsons* has satirized teachers in ways both humorous and painful. She is the boring pedagogue, assigning book reports and passing out worksheets while children gaze longingly out the window. She is the uncaring cynic who smokes a cigarette and offers the monotone objection of "No, stop, think of the children," when Bart threatens to destroy the school. She is the bitter old maid: "Oh, don't worry, children. Most of you will never fall in love but will marry out of fear of dying alone." She is the disillusioned intellectual: "Some of you may discover a wonderful vocation you'd never even imagined. Others may find out life isn't fair; in spite of your masters from Bryn Mawr, you might end up a glorified babysitter to a bunch of dead-eyed fourth graders." Occasionally, she is even the social critic, subtly ridiculing standardized testing by assuring her students that "these tests will have no effect on your grades. They merely determine your future social status and financial success."

Obviously, the writers are playing to the audience with their portrayal of Mrs. Krabappel, a portrayal that is recognizable because it trades on so many established stereotypes. We can all point to teachers who bear enough of a resemblance to the many faces of Edna to make the fictional familiar. We recognize the pedagogue in *Harry Potter* and the cynic in *Glee*, the old maid in *Calvin and Hobbes* and the intellectual in *Finding Forrester*, even the critic in *Teachers*. Mrs. Krabappel can't embody every version of the teacher, however, because there are so many more. There's the rebellious outsider in *School of Rock*, the righteous novice in *The Ron Clark Story*, the harsh disciplinarian in *Miss Nelson Is Missing*. We know the saints in *Matilda* and *Boy Meets World* as well as the sinners in *Half Nelson* and *Boston Public*. We can separate the savior in *Music of the Heart* from the scapegoat in *The Children's Hour* from the schoolmarm of the *Little House* books.

We watch hundreds of movies and television shows, read countless books and comics, see numerous cartoons and editorials—and so many include a teacher in their narrative. (My mother's television preferences introduced me to Miss Crump and Miss Beadle.) We spend a minimum of 12 years in school classrooms interacting with dozens of teachers, for better, for worse, for richer, for poorer, in sickness and in health. Teachers—real and representational—are everywhere, so embedded in our daily lives that we learn as much about teachers from the fictional as from the factual.

And we make meaning from our interactions with teachers in everyday life and popular culture, participating in a "public pedagogy" that has the ability to "reproduce or challenge [our] commonsensical and oppressive configurations of reality" (Sandlin, O'Malley & Burdick, 2011, p. 343). We recognize our chorus teacher in Monsieur Mathieu; we see our math teacher reflected in Mr. Escalante; we compare our elementary teachers with Miss Frizzle. All of these teachers "overlap, contrast, amplify, address, or confirm each other as they compete for our attention" (Mitchell & Weber, 1999, p. 167), solidifying our understanding of who teachers are and what they do.

We may be watching these fictional teachers as entertainment but they exert a great deal of influence over how we make sense of teachers—especially over those who wish to follow in their footsteps. To dismiss fictional teachers as simple figures of entertainment is to dismiss the power they have over preservice teachers' understandings of being and becoming a teacher.

Remember, Snow White Choked on the Apple

Ask preservice teachers to share why they want to teach—as I do in my position as a teacher educator—and they will share how specific people have affected their choice of profession. Many will relate stories of favorite English teachers or creative elementary teachers; they will remember the 4th grade teacher who praised their writing ability or the 10th grade teacher who came to their basketball games. They will also tell you they want to inspire students like Mr. Keating and encourage teenagers like Ms. Gruwell. They will reference the importance of caring, like Miss Stacy, and the need to challenge, like Professor Lupin. They might even refer to the impact of poor teachers: they don't want to be like Sue Sylvester or Ferris Bueller's history teacher. I'm certainly not surprised by these fictional influences—I've seen the movies and read the books, too. Even Mrs. Krabappel was inspired by a teacher on the big screen, after all: "You have crushed my dreams of teaching ever since I saw *To Sir, With Love* as a little girl."

We develop understandings about teachers and teaching through what we absorb, personally and representationally (Bulman, 2015; Cohen & Scheer, 1997; Dalton, 2010; Harris, 2009; Heilman, 2001; Joseph & Burnaford, 2001; Labaree, 2000; Liston & Renga, 2015; Lortie, 2002; Weber & Mitchell, 1995). This apprenticeship of observation (Lortie, 2002) then allows preservice teachers to construct an interpretation of the teacher that informs their actions and beliefs, from how to interact with students to what to do in the classroom to why to enter the classroom in the first place. In essence, they are educated while they are entertained, taught by the images, ideas and ideologies (Giroux, 2001) they ingest to see the teacher in certain ways. While Giroux (2001) focuses on the specific medium of film, his assessment of its power is applicable to all forms of fiction: "a powerful teaching machine that intentionally tries to influence the production of meaning, subject positions, identities, and experience" (p. 586).

Preservice teachers see the saviors, the teachers who, against all odds, can work wonders with students, reorienting the difficult, engaging the disinterested, inspiring the disaffected. These teachers are solitary soldiers fighting for their students in order "to win them over to a better life, all the while doing battle with . . . idiot colleagues, the dull-witted administration, and the dangerously backward parents" (Ayers, 2001, p. 201). They are outsiders to the system, pouring heart and soul into their classroom, able to reach the most troubled adolescent through sheer willpower, unlimited love and irresistible personalities—and they can do all this on their own, thank you very much. As Bulman (2015) succinctly explains, these rebels

> do not need teacher training, smaller class sizes, a supportive staff, strong administrative leadership, parental participation, technological tools, corporate partnership, school restructuring, a higher salary, a long school day, charter schools, tuition vouchers, or more financial resources. All they need to bring to the classroom is discipline, tough love, high expectations, and a little good old-fashioned middle-class common sense about individual achievement and personal responsibility.
>
> *(p. 41)*

Preservice teachers see the scapegoats, the teachers who personify the perceived ills of education, from low expectations to crumbling infrastructure to lack of ability. These teachers don't inspire, they ignore; they don't connect, they control. Rather than young and sprightly educators with boundless energy in the classroom, they are decrepit and distanced pedagogues. They make no effort to reach students; they are there to collect a paycheck with as little expenditure of time and effort as possible. Their classrooms are dull, their teaching is dreary; their interest is weak, their students are weary. If they are urban teachers, in particular, they illustrate the problems of the urban school: "uncaring, cynical, incompetent, and ineffective" (Bulman, 2015, p. 39).

Preservice teachers also see the schoolmarms. The lone woman committed to a life circumscribed by the one-room schoolhouse has altered only in context and gender. These schoolmarms and misters inhabit their identity as teachers; they evince no other existence beyond the classroom walls and no other interests than their students. Their commitment to the classroom makes them "bright lights in schools of darkness" (Dalton, 2010, p. 27); if not shining examples, they are reflected warnings. Sometimes saviors, sometimes not; sometimes sexual, sometimes not; sometimes good, sometimes not—these teachers embody their teacher-ness, situated in the recognizable accouterments of education: the red pen, the shiny apple, the scribbled blackboard, the love of subject, the lack of sartorial style.

Through their viewing and reading—and experiences—preservice teachers "are exposed to both right and left wing images of teaching, image-texts that can be agents of change and subversion, or conversely, unnoticed but powerful agents of reproduction and conservatism" (Mitchell & Weber, 1999, p. 170); these implausible and contradictory images too often convince preservice teachers that they understand teachers and teaching. What they learn, however, is "intuitive and imitative rather than explicit and analytical" (Lortie, 2002, p. 62). The teachers that they find in movies and books may speak *to* them but they don't speak *for* them because these teachers do not—perhaps, cannot—portray the complex professional in a complicated profession. That is the difficult task of teacher educators.

When the Things We Know Aren't the Things We See

We know that preservice teachers enter a profession of contradictions:

> It is honored and disdained, praised as "dedicated service" and lampooned as "easy work." It is permeated with the rhetoric of professionalism, yet features incomes below those earned by workers with considerably less education. It is middle-class work in which more and more participants use bargaining strategies developed by wage-earners in factories.
>
> *(Lortie, 2002, p. 10)*

We know that preservice teachers grapple with ill-defined issues of content, instruction, assessment, expectation, responsibility; we understand that teachers navigate multilayered matters with learners, workload, relationships, emotions, identity (Alsup, 2006; Danielewicz, 2001; Darling-Hammond & Bransford, 2005; Labaree, 2000; Shoffner, 2011; Shoffner & Brown, 2010; Zembylas, 2007). The complexity of teaching means that there are few hard-and-fast rules for preservice teachers to follow as they learn how to educate, adapt and evolve; unlike the rigid capitalistic consumer approach now dominating school reform, preservice teachers learn that teaching is fluid, responsive, flexible, attentive. As Labaree (2000) eloquently explains, teacher education must engage "ordinary college students with the imponderable so that they can teach the irrepressible in a manner that pleases the irreconcilable, and all without knowing clearly either the purposes or the consequences of their actions" (p. 231).

We know that preservice teachers struggle to integrate what they know and believe about teaching into what they (are allowed to) do and say in the classroom. Once they leave their teacher educators behind, the imponderable, irrepressible and irreconcilable require them to react in real time—literally, thinking on their feet—using the knowledge, skills and dispositions (re)formed and refined before they entered the classroom. As Danielewicz (2001) outlines with precision and honesty, the "complex and delicate" (p. 9) act of teaching

> demands that teachers analyze the situation, consider the variables of students, texts, knowledge, abilities, and goals to formulate an approach to teaching, and then to carry it out—every day, minute to minute, within the ever-shifting context of the classroom. It requires having empathy for students, a knowledge of one's field, a sense of how learning occurs, the ability to generate a practice out of an idea, and the power to evaluate instantaneously whether it's going well or needs adjusting. Moreover, teaching depends on the teacher's capacity to constantly think ahead, to follow hunches, and usually, on top of all this, to perform convincingly for an audience, sometimes lecturing but always being the leader, directing activities and managing time efficiently.
>
> *(pp. 9–10)*

Preservice teachers rarely see teachers—their own or those represented in fiction and film—in this context. They don't observe teachers planning lessons or grading papers, rearranging desks or putting up bulletin boards, attending faculty meetings or sitting in workshops. They aren't privy to the discussions needed to arrange the upcoming field trip or reduce the number of days given to test preparation. They don't notice how lunch duties overlap with planning periods and parent meetings cut into dinners and new books result in fewer trips to Starbucks. They see the outcome, not the process—whether sitting in a classroom, a theater or a living room—and they want to replicate that outcome when they finally enter their own classroom. The fictional world of the teacher doesn't include the mundane—and why would it: I don't want to grade hundreds of essays, much less watch someone else do it—because the extraordinary is so much more interesting.

But these fictional representations of teachers trade on the very things preservice teachers learn to do. Real teachers connect to their students and engage them in the classroom, be it learning multiplication tables, understanding persuasive argument or applying the periodic table. They do so by understanding their subject matter, planning meaningful curriculum, creating authentic assessments (Darling-Hammond & Bransford, 2005), building relationships, enacting culturally relevant pedagogy (Gay, 2000) and engaging in reflection (Shoffner, 2009, 2011; Shoffner & Brown, 2010; Zeichner & Liston, 2013). Real teachers care about their students, in ways seen and unseen (Gay, 2000; Noddings, 1992; Rogers & Webb, 1991), because "teaching involves caring deeply about students as human beings and, at the same time, caring just as deeply that all students have rich opportunities to learn academically challenging material that will maximize their life chances" (Cochran-Smith, 2003, p. 372). Real teachers are creative and charismatic; they advocate for opportunity and fairness; they know how to laugh with and cry for. Real teachers are also collaborative, responsible, flexible—because they are professionals, possessing the knowledge, skills and dispositions that guide their teaching and their students' learning.

Real Learning With Reel Teachers

This book explores what it means to become a teacher in the confines of a fictionalized world. Preservice teachers are surrounded by representations of good, bad and indifferent teachers that shape their understandings of the teachers they wish to be. Ignoring the influence these constructs may have on beginning teachers is disingenuous; accepting their influence, however, provides an opportunity. By leveraging these fictional representations, teacher educators have a pedagogical opportunity (Trier, 2001) to problematize and expand preservice teachers' understandings of teachers and teaching. This book offers one such opportunity through chapters that critically analyze familiar representations of teachers in popular culture in order to engage preservice teachers in what they know and believe about teaching.

In Part I, "Identifying With the Teacher Image," six authors explore the fictional teacher, writ large, to consider the implications of these representations for preservice teachers' identity development. The opening chapter by Dawan Coombs and Jonathan Ostenson connects the fictional world of Harry Potter to the real world of teacher education through a pedagogical book club. Engaging their preservice teachers in discussion of the books offers the opportunity to apply their evolving understanding of teaching to their own development as teachers. Sheryl Long and Carol Pope, Jason Whitney and Nalova Westbrook share ways in which they have used film to engage their students with different constructions of the teacher. In detailing the approaches they have used in their coursework, they provide specific ways by which preservice teachers can examine images of the teacher and apply that examination to their own professional development. Joseph Rodríguez approaches teacher identity through the lens of short fiction, where the interactions between fictional teachers and their students encourage preservice teachers to consider how classroom relationships may impact their identity and their students' learning. Mark Lewis and Ian Renga turn to film to analyze teacher-student relationships and the elements that impact these fictional interactions, providing preservice teachers with an alternate reading of the relationships they may form in the future.

Part II, "Constructing the Teacher With Content," explores the teacher with more specificity, as five authors look closely at the ways fictional teachers represent the teaching of factual subject matter. Benjamin Boche considers the teaching of the English language arts broadly, analyzing the English teachers found in three young adult novels using the professional standards used to prepare secondary English teachers; in doing so, he considers the pedagogical implications of this analysis for preservice teachers. Shelbie Witte addresses English more narrowly, focusing on how she uses a variety of films to engage her preservice English teachers in examinations of literacy values and pedagogies. Amanda Jansen and Charles Hohensee explore the teaching of mathematics in popular films; as preservice teachers discuss and reflect on these films, they have the chance to develop awareness of the values they bring to their own mathematics teaching. Carol Anne Smith looks at the fictional portrayals of physical education teachers and the stereotypes they perpetuate before considering how preservice teachers can learn from these representations. Sarah Fischer concludes this section with her examination of the *Miss Malarkey* series; the fictional 1st grade teacher offers elementary preservice teachers a lens through which to consider their future profession.

Part III, "Imaging the Teacher as Savior," focuses specifically on the familiar character of the teacher savior. In this section, four authors critique the construct of the heroic teacher and consider the implications of this ubiquitous image for preservice teachers. Carey Applegate explores the teacher savior in the seminal films *Dangerous Minds* and *Freedom Writers* through the metaphors connected to war and mission work. Chea Parton examines the revisionist film *Detachment* as a counternarrative that both reifies and revises the teacher savior image. Ashley Boyd focuses on the teacher savior in *Won't Back Down*, considering how the film reinforces the trope while advancing a political agenda. In contrast, Walter Squire analyzes *Chalk*, a film that pushes against the teacher savior stereotype through its presentation of teachers as regular, often flawed, people.

Finally, Part IV, "The Teacher Construct as Commentary," examines the ways in which teacher films represent and shape current educational issues. Patrick Shannon addresses the contested field of reading education, using film to engage his preservice teachers with the educational and political issues informing their future literacy teaching. Patrick and Ewa McGrail examine the film *Bad Teacher*, positing that the film's portrayal of teachers illustrates societal cynicism toward education while offering opportunities for preservice teachers to examine their understandings of and beliefs about the profession they wish to enter. Moving away from fictional portrayals of teachers, Christian Goering, Jen Dean and Brandon Flammang analyze three education documentaries that directly and indirectly focus on teacher accountability, encouraging preservice teachers to recognize the fiction found within nonfiction narratives. Jeff Spanke provides the concluding chapter that, appropriately, focuses on the survival of teachers in today's world. Drawing on the television show *Falling Skies*, he compares the forces currently shaping education to that of an alien invasion; if we wish to survive, teacher educators must prepare preservice teachers for the realities of the future rather than the fictions of the past.

As the chapters in this book reveal, we *can* learn from fictional teachers; in fact, we can learn quite a lot when we pause to consider the representations of teachers that surround us in our movies and novels and television shows and cartoons. We *do* learn, however, from real teachers: the ones who try again when students don't understand; the ones who forget to return the papers sitting on the dining room table; the ones who go to the school play on Friday night; the ones who step outside the room for just one minute before they lose their temper; the ones who show up every day, in every class, to work with every student.

Fictional teachers are larger than life; real teachers are life-sized. Fictional teachers entertain; real teachers educate. We learn from real people doing real work in the real world. They aren't saviors, saints, sinners, scapegoats or schoolmarms. They are teachers—and they are extraordinary.

References

Alsup, J. (2006). *Teacher identity discourses: Negotiating personal and professional spaces*. Mahwah, NJ: Lawrence Erlbaum.

Ayers, W. (2001). A teacher ain't nothin' but a hero: Teachers and teaching in film. In P. B. Joseph & G. E. Burnaford (Eds.), *Images of school teachers in America* (2nd ed., pp. 201–210). Mahwah, NJ: Lawrence Erlbaum.

Bulman, R. C. (2015). *Hollywood goes to high school: Cinema, schools, and American culture* (2nd ed.). New York, NY: Worth.

Cochran-Smith, M. (2003). Sometimes it's not about the money: Teaching and heart. *Journal of Teacher Education, 54*(5), 371–375.

Cohen, R. M., & Scheer, S. (1997). *The work of teachers in America: A social history through stories.* Mahwah, NJ: Lawrence Erlbaum.

Dalton, M. M. (2010). *The Hollywood curriculum: Teachers in the movies* (2nd ed.). New York, NY: Peter Lang.

Danielewicz, J. (2001). *Teaching selves: Identity, pedagogy, and teacher education.* Albany: State University of New York Press.

Darling-Hammond, L., & Bransford, J. (2005). *Preparing teachers for a changing world: What teachers should learn and be able to do.* San Francisco, CA: Jossey-Bass.

Gay, G. (2000). *Culturally responsive teaching: Theory, research, and practice.* New York, NY: Teachers College Press.

Giroux, H. (2001). Breaking into the movies: Pedagogy and the politics of film. *JAC: A Journal of Composition Theory, 21*(3), 583–598.

Groening, M., & Brooks, J. L. (Producers). (1989–2015). *The Simpsons* [Television series]. Los Angeles, CA: Fox.

Harris, A. (2009). The good teacher: Images of teachers in popular culture. *English Drama Media, 14,* 11–18.

Heilman, R. B. (2001). The great-teacher myth. *American Scholar, 42,* 417–423.

Joseph, P. B., & Burnaford, G. E. (2001). *Images of schoolteachers in America.* New York, NY: Routledge.

Kantor, K., Kantor, N. L., Kantor, J., Eaton, M., & Kantor, B. (2001). "I will not expose the ignorance of the faculty": *The Simpsons* as social satire. In P. B. Joseph & G. E. Burnaford (Eds.), *Images of schoolteachers in America* (2nd ed., pp. 185–200). Mahwah, NJ: Lawrence Erlbaum.

Labaree, D. F. (2000). On the nature of teaching and teacher education: Difficult practices that look easy. *Journal of Teacher Education, 51*(3), 228–233.

Liston, D., & Renga, I. P. (Eds.). (2015). *Teaching, learning, and schooling in film: Reel education.* New York, NY: Routledge,

Lortie, D. C. (2002). *Schoolteacher: A sociological study* (Vol. 2). Chicago, IL: University of Chicago Press.

Martin, S. (2008). *Born standing up: A comic's life.* New York, NY: Scribner.

Mitchell, C., & Weber, S. (1999). *Reinventing ourselves as teachers: Beyond nostalgia.* Philadelphia, PA: Falmer.

Noddings, N. (1992). *The challenge to care in schools: An alternative approach to education.* New York, NY: Teachers College Press.

Rogers, D., & Webb, J. (1991). The ethic of caring in teacher education. *Journal of Teacher Education, 42*(3), 173–181.

Sandlin, J. A., O'Malley, M. P., & Burdick, J. (2011). Mapping the complexity of public pedagogy scholarship: 1894–2010. *Review of Educational Research, 81*(3), 338–375.

Shoffner, M. (2009). The place of the personal: Exploring the affective domain through reflection in teacher preparation. *Teaching and Teacher Education, 25*(6), 783–789.

Shoffner, M. (2011). Considering the first year: Reflection as a means to address beginning teachers' concerns. *Teachers and Teaching: Theory and Practice, 17*(4), 417–433.

Shoffner, M., & Brown, M. (2010). From understanding to application: The difficulty of culturally responsive teaching as a beginning English teacher. In L. Scherff & K. Spector (Eds.), *Culturally relevant pedagogy: Clashes and confrontations* (pp. 89–112). Lanham, MD: Rowman & Littlefield.

Trier, J. (2001). The cinematic representation of the personal and professional lives of teachers. *Teacher Education Quarterly, 28*(3), 127–142.

Weber, S., & Mitchell, C. (1995). *"That's funny, you don't look like a teacher": Interrogating images, identity and popular culture.* New York, NY: Routledge.

Zeichner, K., & Liston, D. (2013). *Reflective teaching: An introduction* (2nd ed.). New York, NY: Routledge.

Zembylas, M. (2007). Emotional ecology: The intersection of emotional knowledge and pedagogical content knowledge in teaching. *Teaching and Teacher Education, 23*(4), 355–367.

PART I

Identifying With the Teacher Image

We teachers are rather good at magic, you know.

—Professor Minerva McGonagall

Lord, we know what we are, but know not what we may be.

—Ophelia

Of course it is happening inside your head, Harry, but why on earth should that mean that it is not real?

—Professor Albus Percival Wulfric Brian Dumbledore

1

LOOKING INTO THE MIRROR OF ERISED

Transacting With Representations of Hogwarts' Teachers and Pedagogy

Dawan Coombs
Jonathan Ostenson

The Mirror of Erised, a magical device introduced in *Harry Potter and the Sorcerer's Stone* (Rowling, 1997), shows those who look into it their heart's deepest desire. When the orphan Harry looks into the mirror, he sees his dead parents and relatives; Ron, the youngest brother from a large family, sees himself as captain of the house Quidditch team, emerging from the shadows of his siblings. If we, as teacher educators, were to look into the mirror, we might see our preservice teachers immersed in the field, gaining valuable experience with students in classrooms. Our preservice teachers might see clear-cut, easily applicable solutions to the challenges they expect to face in the classroom as practicing teachers.

Unfortunately, achieving these desires requires more than a longing gaze and wishful thinking. Still, we find the Mirror of Erised a fitting metaphor for the journey we took with our preservice teachers when we invited them to reread the *Harry Potter* series (Rowling, 1997–2007) through the eyes of a future teacher. Reflecting on representations of teachers and teaching, however fanciful they might be, helped our preservice teachers consider the realities of what they ultimately wanted to become as classroom teachers. In this chapter, we examine how representations of teachers and teaching portrayed in the series allowed our preservice teachers to apply learning from their methods courses to the Hogwarts context while deepening their understandings of the discipline. We conclude with a discussion of potential implications of this work for teacher education programs, particularly how transacting with representations of teachers in young adult literature may influence preservice teachers' perceptions of their own ultimate roles.

Context of the Issues

Many children's and young adult texts embody the notion of "erziehungsroman" or the "school story," showcasing experiences of students, schools and education as part of the journey into adulthood (Atwood & Lee, 2007). The *Harry Potter* series embodies this concept well; amidst the fantasy-filled adventures of Harry and his friends, their stories provide fodder for discussion about real-life educational issues (Mullen, 2000). Multiple books in the series exemplify "the good, the bad and the ugly" (Booth & Booth, 2003, p. 313) in student-centered education as the Hogwarts teachers and system wrestle with principles such as differentiated instruction, cooperative learning, mentoring and Vygotskian social constructivist theories of modeling, scaffolding and relevance. Representative of actual student experiences with teachers, classes and individuals (Houston, 2011), the narratives also invite readers to contemplate moral issues in education (Glanzer, 2008) and to examine representations of educational systems, faculty evaluation and academic freedom (Sheppard, 2008).

Studies document the use of erziehungsroman literature as a means for preservice and practicing teachers to explore issues of diversity and teenage experience (Brindley & Laframboise, 2002; DeGroot, 2011; Mason, 2010), culture and pedagogy (Laframboise & Griffith, 1997) in conjunction with professional development (Back, Choate & Parker, 2011). We envisioned the *Harry Potter* texts working in similar ways. As the preservice teachers read through their "teacher lens"—developed as a result of semesters in methods courses and classroom observations—they would be better able to attend to details overlooked or seemingly insignificant in previous readings.

This notion of attending finds a theoretical basis in Rosenblatt's (1995) transactional theory that explains how readers may produce different interpretations of the same text at different times in their lives, based on the conditions under which the text is encountered. She explains that these conditions may make readers "especially receptive or especially impervious to what the work offers" (p. 35). For our preservice teachers, being in the midst of their pedagogical training and on the cusp of their student teaching provided the conditions that allowed them to transact with ideas in new ways. Rosenblatt (1995) explained that readers approach texts with their own unique "personality traits, memories of past events, present needs and preoccupations" (p. 30) that influence how they respond to characters, situations and ideas presented in the text. In other words, meaning comes not just from the printed words but also from what readers bring to their reading.

Given this theory, we chose the *Harry Potter* series (Rowling, 1997–2007) in part because our preservice teachers grew up alongside Harry, Ron and Hermione as members of the Harry Potter Generation (Browne, 2009; Houston, 2011). Through multiple readings of the books, viewings of the movies and even participation in fan sites like Pottermore.com, their intense attachment and interest provided motivation to participate in the project and engage in dialogue with one another. More importantly, their immersion in the world of Harry Potter created a strong context within which to productively reflect on issues of teachers and teaching. Our conception of productive reflection comes from Moore-Russo and Wilsey (2014), who characterized reflection as productive when it considers teaching and learning in relation to the environment, the students' needs, the subject and the teachers' expectations; compares and builds on past experiences, others' perspectives, educational theories and educational research; and emphasizes and integrates a variety of aspects of teaching.

The Harry Potter Book Club

During the 2013 fall semester, we invited all preservice English teachers enrolled in the methods courses at our university to join a book club examining portrayals of teachers and teaching in the Harry Potter series. Of those invited, Kelly, Natalie, Wendy, Rachel, Thomas and Scott (all names are pseudonyms) committed to reread the series with us. Our group of four women and two men, all White college students between the ages of 20 and 24, represented a range of socioeconomic backgrounds. All were accepted into the English teaching program but represented a range of abilities and academic achievement. They were not compensated for participating in the group, aside from what they gained in the discussions and exploration.

The club focused on one book in the series each month and met for a total of six 90-minute sessions. Each meeting began with the prompt, "What teaching and learning practices did you observe in the book?" which launched a free-flowing discussion, with preservice teachers responding to the question, referencing markings or annotations in their books and sharing insights they had while reading.

As researchers, our role consisted primarily of noting major topics and directions of discussion, recording observations of interactions and, at times, making connections between the discussion and educational research; on rare occasions, we highlighted significant insights we had while reading. Occasionally we asked follow-up questions to clarify a comment; at other times, we answered questions posed by the preservice teachers. Throughout, our main goal was to create a forum for them to discuss and explore their reactions, insights and connections.

Each meeting was audio-recorded and later transcribed by an undergraduate research assistant. We coded the transcripts, our observations and participant feedback and then conducted a thematic analysis of the data (Braun & Clarke, 2006), identifying themes that resonated in the group's analysis of the books. Through this analysis, we identified ways in which the preservice teachers explored representations of teaching and how they applied those to their future experiences.

Transacting With Representations of Teaching

The preservice teachers engaged most frequently and meaningfully with three major representations of teachers and teaching: pedagogy, curriculum and students. In the sections that follow, we discuss the significance of these transactions for their understandings of the role of the teacher.

Representations of Pedagogy

The pedagogical approaches of various Hogwarts teachers became the focus of numerous book club discussions. For our preservice teachers, Lupin (Defense Against the Dark Arts professor by day, werewolf by night) and his nurturing pedagogy often represented approaches worth emulating, while the methods of Snape, Umbridge, Trelawney, Hagrid and even Dumbledore (at times) proved problematic. In a sense, the characters served as case studies where our preservice teachers could apply their own experiences as they critiqued. For example, Natalie explained,

> A lot of teachers at Hogwarts are there not because of their teaching ability. Like Hagrid—I mean, I love the guy—but he's a terrible teacher . . . He has no training, he has no curriculum, there's no oversight. He apparently can do whatever he wants, which, as much as I love Hagrid, putting 13-year-olds in front of deadly beasts is probably not your best plan.

Concerns about preparation and training echoed throughout our discussions. As seen in Natalie's comment, we observed preservice teachers taking on the role of classroom observer, critiquing teachers' approaches and philosophies represented in the narrative while seeking to separate themselves from their personal feelings or sympathies for individual characters. In this way, they interrogated teacher intervention in students' learning, the challenges teachers extended to students and the extent to which these activities motivated students.

Our preservice teachers quickly identified less effective teaching approaches in opposition to the student-centered, constructivist frameworks they were exposed to in their coursework. Professor Binns's lecture-based history class was an obvious example, but other professors' efforts fell into this category as well. During a discussion about one of Snape's lessons, Thomas explained his understanding of student-centered versus teacher-centered approaches to instruction:

> When Hermione tries to actually answer [Snape's] question . . . he says, "I was under the impression that I am teaching this lesson, not you." It's so against the way we should teach. [His approach is] the old standard way of teaching with lecture: The teacher knows everything, and the students are helpless . . . He refuses any attempt at the students trying to teach each other.

In contrast, Lupin's methods provided multiple examples of student-centered teaching and learning. In one lesson, Lupin challenges the self-doubting Neville Longbottom to defend himself against a fearsome boggart; Lupin clearly explains the steps of the defensive spell and even intercedes a bit when necessary but allows Neville to successfully dispel the creature. This narrative event provided an opportunity for our preservice teachers to consider how Lupin positioned students as competent learners.

Dumbledore's methods, on the other hand, elicited more ambivalent responses from the preservice teachers. They criticized Dumbledore's absence at key moments in the book, while simultaneously wondering if this absence represented a teaching technique by not stepping in, even when students seemed in dire straits (as with the fight with the mountain troll in the girls' bathroom). They believed that Dumbledore displayed trust and confidence in students by allowing them to learn independently through hands-on, trial-and-error experiences, but they wondered about his methods. The tension they expressed in these discussions about Dumbledore revealed their efforts to integrate their own developing pedagogical understandings with the choices of these fictional teachers. At the same time, our preservice teachers became increasingly aware of how their expectations could inform the treatment of their future students. In speaking of Lupin's confidence in Neville, Thomas explained what it suggested about his own interactions with students:

> I think expectations are important not only for our students, because they'll feel a sense of empowerment if we at least make our [high] expectations known. But also, even subconsciously we treat people differently, depending on our expectations.

This excerpt is representative of multiple instances throughout the meetings where Thomas wrestled with his responsibility to set high expectations. Many of the other preservice teachers also discussed moments in the novels when the characters were asked to accomplish feats that seemed beyond their ability and the role these tasks played in their learning.

As teacher educators, we recognize that the motif of adolescents facing challenges alone so they can grow and mature also has pedagogical implications that point toward teacher expectations for students and the challenges they provide for student growth. We were gratified to hear our preservice teachers make that same connection in their analysis of Hogwarts teachers. Our preservice teachers drew contrasts between teachers like Snape, Trelawney and Umbridge, who demonstrated explicit doubt in students' potential for success because they lacked "the gift" for a particular sort of magic, and teachers like Lupin and Dumbledore, who pushed students to do hard things and provided support that enabled students to succeed. For example, after discussing why Lupin would challenge Harry to learn a particularly difficult spell that causes him to pass out, Scott explained,

> I also think that failure is an important part of learning . . . a lot of times I think we do students a disservice if we're not putting them in situations where we know they're going to fail. It can be really hard, but I think you can learn so much in those situations and I didn't have a lot of situations like that in high school.

Here, Scott brings his own school experiences, as well as his beliefs, into dialogue with the events portrayed in the book. Natalie echoed Scott's idea when she concluded, "When the student has a good reason for learning and really believes they can do it, then maybe it doesn't even matter what the teacher thinks," suggesting the critical importance of student motivation. Rachel also noted that when Harry and others had a clear purpose for their learning, they experienced greater success, which she connected to her coursework:

> In my practicum class we were talking about lesson plans and the objectives that we have and the "Students will be able to" phrase. Well, [my methods professor] mentioned you should tell your students what this phrase is so that they know what they're supposed to learn . . . so they have some type of start as to where they should go.

Inspired by the innate curiosity displayed by Harry and company, Scott linked the conversation back to motivation as he referenced a TED Talk he watched about the relationship between curiosity and learning:

> The greatest gateway to real learning is curiosity . . . No one inquires about something because they are *asked* to inquire. That's not inquiry, that's an assignment . . . But how can we make kids curious? Like really, sincerely curious, where they want to inquire about something?

His question, we feel, is a significant one, arising from the intersection of his own experience, his education and his reading of the books. Our preservice teachers often referred to the independent learning that Harry, Ron and Hermione engaged in outside of class to accomplish meaningful, relevant tasks: saving the hippogriff required significant library research, creating a polyjuice potion required creative problem solving and forming Dumbledore's Army to supplement the school's defensive instruction showed self-directed learning at its best.

Representations of Curriculum

As often as they explored questions of teacher practice, our preservice teachers also explored questions related to curriculum. Of particular concern was the depth of content knowledge teachers needed. During our discussion of Gilderoy Lockhart, the famous (but fraudulent) writer-turned-teacher, Kellie's comment typified their concerns:

> [We need] to know our subject enough that we can confidently instruct [students]; that's a parallel [to the book] that I found, that I want to be able to know answers to grammar questions or think thematically about . . . the novel we're reading so that my students can look to me and count on me.

They shared fears about the consequences of not possessing strong content knowledge, from embarrassing themselves to actually harming students' development and learning. In critiquing Lockhart, Natalie commented, "I think what makes him so destructive as a teacher is that he pretends to know things but he really doesn't and that's, like, a horrible thing for a teacher."

Looking ahead to decisions they would be asked to make about curriculum, these preservice teachers expressed concerns about content at Hogwarts, particularly in relation to the troublesome Defense Against the Dark Arts class. They explored the limitations of decisions made by teachers like Umbridge, who focused primarily on the theory behind what is, in the world of Harry Potter, a very practical art; in contrast, they praised the practices of Lupin and Mad Eye Moody, who engaged students in hands-on practical applications of the art.

As at Hogwarts, where curriculum focuses on potentially destructive magical forces, these preservice teachers will one day make choices about books that could expose their students to potentially troublesome topics. The power inherent in literature was not new to them, but the Hogwarts context invited them to reflect on their role in these choices. As Natalie aptly put it,

> There is a line, and books do have a lot of power, and sometimes that power is too powerful for teenagers . . . We get really excited about our rights [to choose any book we want to teach] but sometimes we forget about our responsibility, too.

Examining the choices of Hogwarts teachers helped our preservice teachers consider their responsibility to make informed and purposeful decisions about content in their own classrooms.

Our preservice teachers also focused on what was *not* taught at Hogwarts and, in so doing, engaged in meaningful reflection about their ethical responsibilities. They noted the primarily vocational focus of coursework at the expense of classes in the arts or the ethics of magic. The history class (the only nonvocational course described in the series) does not teach about the consequences of historical actions, focusing instead on the memorization of noteworthy dates, battles and people. Our preservice teachers applied this observation to the role of arts and humanities in schools and to concerns about our state standards. Scott exemplified these concerns when he wondered if teachers "think [the standards] limit them in a sense like, 'Oh, then I can't have an objective like develop empathy. What does that have to do with the [standard]?'" Natalie expressed similar concerns when talking about a unit she was designing for her capstone methods class, in which she wanted to embed an exploration of choice and consequence, but she worried that she was overstepping her bounds by including this content.

Representations of Students

The book club also allowed the preservice teachers to consider how decisions about pedagogy and curriculum are not made in a vacuum but informed by students' needs and their lived experiences. During their discussions, they frequently explored how teachers seek to (or fail to) understand their students based on assumptions.

As younger readers, our preservice teachers had, understandably, related most to characters like Harry or Hermione; even reading through a teacher lens, they often expressed similar sympathies. As older readers and preservice teachers, however, they shared slightly different interpretations. Some participants praised Dumbledore's awareness of Harry's needs (given that he would ultimately face Voldemort) while others observed this attention came at the expense of other students, such as Malfoy or Ron. They showed a growing awareness of the difficult choices teachers make when faced with limited resources and time.

This rereading caused these preservice teachers to reflect on their own tendencies to favor some students over others, especially those who would share predilections for reading and writing or who embodied the characteristics of "good students." These discussions became particularly involved when Harry was first labeled (in an "ah-ha" moment for our preservice teachers) an "at-risk" student, causing them to think critically about labels placed on students and their influence on teachers. Subsequent discussions focused on the home-school connection and its influence on learning at Hogwarts. The preservice teachers were eager to give Harry the benefit of the doubt when he broke rules but were less forgiving of Malfoy's malfeasance. As Wendy noted, "[Harry] is easy to sympathize with because of his extenuating circumstance, which is why it gets emotionally difficult" when accounting for students' backgrounds in classroom decision-making. However, Thomas pushed back when he asked, "Could Malfoy have turned out different? . . . If he had the opportunity and a teacher really showed that they believed in him and wanted to actually help him?"

These tensions engaged our preservice teachers in multilayered, critical examinations of students and teaching. For example, our preservice teachers showed distress over the actions of teachers like Slughorn, who exploited his position at Hogwarts by inviting students with the potential to further his career into his exclusive club. Preservice teachers connected this to their coursework in adolescent development, as Scott noted, "Teachers are involved with human beings at a very delicate time in their mental and cognitive and emotional growth." Their concerns about actions like Slughorn's acknowledged the vulnerable nature of many of the students with whom teachers work.

While recognizing students' vulnerabilities, these preservice teachers also acknowledged the great potential of the teens with whom they would soon be working. They showed confidence in teens' abilities, as when they discussed the very adept learning displayed by Harry, Ron and Hermione outside the classroom. At one point, Natalie connected her experience as a younger reader and her current position as a future teacher: "When I was growing up reading *Harry Potter*, I always felt like, 'Look what Harry and Hermione and Ron can do and they're only the same age as I am.'" In this reading, though, recognizing that many adults (teachers included) are often dismissive of what teens can do, she noted that teachers are "in a position where we do have an opportunity to help them empower themselves, and ... I think that we should help them to recognize their own ability. Like Harry." The high expectations essential to good teaching are born from a confidence in teens' abilities in the classroom, a confidence that these preservice teachers could see in these fictional characters as well as their future students.

Life After Hogwarts (or From the Figurative to the Literal)

As teacher educators, we recognize our responsibility to maximize opportunities for preservice teachers to engage in reflective thinking about teacher practices and the development of their teacher identities. Classroom observations and field experiences provide invaluable opportunities but alone are not enough to engage preservice teachers in the self-reflection and analysis vital for their development. Our purpose in inviting preservice teachers to join us in rereading the Harry Potter series was to provide an additional—and familiar—space for reflective thinking about teaching.

As young readers, our preservice teachers saw themselves reflected in the characters of Harry, Ron and Hermione; in the present, on the cusp of student teaching, they saw themselves reflected in Lupin, McGonagall and Dumbledore. In a sense, the books became a Mirror of Erised for them; they saw reflected in their reading those things they most cared about. In Rowling's imagined world, characters could become hopelessly lost in the vain imaginings inspired by the mirror, but for our participants, the reflections they engaged with empowered them and even informed their actions as student teachers. In a follow-up interview conducted during her student teaching, Natalie shared how this had happened for her:

> [My supervisor] came to observe one of my classes and pointed out that even though I was really trying, many of my students just were not engaged in the activities we were doing. I remembered our discussions [from book club] about Lupin and how he was such a star at doing some of the things I was struggling to incorporate—questioning, inquiry and movement. After that, when I sat down to plan a lesson, I would ask myself, "How would Lupin teach this?" Which is totally nerdy, but it really did help me figure things out a little better!

We feel gratified to see this literature help our preservice teachers begin to make sense of the complexities of our discipline. Four of our six participants became so interested in some aspects of our discussion that they engaged in additional scholarly research and presented their work at an undergraduate research roundtable at the 2014 meeting of the National Council of Teachers of English (Alder &

Sommerville, 2014; Westenskow & Johnson, 2014). Natalie, for instance, chose to look at lesson planning and how her understanding of that process was influenced by her study of the books.

Their familiarity with the series undoubtedly provided a meaningful context for our preservice teachers' interpretations, an element often missing from case studies or even classroom observations. We saw that fiction holds a tremendous power to excite the mind and create vivid worlds in which preservice teachers encounter these representations, as Coles (2004) also observed in his graduate courses that used fiction in similar ways. We encourage teacher educators to consider how school stories like Harry Potter's might be integrated into methods courses in ways similar to field experiences or case studies. For example, beyond merely presenting the angst of preteen and teenage life, novels like *The Wednesday Wars* (Schmidt, 2007) also portray teachers and pedagogy through the eyes of students; the follow-up novel, *Okay for Now* (Schmidt, 2011), shows how home life plays a critical role in a student's school identity. Similarly, *Don't You Dare Read This, Mrs. Dunphrey* (Haddix, 1996) provides opportunities for extensive discussion about the teacher's role in reading and assessing student writing, as well as responsibilities to support students amidst intense personal challenges. Novels such as *Speak* (Anderson, 1999), *No More Dead Dogs* (Korman, 2002), *Schooled* (Korman, 2007) and *Tears of a Tiger* (Draper, 1994) provide vignettes that highlight the ironies, shortcomings and complexities of the educational system, in addition to exposés on student behavior.

Critically examining the fictional world of Hogwarts provided our preservice teachers with meaningful insights into their teacher roles and identities, in line with the powerful role that personal narratives have demonstrated in the development of teachers (Alsup, 2006). Exploring their responses to the teachers and teaching in this magical school invited them to interrogate their own developing identities and understandings of pedagogy. As important as we find it to be to provide "real-life" encounters with such things in the classroom, we should not overlook the power of imagined worlds to provide those encounters as well.

References

Alder, R., & Sommerville, W. (2014, November). From Potter to pedagogy: True scholarly research inspired by fiction. In A. Brown & L. Rodesiler (Chairs), *The future is now: Exploring 21st century teaching ideas with the next generation of English teachers*. Research roundtable presented at the 104th National Council of Teachers of English Conference, National Harbor, MD.

Alsup, J. (2006). *Teacher identity discourses: Negotiating personal and professional spaces*. Mahwah, NJ: Lawrence Erlbaum.

Anderson, L. H. (1999). *Speak*. New York, NY: Farrar Straus Giroux.

Atwood, T., & Lee, W. (2007). The price of deviance: Schoolhouse gothic in prep school literature. *Children's Literature, 35*(1), 101–126.

Back, J., Choate, L., & Parker, B. (2011). Young adult literature and professional development. *Theory Into Practice, 50*, 198–205.

Booth, M., & Booth, G. (2003). What American schools can learn from Hogwarts School of Witchcraft and Wizardry. *The Phi Delta Kappan, 85*(4), 310–315.

Braun, V., & Clarke, V. (2006). Using thematic analysis in psychology. *Qualitative Research in Psychology, 3*, 77–101.

Brindley, R., & Laframboise, K. (2002). The need to do more: Promoting multiple perspectives in preservice teacher education through children's literature. *Teaching and Teacher Education, 18*, 405–420.

Browne, D. (2009, July 22). Harry Potter is their Peter Pan. *New York Times*. Retrieved from http://www.nytimes.com/2009/07/23/fashion/23nostalgia.html

Coles, R. (Ed.). (2004). *An anthology on the power of learning and literature: Teaching stories.* New York, NY: The Modern Library.

DeGroot, A. (2011). Talking about texts: Examining the role of interventions in preservice teachers' discussions of young adult multicultural literature. *Journal of Multiculturalism in Education, 7*, 1–31.

Draper, S. (1994). *Tears of a tiger.* New York, NY: Simon Pulse.

Glanzer, P. (2008). Harry Potter's provocative moral world: Is there a place for good and evil in moral education? *The Phi Delta Kappan, 89*(7), 525–528.

Haddix, M. P. (1996). *Don't you dare read this, Mrs. Dunphrey.* New York, NY: Simon Pulse.

Houston, K. (2011). Teaching the Harry Potter generation. *Networks: An On-line Journal for Teacher Research, 13*(2), 1–5.

Korman, G. (2002). *No more dead dogs.* New York, NY: Hyperion.

Korman, G. (2007). *Schooled.* New York, NY: Scholastic.

Laframboise, K., & Griffith, P. (1997). Using literature cases to examine diversity issues with preservice teachers. *Teaching and Teacher Education, 13*(4), 369–382.

Mason, K. (2010). From pre-service teacher to trusted adult: Sexual orientation and gender variance in an online YAL book club. *The ALAN Review, 38*(1), 7–14.

Moore-Russo, D., & Wilsey, J. (2014). Delving into the meaning of productive reflection: A study of future teachers' reflections on representations of teaching. *Teaching and Teacher Education, 37*, 76–90.

Mullen, A. (2000). Harry Potter's school days: Tom Brown, Harry Potter & other schoolboy heroes. *The Hudson Review, 53*(1), 127–135.

Rosenblatt, L. (1995). *Literature as exploration.* New York, NY: MLA.

Rowling, J. K. (1997). *Harry Potter and the sorcerer's stone.* New York, NY: Scholastic.

Rowling, J. K. (1997–2007). *Harry Potter* (Vols. 1–7). New York, NY: Scholastic.

Schmidt, G. (2007). *The Wednesday wars.* New York, NY: Houghton Mifflin Harcourt Books for Young Readers.

Schmidt, G. (2011). *Okay for now.* New York, NY: Houghton Mifflin Harcourt Books for Young Readers.

Sheppard, J. (2008). Faculty forum: Harry Potter and the sinister measures of merit. *Academe, 94*(1), 62.

Westenskow, N., & Johnson, K. (2014, November). Lupin versus Umbridge: Planning and pedagogy. In A. Brown & L. Rodesiler (Chairs), *The future is now: Exploring 21st century teaching ideas with the next generation of English teachers.* Research roundtable presented at the 104th National Council of Teachers of English Conference, National Harbor, MD.

2

PLAYING THE ROLE OF TEACHER

Using Film to Explore Teacher Identities

Sheryl Long
Carol A. Pope

Preservice teachers, who have typically spent more than 12 years as students, have had extensive experiences as observers of the school environment and of the ways in which teachers operate in that environment. Through what Lortie (1975) has called an "apprenticeship of observation," they have developed concepts of who a teacher is and what a teacher does. Thus, their understandings of the teaching profession are strongly influenced by their prior beliefs or "psychologically held understandings, premises, or propositions about the world that are felt to be true" (Richardson, 1996, p. 123). They bring these beliefs with them to their teacher education programs, where they find these beliefs challenged by the multiple perspectives they encounter in new settings. While this process may create discomfort, it is vital to becoming a teacher. Much like an actor preparing to play a new character, these preservice teachers must study the role of teacher carefully so that they can assume this identity for themselves.

In this chapter, we discuss our pedagogical approach to using film to help preservice teachers examine, challenge and reshape their perceptions of teacher identity. This method is strongly guided by reader response theory and the belief that readers create meaning from their interactions with a text—in this case, a film narrative. Building on the concept of the interpretive community—a group of readers who employ similar interpretive strategies (Fish, 1980)—we argue that our classroom communities function as interpretive communities and that our pedagogical approaches shape the interpretive strategies employed within these communities.

Teacher Identity

Within the field of teacher education, there are multiple approaches to defining *teacher identity* (Olsen, 2008). However, in reviewing the related literature, Rodgers and Scott (2008) have found that most discussions of teacher identity are characterized by the following four assumptions:

> (1) that identity is dependent upon and formed within multiple contexts which bring social, cultural, political and historical forces to bear upon that formation; (2) that identity is formed in relationship with others and involves emotions; (3) that identity is shifting, unstable and multiple; and (4) that identity involves the construction and reconstruction of meaning through stories over time.
>
> *(p. 733)*

These assumptions suggest teacher identity is not a fixed concept but rather "a moving intersection of the inner and outer forces" (Palmer, 2007, p. 14). Teacher identity should be seen as situated within contexts (Hoffman-Kipp, 2008; Smagorinksy, Cook, Moore, Jackson & Fry, 2004; Stockinger, 2007), which include the school settings in which teachers work as well as the larger sociopolitical contexts in which they operate. For preservice teachers, the teacher education program provides multiple contexts for identity formation, including college/university community, classroom settings, student cohorts and field settings.

These assumptions also indicate the importance of stories to the formation of teacher identity. Rodgers and Scott (2008) explain that teacher identity can be seen as "both interpreted and constructed through the stories that one tells oneself and that others tell" (p. 737). Teacher preparation programs support preservice teachers in their process of identity formation by developing "instructional programs that guide preservice teachers to examine their past and present experiences through multiple lenses, to help them step out of their personal visions and explore other ways of thinking about and interpreting their experience" (Stockinger, 2007, p. 204). Although preservice teachers have developed an understanding of teacher identity that is largely based on their prior beliefs, they may not understand how or the extent to which their experiences have shaped their beliefs about teaching. As they participate in a teacher preparation program, they gain new experiences that influence their concepts of teacher identity; they develop new personal stories and, through their involvement with new people and settings, they are exposed to a variety of narratives about school and teaching. In order to interrogate their understandings about teacher identity, they need opportunities to articulate and make meaning of their personal stories and the stories they encounter from others.

The Influence of the Interpretive Community

In our work with preservice teachers, we work to create environments that support the exploration and interpretation of prior experience and to help preservice teachers look beyond themselves so that they can learn from the experiences of others. In the projects we describe here, preservice teachers are enrolled in master's programs from a number of content areas, including elementary, English language arts, social studies, mathematics and instructional technology. Within these programs, preservice teachers take classes along with practicing teachers who are pursuing advanced degrees in teaching. We are tasked with fostering the development of dynamic classroom communities that support our belief in constructivist theories of teaching and learning (Powell & Kalina, 2009) and with providing the means for our students to explore practical teaching knowledge and personal knowledge (Clandinin, 1985). These classroom communities function as more than simply settings in which learning can occur; they become contexts that influence personal knowledge.

Because our work with teacher identity centers on the analysis of narrative texts, we can best describe our approach as being guided by theories of reader response, which establish that the reader is an active participant in the reading process and, therefore, helps to create the meaning of the text (Bressler, 2003). Within these classroom communities, students interact with each other and their instructors, with their personal stories of teaching and with others' stories about teaching. The teaching narratives serve as the texts to be "read" or interpreted. Each individual brings prior experiences, understandings and concepts that influence how the individual interacts and creates meaning from the text. In this way, the process of making meaning from a narrative becomes a transaction between reader and text (Rosenblatt, 1983). Yet as members of the same community, their engagement with the text is also directed by the shared values of the teacher education program and the practices emphasized by us as their instructors. Therefore, when the teacher education program emphasizes appreciation of diversity or teacher leadership through its overall policies and in its individual courses, students view the texts through these lenses. Their understandings of a text are affected by commonly shared interpretive strategies, and so they become an interpretive community (Fish, 1980). When encouraged to examine their personal stories in this setting, preservice teachers begin to apply the interpretive strategies of the community to construct new or expanded understandings of their experiences and beliefs as well as to use these strategies to analyze teaching narratives told by others.

Film as Tool for Exploring Teacher Identity

Film offers an excellent text for examining narrative representations of teachers because it is a text with which most students have extensive experience as well as a text they are capable of comprehending with ease. Viewers make meaning or *read* a film by engaging in a multimodal experience that involves the use of visual, auditory, spatial and musical cues (Young, Long & Myers, 2010). Just as readers of print engage in a transactional process, so, too, do the readers of a film. Because of its "dynamic, experiential context" (Berger, 1978, p. 145), film lends itself to a reader response analysis; it logically follows, then, that "film can be used to help future teachers to examine their beliefs and perceptions of teachers" (Ryan & Townsend, 2012, p. 241).

By asking preservice teachers to engage with film representations of teachers, we allow them to study a wide array of teaching personalities and approaches, from the mundane to the extraordinary. They respond intellectually and emotionally to these narratives, and they expand their understandings of the contexts in which teachers function. These narratives become part of the collection of teacher stories they carry with them and offer a source of comparison for their individual stories of personal experiences. Thus they enrich and support the ongoing process of identity formation.

Our approach to using film is based on the "film talk" strategy developed by Carol. Similar to the popular book talk assignments given in English language arts classes, students select a film related to a designated topic and prepare a presentation that explains the film's relevance to class content. Carol has used variations of this assignment in several classes, and it has become an integral part of her Teachers as Leaders course. Sheryl learned this approach when she was Carol's student and later adapted it for her Diversity in Education course. The film talk strategy has proven especially effective in these two courses that focus so strongly on teacher identity.

Addressing Diversity Through Film

Sheryl's Diversity in Education class involves understanding individual and group differences and, as such, requires examining the beliefs and values of others. More importantly, it requires looking within and examining personal beliefs and values. Research has shown explicit connections between student achievement and teacher expectations; therefore, it is essential that teachers examine and overcome any biases that would undermine positive perceptions of students (Bennett, 2011). Personal values and beliefs help to shape teachers' worldviews, which can be expanded by examining the lenses used to view the world (Bennett, 2011). As a result, the Diversity in Education course focuses considerable attention on teacher identity, both individually and within groups.

The approach to this process is largely narrative-driven, as illustrated by the three major projects: a semester-long reflective journal, an analysis of diversity in children's literature and a film talk. Because the reflective journal requires intensive exploration of existing values, beliefs and biases, the students, including both preservice and practicing teachers, sometimes find this assignment to be an uncomfortable and risky experience. However, the children's literature analysis and the film talk offer safer ways of engaging with narratives, for they focus on outside narratives.

The purpose of the Diversity in Film Talk is to give students a text for examining representations of individual and group differences and how teachers respond to those differences. Depending on the size of the class, the students work either individually or in pairs to select a film that presents a teacher addressing or responding to an issue of diversity. The students view the film in its entirety and select a 7–10-minute scene that serves as the main text of their film talk. They prepare a presentation for the class in which they set up and share the film clip and briefly outline for their classmates the main issue(s) of diversity they see highlighted in the film and what they believe to be the essential understandings the film offers. After presenting the clip and providing these talking points, they lead their classmates in a discussion (10–12 minutes) of the worldview demonstrated by the teacher and how that worldview was challenged/reinforced through the film's events.

As students initially respond to these films, they analyze (even judge) the teacher by their own teacher values, filtering their understanding of the teacher through their experiences and their nascent teacher identities. As they engage with their classmates, however, they apply the values of the community either to justify their understandings or to revise them. As indicated in journal writings and daily exit slips, each student learns from the experiences and interpretations of others: The preservice teachers see the film teacher through the eyes of their more experienced classmates, and the practicing teachers adopt the perspectives of novice teachers. This interaction does not dictate that all students have the same interpretation but it does help them to apply shared strategies. Each student is free to form her own understanding, just as she will assume her own teacher identity, but the interpretive community functions to ensure that these understandings result from meaningful discussions and in-depth evaluations.

The most common theme in the film talks is personal and professional growth. For example, one student explained in her presentation of *Beyond the Blackboard* (Gottlieb et al., 2011),

> Stacey begins the film as a new teacher overwhelmed by the poverty of her students. She has to learn to make good teaching choices, but she also has to learn to handle the stress of working with students who need so much.

She continued to explore this theme in her reflective journal:

> I used to think about how hard it would be to get all my lesson plans and grading done, but lately I worry more about how I will handle it when students don't have enough to eat or can't pay for field trips. I guess that's just part of the job, and you can't let that stop you.

The preservice teacher revealed her growing understanding of how a teacher can be burdened by the needs of her students, but she also indicated a developing sense of resilience, developing an identity not only as a teacher who cares for her students but also as a teacher who perseveres (Stanford, 2001).

Another preservice teacher also addressed the theme of personal and professional growth in her discussion of *Like Stars on Earth* (Bijili et al., 2007). She explained that the film focuses on the experiences of Ishaan, a young boy who has a learning disability and struggles with school. She highlighted the strengths of the art teacher who empathizes with Ishaan and nurtures his artistic nature, but she does not condemn the teachers who dismiss Ishaan as lazy. Instead, she determined that these teachers have an opportunity to understand "there is more to teaching than just books and rigid procedures." She explained that teachers should be as accepting of learning differences as they are of cultural differences and that they should assume responsibility when they treat students unfairly. In the ensuing class discussion, several of the practicing teachers in the class responded by sharing stories of times when they felt they had failed in their acceptance of students' learning differences. A veteran elementary teacher with 20 years of classroom experience revealed to her classmates that early in her career, she had resented how hard she had to work to help students who seemed unable to learn. Later in her journal, the teacher wrote of the shame she felt about her prior attitudes and that she had hesitated to share this story with her classmates but believed she should because it revealed how teachers grow throughout their careers. The interaction between all class members showed a willingness to examine self and to be vulnerable in revealing their thoughts—and their possible weaknesses—to each other. Vulnerability has been found to be a consistent element in analyses of the narratives of experienced teachers (Kelchtermans, 2005). Teachers often feel personal accountability for the welfare and education of their students, even as they lack control of many of the forces that impact that welfare and education (Kelchtermans, 2005). Preservice teachers can benefit from seeing that vulnerability in the stories told by their classmates and through these stories learn how to negotiate that state.

In selecting films, students often look for the teacher figure in settings other than the traditional classroom; the most notable example is the sports coach, frequently described as a teaching colleague. In their film talk, two preservice teachers opened their presentation of *Remember the Titans* (Bruckheimer et al., 2000) by acknowledging that the film is about Coach Herman Boone and the challenges he faces when coaching a newly integrated football team. They point to the significance of his team's success and say that it "opens the door to more open relationships between different groups of students." However, they focused on the relationship between Boone and his assistant, Coach Yoast. They compared the coaching partnership to a professional learning community because "they are planning and working together to teach their players just like teachers do." Although the relationship is sometimes strained by racial tensions and conflicts in the community, the two men develop a profound respect for each other. Seeing this relationship develop and discussing it within their classroom community allowed the students to explore how issues of diversity impact teachers' relationships with colleagues, how teachers function effectively as teams and how different worldviews can make those teaching teams stronger.

At the heart of the Diversity in Education course is the goal of becoming teachers who create "classroom environments where students are respected, cared for, and encouraged to develop their fullest potential" (Bennett, 2011, p. 317). We begin the class with the knowledge that we are as interested in personal self-growth as we are in improving teaching and learning, and we engage in activities that help us examine our beliefs and values for our strengths and weaknesses with the understanding that this process is likely to alter concepts of teacher identity. The film talks become part of a reciprocal process by which the students examine the film narratives and, in response to these stories, reflect on their beliefs and experiences. Within their classroom community, they develop new contexts for their understanding of teacher identity, and they work to reconcile their developing knowledge into new concepts of personal and professional identity. Ultimately, these evolving identities will become internal compasses that guide them as they work to establish just and equitable classroom and school environments (Bennett, 2011).

Teacher Leaders in Film

Carol's Teachers as Leaders graduate class contains a mixture of preservice, new and experienced teachers. The course explores "what it means to be a teacher leader in various environments" with the goal of supporting "the development of informed thoughtful teachers who are prepared for the leadership roles they will assume as part of their professional responsibility and opportunity" (Pope, 2015, p. 1). As evidenced by national teaching standards, teachers today are expected not only to be competent professionals who know their discipline and content pedagogy but also to be learners and leaders in their classrooms, schools, school systems, local communities and the larger national and global educational community (Council of Chief State School Officers, 2011).

No doubt this description includes some pretty heady concepts, so the class—in true constructivist philosophy—provides experiences that scaffold the individual development and vision of teacher leaders. Readings, assignments, class conversations and personal leadership logs, in concert with weekly electronic discussions, serve as the foundation for those visions. The framework for the class aligns with that of Katzenmeyer and Moller's (2009) *Awakening the Sleeping Giant: Helping Teachers Develop as Leaders*, a text that moves from self-awareness as a teacher leader to issues of culture, strategies for leading and, finally, creation of the personal plan of action. A critical element of our process of studying, reading, observing and making connections is to bring the "outside in" to our class; we not only interview teacher leaders but also observe leadership boards in action and, in an outside-class activity, we introduce ourselves to strangers and ask them to envision themselves in their own futures. Such experiences open us to the role of teacher leaders in education and in the world.

To the existing litany of experiences and discussions in the class, students work in pairs to review a number of teacher films and select one that represents a positive or negative example of a teacher leader. Each group gets 20 minutes to present a clip from the selected film and to discuss its portrayal of teacher leadership. They relate these characteristics to those defined by the class, examined in our readings and addressed in our discussions. They also explore what teachers and other viewers can understand from the film's message about leadership and the value of the teacher.

These weekly presentations, accompanied by a written review covering these topics in more detail, have become a linchpin in our class; they foster in-depth explorations of the potential and challenges for teachers as leaders. The assignment and attendant discussion are meant to be analytic, not a critique of the teacher leadership representation; this focus is sometimes hard to achieve because students understandably think that a film romanticizes or even demonizes the teacher. However, when students explore deeply, they recognize that certain qualities of teacher leadership exist in each of them, in many of their models or prior teachers, in the burgeoning visions of themselves and in their identities.

Each semester as we view and discuss 12–15 film talks, the classroom becomes an interpretive community (Fish, 1980). The students both experience and respond aesthetically to the films as texts and, in turn, create a new class text over time (Rosenblatt, 1983) as they consider the messages of the films as explorations of teacher leadership. Presenters often focus on diverse elements of teacher leadership that we have collaboratively discussed, defined and even role-played—for example, how teacher leaders develop, the qualities of teacher leaders, the passion of teacher leaders, the impact of culture and the power of advocacy.

One of the more memorable films that emerges each year is the true story of high school teacher Erin Gruwell, as represented by the film *Freedom Writers* (DeVito et al., 2007). In her presentation and discussion, a student chose to focus on the impact of culture in this film: "the culture of the school and the culture from which Ms. Gruwell's students enter the classroom." Because of the existing cultures, Ms. Gruwell found it difficult to engage students, to get challenging books for them to read with which they could identify and to find like-minded teachers who could see the potential of her students. After a number of missteps, Ms. Gruwell used writing of personal story, students' pain about gang violence and the loss of family and friends to that violence, as well as their curiosity about the Holocaust violence, to motivate her students. In the student's viewing of this film, she connected Barth's (2001) message that "to change the culture requires that we first be aware of the culture, the way things are here" (p. 8). Erin Gruwell had to learn the culture through a series of painful encounters in order to find a way to shift the culture with and for her students. She moved from reflecting and refracting (Pope, 1999) about her own role and its relationship to the real students in her classroom to "craft knowledge" (Barth, 2001, p. 56) as she made meaning of her war stories and learned from them in order to emerge as a teacher leader.

Because we read and reference throughout our Teachers as Leaders class the importance of being advocates for our students, teachers, parents and education, the theme of advocacy often emerges in the presentations and discussions of the films. In the ever-popular *Boy Meets World* (Jacobs, 1993–2000), Mr. Feeny, as described by one student, advocates for students by holding them to standards while also challenging, befriending and taking risks with them. He challenges Cory, who thinks anybody can teach, to teach a class on Anne Frank and get students to pass the test. Of course, Cory discovers the layers of challenges that accompany teacher leadership and appreciates the issues that Mr. Feeny discusses with his class about student behavior and teacher pay. The student suggested that Mr. Feeny represents well what most teachers want, as explained by Barth (2001): "We care deeply about our important place in the lives of students. To put it simply: in addition to a brain, we have a heart—and we want to put it to use promoting young people's learning" (p. xxxv). Mr. Feeny refuses to give up on teaching or students; he advocates for them at every turn.

Each of these film presentations precipitates extensive conversation about the qualities of teacher leadership they reflect, the controversial issues surrounding them, the commitment it takes to be a teacher leader and the concern undergirding these discussions—that is, "Do I have what it takes?" While they enjoy the film searches, the presentations and the explorations, students can be understandably overwhelmed by the tensions, the goals and the images in film. As stated earlier, it is easy for them to dismiss the whole teacher leadership concept and make it just an ideal as represented by the movies or television, produced only for monetary gain.

In response to these concerns, we reach back into the treasure trove of our experiences as students who have had teacher leaders in our lives, to the lives of the experienced teachers in the class who readily describe the moments when they see and know they have made a difference as a classroom or school leader, to our readings and ongoing analyses of the research and literature on the impact of teacher leadership. We revisit the points that there are many ways we can be teacher leaders, that our energy and priorities can come in cycles that reflect our personal and professional circumstances, that we are never perfect. What we *can* do is find ways to support our developing selves, to open our door to colleagues and build relationships, to stay healthy, to build our craft knowledge and to learn strategies for empowerment (Zemelman & Ross, 2009).

As might be expected, it is not always easy to see in a process-oriented class like Teachers as Leaders the impact and transfer of film stories' messages to actual implementation. To provide students a possible plan or structure for their own future development as teacher leaders, Carol asks them to build a plan of action at the end of the semester for their goals and strategies for implementation. Inevitably, they describe how they intend to embrace parts of the film characters' qualities and integrate them into their behaviors. They talk about commitment to students, learning about cultures, finding ways of being a part of, yet not afraid to push, existing ways of doing things. Of course, they have ideals (e.g., "I want to be like Erin Gruwell"), but, most of all, the themes that emerge involve "I'm thinking about myself differently now. I see where and how I can make a difference because it is an extension of who I am, where I started in this class, my own readiness to be a teacher leader." They speak of their ability to make friends (i.e., build professional relationships) (Zemelman & Ross, 2009); an interest in doing collaborative classroom-based research; the ease with which they contribute to meetings and are willing to negotiate for the good of students (Barth, 2001; Pope, 1999; Zemelman & Ross, 2009); their ability to be reflective practitioners who can now take students into account and share those successes and failures with trusted others (i.e., make craft knowledge) (Barth, 2001; Katzenmeyer & Moller, 2009; Pope, 1999) and the fact that they are good listeners (Pope, 1999). These qualities and behaviors are ones the literature associates with teacher leadership; they are characteristics that build a sense of self and a recognition of one's own identity as a developing professional.

Conclusion

Teacher identity is not a fixed concept but rather one that evolves within contexts. While preservice teachers may enter their teacher preparation programs with notions of teacher identity that are significantly shaped by their prior beliefs, their understandings of teacher identity are malleable and can be influenced by the theories, practices and settings they experience while in these programs. Stories are integral to teacher identity, for through stories, teachers and preservice teachers shape and reshape concepts of teacher identity (Rodgers & Scott, 2008). These stories are not limited to the individual stories of self but also include stories that are experienced through others' retelling. For that reason, we can support preservice teachers in their examination of teacher identity by providing them with a wide range of stories to examine.

Film offers an excellent source for these stories. Even as we provide these narratives to examine, we also give frames for interpreting and analyzing these texts within the classroom communities, from the abstract qualities of diversity and teacher leadership to our understandings of reader response theory and the transactional process of reading. Students engage with the teachers in film though the lens of personal beliefs and through the lens of established community understandings. Interaction with these texts and with each other influences the meaning that they create from texts—and the understandings they have of what it means to play the role of teacher.

References

Barth, R. S. (2001). *Learning by heart*. San Francisco, CA: Jossey-Bass.

Bennett, C. L. (2011). *Comprehensive multicultural education: Theory and practice* (7th ed.). Upper Saddle River, NJ: Pearson.

Berger, C. (1978). Viewing as action: Film and reader response theory. *Literature Film Quarterly, 6*(2), 144–151.

Bijili, A., Bijili, S. K., Khan, A., Ram, S., Rao, B. S., . . . Shroff, M., (Producers) & Khan, A. (Director). (2007). *Like stars on earth* [Motion picture]. India: Aamir Khan Productions.

Bressler, C. E. (2003). *Literary criticism: An introduction to theory and practice.* Upper Saddle River, NJ: Prentice Hall.

Bruckheimer, J., Flynn, M., Krug-Worthington, J., Oman, C., Sandston, P., Stenson, M. (Producer), & Yakin, B. (Director). (2000). *Remember the titans* [Motion picture]. United States: Walt Disney Pictures.

Clandinin, D. J. (1985). Personal practical knowledge: A study of teachers' classroom images. *Curriculum Inquiry, 15*(4), 361–385.

Council of Chief State School Officers. (2011, April). *Interstate Teacher Assessment and Support Consortium (InTASC) model core teaching standards: A resource for state dialogue.* Washington, DC: Council of Chief State School Officers.

DeVito, D., Durning, T., Glick-Franzheim, J., Levine, D., Morales, N., . . . Swank, H. (Producer) & LaGravenese, R. (Director). (2007). *Freedom writers* [Motion picture]. United States: Paramount Pictures.

Fish, S. (1980). *Is there a text in this class?* Cambridge, MA: Harvard University Press.

Gottlieb, A., Johann, C., McClaren, S., Molen, G. R., Shields, B. (Producers), & Bleckner, J. (Director). (2011). *Beyond the blackboard* [Motion picture]. United States: Hallmark Hall of Fame.

Hoffman-Kipp, P. (2008). Actualizing democracy: The praxis of teacher identity construction. *Teacher Education Quarterly, 35*(3), 151–164.

Jacobs, M. (Producer). (1993–2000). *Boy meets world* [Television series]. Hollywood, CA: American Broadcasting Company.

Katzenmeyer, M., & Moller, G. (2009). *Awakening the sleeping giant: Helping teachers develop as leaders* (3rd ed.). Thousand Oaks, CA: Corwin Press.

Kelchtermans, G. (2005). Teachers' emotions in educational reforms: Self-understanding, vulnerable commitment and micropolitical literacy. *Teaching and Teacher Education, 21*, 995–1006. DOI: 10.1016/j.tate.2005.06.009

Lortie, D. C. (1975). *Schoolteacher: A psychological study.* Chicago, IL: University of Chicago Press.

Olsen, B. (2008). Introducing teacher identity and this volume. *Teacher Education Quarterly, 35*(3), 3–6.

Palmer, P. J. (2007). *The courage to teach: Exploring the inner landscape of a teacher's life* (10th anniversary ed.). San Francisco, CA: Jossey-Bass.

Pope, C. A. (1999). Reflection and refraction. *English Education, 31*(3), 177–200.

Pope, C. A. (2015). *Teachers as leaders* [Course syllabus]. Department of Curriculum, Instruction and Counselor Education, College of Education, North Carolina State University, Raleigh, NC.

Powell, K. C., & Kalina, C. J. (2009). Cognitive and social constructivism: Developing tools for an effective classroom. *Education, 130*(2), 241–250.

Richardson, V. (1996). The role of attitudes and beliefs in learning to teach. In J. P. Sikula (Ed.), *Handbook of research on teacher education* (2nd ed., pp. 121–136). New York, NY: Macmillan.

Rodgers, C. R., & Scott, K. H. (2008). The development of the personal self and professional identity in learning to teach. In M. Cochran-Smith, S. Feiman-Nemser, D. J. McIntyre & K. E. Demers (Eds.), *Handbook of research on teacher education* (3rd ed., pp. 732–755). New York, NY: Routledge.

Rosenblatt, L. (1983). *Literature as exploration* (4th ed.). New York, NY: Modern Language Association.

Ryan, P. A., & Townsend, J. S. (2012). Promoting critical reflection in teacher education through popular media. *Action in Teacher Education, 34*(3), 230–248. DOI: 10.1080/01626620.2012.694019

Smagorinsky, P., Cook, L. S., Jackson, A. Y., Fry, P. G., & Moore, C. (2004). Tension in learning to teach: Accommodation and the development of a teaching identity. *Journal of Teacher Education, 55*(1), 8–24.

Stanford, B. H. (2001). Reflections of resilient, persevering urban teachers. *Teacher Education Quarterly, 23*(3), 75–87.

Stockinger, P. S. (2007). Living in, learning from, looking back, breaking through in the English language arts methods course: A case study of two preservice teachers. *English Education, 39*(3), 201–225. Retrieved from http://www.ncte.org/journals/ee

Young, C. A., Long, S., & Myers, J. (2010). Editorial: Enhancing English language arts education with digital video. *Contemporary Issues in Technology and Teacher Education, 10*(1), 7–19. Retrieved from http://www.citejournal.org/vol14/iss4

Zemelman, S., & Ross, H. (2009). *13 steps to teacher empowerment: Taking a more active role in your school community*. Portsmouth, NH: Heinemann.

3

THE ROLE OF THE TEACHER, REAL AND IMAGINED

Jason Whitney

School movies provide preservice teachers with a means of entry into a field and a line of work that grows more complex, contested and politicized with every passing year (Cochran-Smith, 2006; Debray, 2006; Giroux, 1983; MacArthur, 2012; Sandholtz, 2011; Tikly, 2004). Teachers in the 21st century enter their profession in an era in which there is little agreement about the dispositions and knowledge a teacher should possess, in part because there is little agreement about the purposes of education. It is difficult for anyone—but especially for beginners in the field—to distinguish between what is real and what is imaginary in education, what information is reliable and what constitutes misinformation about teaching. Society has a particularly unstable valuation of teachers in addition to incomplete and contradictory understandings of the kinds of work they do, in part because there is no single concept of what effective teaching practice should look like. By unpacking the theoretical and cultural constructs behind a wide range of teacher movies, however, preservice teachers have the opportunity to examine these complex issues from the varied presentations of the individuals who show up to do the work of teaching in schools.

Preservice teachers need to examine prior beliefs and expectations of what teaching will involve (Britzman, 2007; Buchmann & Schwille, 1983), while the increasingly multimodal nature of learning (Britzman, 2007; Gee, 2008; NCTE, 2008; New London Group, 1996; Swenson, Young, McGrail, Rozema & Whitin, 2006) encourages the use of film in the classroom. To integrate these two concepts, teacher educators have often turned to school films. Trier (2006) used school films as a launching point for his preservice teachers' analysis of various social theories, while Grant (2002) utilized films as "starting points for reflection about learning and teaching, diversity, and working in educational communities" (p.77) in order to challenge preservice teachers' beliefs about teaching in urban schools. Takahashi (1996) described the use of film to broaden preservice teachers' multicultural perspectives; Fontaine (2010) argued that school films may help preservice teachers "name and therefore see their world, to challenge them to perceive its injustices in new ways, and to inspire them" (pp. 67–68).

In this chapter, I describe my approach to a film-based course for preservice teachers. In my course, I organize a range of films into six subgenres, providing preservice teachers with contextual understandings (Bordwell & Thompson, 2008) of how these subgenres emerge, the reasons these films are produced and the motives people have for watching them. Following a screening of a film or television show in its entirety or through clips, preservice teachers first consider how the teacher is portrayed and whether there is any reality in the depiction before considering what approaches and/or methods the teacher offers and the constraints under which the teacher operates. They next describe their impressions of the students in the teacher's classroom and consider the extent to which the presentation of these students seems real or fictional. They then consider the intended audience for the film and the experience the audience is expected to have. Next, preservice teachers consider to what extent the film may have distorted reality in favor of convenient stereotypes and sensationalized educational topics as well as the purposes these distortions might serve. For example, I may ask what societal—even global—concerns the film takes on and what commentary, if any, the film is making about sex, race, class, socioeconomic status and the achievement gap; when a film is silent on these issues, I ask whether this is a stance in its own right. Lastly, the preservice teachers consider how the film has influenced popular and current beliefs about teachers and whether these beliefs help or harm the profession.

The Dinosaur/The Icon

This teacher movie subgenre sets up many of the stereotypes and the expectations that are subverted in other such films, presenting teachers as filling a conservative role within a traditional profession. At worst, the dinosaur is a living anachronism, a parody of himself, droning on, boring even himself, like the burned-out (but sadly, all too familiar) economics teacher droning "Bueller? Bueller?" in *Ferris Bueller's Day Off* (Chinich & Hughes, 1986). At best, the dinosaur is a beloved icon, the provider of a certain nostalgic gravity around which a body of fond memories assemble, often the symbolic soul of the school. When considering these films, preservice teachers contend with what this presentation of teacher means for them personally: The job may be asking that they subvert a part of their identity (not to mention a part of their sexuality) in service to various expectations of teachers that are widely held within American culture.

The first film we encounter is *Goodbye, Mr. Chips* (Wood & Franklin, 1939), which models teaching as respectable and deserving of respect, even from those of the highest societal rank. In this film, teaching is an appropriately masculine role for men, and Mr. Chips's support for "tradition and love of the past" is an appropriate outcome for education. The iconic teacher is so powerful within teaching culture that legions of preservice teachers often worry about their futures in terms of the filmic life situations invented in *Goodbye, Mr. Chips*, many of which have become stock through repetition in countless films. How will they face the unruly mob of students? How will they exercise discipline judiciously? What novel methods will they employ? Like Mr. Chips's threadbare coat and decency, what will be their signature? For what will they become known and celebrated? What will be their podium moments, the significant speeches of their careers?

The other dinosaur we consider is the iconic Mr. Hand from *Fast Times at Ridgemont High* (Azoff, Erickson, Linson & Heckerling, 1982), who models both the affordances and the ridiculousness of a curriculum-driven authoritative lecturer teaching an especially irrelevant U.S. history curriculum (who wouldn't spend three weeks on the Platt Amendment?). Mr. Hand masquerades as a successful teacher by maintaining order and attempting to transmit official knowledge from one generation to the next; he sees himself as a bastion of academic rigor and his students mostly play along, with the exception of Spicoli, a conspicuous mascot for '80s youth culture. In the final "righteous" minutes of the film, Mr. Hand acknowledges that he gets it, that the joke is on him, that he's already losing the battle to a youth culture so vigorous and powerful that it supplies a sort of silent laugh track to his every action. Tellingly, when Mr. Hand visits Spicoli's house, he ignores his student's bong and pornography in order to claim what he can—*his* time, the time Spicoli stole from him. As my students sometimes point out, he would be a stronger teacher if he could acknowledge how inauthentic his class has become for both teacher and student and use that realization to change his methods accordingly. The tragedy of Mr. Hand is that his role has become a farce: His students aren't learning; he knows it, they know it and yet he is powerless to change.

Lastly, we look at Miss Shields from *A Christmas Story* (Clark, Dupont & Goch, 1983), particularly the ways in which she transforms as Ralphie's perception of her changes. She is presented in three different costumes, the first of which is the dedicated Midwestern schoolteacher. Her sense of humor, as evidenced by the slight smile she betrays when collecting novelty teeth from her students, remains concealed, as it were, in a sort of drawer at her wooden desk in the front of the room. In her second guise in Ralphie's imagination, Miss Shields becomes the long-suffering Victorian schoolmarm (sexless, in black, but betraying an involuntary arousal nevertheless as she fans herself and gushes over Ralphie's essay). Lastly, she appears as the cackling witch who would deny Ralphie a BB gun, which is apparently what women become when they don't care about being nice and supporting their students' ambitions. Very elegantly, the film makes a cogent assay of the range of the chief roles available to mainstream female teachers as well as the history of a female-dominated profession (Walsh, 1995).

The Student From Hell

The Student From Hell movies are not a subgenre of inner-city teacher movies but a reworking of the vigilante cop tradition best exemplified by the *Dirty Harry* movies. Similar to the inner-city teacher movies, however, the school's culture is borrowed from movies about prison gangs. A common feature of these films is a tour of the hallways, where the White, Black, Latino and Asian gangs stake out and defend their turf. Surveillance cameras, metal detectors and staff who function as cops walk the hallways. The teachers' job in these films is to rescue the school from the stranglehold of the maniacs who have taken charge, since the schools' other teachers are deadbeats, their administrators are overlenient buck-passers and the legal protections for students are both malignant and confounding. After watching students murder, rape and degrade everything in sight, the audience is expected to delight in the catharsis of revenge as the teacher kills the bad apples, one by one.

A hyperbolic remake of the original Student From Hell movie *Blackboard Jungle* (Berman & Brooks, 1955), *Class of 1984* (Kent, Ross & Lester, 1982) is best known for a scene where a biology teacher cracks and conducts a lesson while holding his students at gunpoint. Less memorable is the lead role of Mr. Norris, a music teacher who avenges the gang rape of his wife and the hospitalization of his star student by slaughtering the school's drug-dealing thugs in a gory showdown that takes place in the school building, which also closely describes the grizzly, violence-soaked actions of the teacher-turned-administrator in *The Principal* (Brodek & Cain, 1987). These films are darkly comic but they also worry my students: What martyr (or masochist) would sign up for duty in such an abusive environment?

An interesting variant is *Election* (Berger et al., 1999), an update to the subgenre in which the student from hell is the overachieving Tracy Flick. Her unprincipled ambition and manipulation by/of adults to advance her interests undo the dedicated teacher Mr. McAllister, who enacts his version of vigilante justice by trying to "lose" two votes for Tracy Flick in order to prevent her from becoming student body president. Unlike the other films shown in this subgenre, *Election* presents the power struggle as covert, disguised and repressed, as much of the power in schools tends to be (Delpit, 1988).

The Cool/Funny Teacher

With so many stock presentations of the teacher locked into our cultural consciousness, the Cool/Funny Teacher is a subgenre that capitalizes on subverting audiences' expectations. In this subgenre, teachers are presented utilizing the same three-part story structure: delivering an expectation, reinforcing the expectation and switching to the unexpected.

In a *Saturday Night Live* skit (Spade, 2015), David Spade fails in his "uncool" adult teaching role for about 30 seconds, only to turn the tables by effectively using snark—a students' weapon—to ridicule and subdue his students. A Key and Peele (2015) sketch features a comic reversal of cultural roles: Key plays a Black substitute teacher who mispronounces his White students' names during roll call and then rages when they correct him, believing their pronunciations too outlandish to be true. In another Key and Peele (2012) clip, a haughty authoritarian substitute teacher demanding respect brings the class under control; when he reaches down for his briefcase, he accidentally rips a huge fart and then exits to loud guffaws.

Elizabeth Halsey in *Bad Teacher* (Dietrich et al., 2011) is an elementary school teacher motivated to earn performance pay in order to afford breast implants. Her basic complaint is that to accept teaching is to settle for mediocrity, which isn't especially funny; what is funny, however, are her attempts to seduce a male trust-fund teacher and her bitter rivalry with the school's other teachers. These interactions expose the other teachers' acquiescence to the demands of the traditional teacher role as grotesque in their infantilized affect, their stilted morality, their sexual incompetence, their disguised privilege and their covert ambitions. The humor arises from the revelation that many teachers are faking the dispositions they are expected to have, while Ms. Halsey retains her cool and becomes moderately effective at teaching (within the context of the film) without sacrificing her authenticity.

In *Chalk* (Akel et al., 2006), a feature-length "mocumentary" set in a suburban Texas high school, the teachers are all subversions. They admit in private that they are incompetent, know nothing about teaching, are sex-starved or pandering for teacher of the year; in public, they try their best to hide their insecurities, which only exacerbates them. *Chalk* mocks the inspirational first-year teacher movies that offer intimate insider perspectives, complete with idealistic (though hackneyed) quotations. *Chalk*, on the other hand, opens by citing a statistic that half of teachers will leave the profession after three years. Although the teachers in *Chalk* desperately try to hold their heads high, they are learning on the job and faking a competence that they don't actually possess while their year becomes progressively more disappointing; they are simply outmatched by the often embarrassing demands of the situations they face. Perhaps the funniest—and most sympathetic—teacher in *Chalk* is Mr. Lowry, who is also the most human of them all. He cannot fake his dread, his inexperience or his confusion. To the preservice teachers in my class, any admission that teachers are real people is surprising; Mr. Lowry's humiliation in requesting a book on classroom management from the librarian gets a big laugh from the preservice teachers.

The Inspirational Teacher

This genre is the idealistic subgenre of films in which teaching is portrayed as a means to a meaningful and worthwhile life. Preservice teachers love these films, as they activate and confirm the idealism that often carried them into the profession in the first place. They are especially welcome after weathering the more cynical Student From Hell movies.

In *Dead Poets Society* (Haft et al., 1989), the teacher ignites a passion for learning and awakens students to their "extraordinary" lives. Although Mr. Keating is cooler and more sophisticated than his students, he is also inspirational and charismatic. His influence may begin in the classroom but his students carry the torch themselves by (re)forming the Dead Poets Society and trying to live the life that Mr. Keating—and romantic poetry—suggests is possible. *Mr. Holland's Opus* (Cort et al., 1995) is more complicated since it features a teacher whose dream job is that of conductor but whose Plan B is that of teacher. Mr. Holland stumbles through his career only to find that teaching was more satisfying and meaningful in retrospect than it was when he was doing it. The release of his frustrated ambition in the surprise performance of his opus at the end is bittersweet, celebrating his teaching career while reminding him of an artistic life he might have had otherwise.

The last inspirational teacher we see is Mr. Lopez from *To Be and To Have* (Burah, Lalou, Sandoz & Philibert, 2002; in French, *Être et Avoir*), who manages to teach all elementary grades in a one-room schoolhouse in Normandy, France. A master teacher on the verge of retirement, he models an ordered decency absent from the rest of the world. His classroom employs a whispered quiet so steady that it serves as a sort of miraculous technology, given his context of multiple groups undertaking multiple activities within the same room. Although he is a male teacher, he eschews aggression and actively coaches his students using conflict resolution skills. It is the small touches—the unscripted conversations, the teachable moments—that demonstrate his mastery of craft. My preservice teachers are particularly moved by a scene that occurs on the last day of school, when Mr. Lopez kisses his students good-bye, and then, with the camera steady on his face, stands in the doorway holding back tears until their playful noises fade to silence.

The Inner-City Teacher

In this subgenre, which includes seminal titles like *To Sir, With Love* (Clavell & Sloan, 1967) and made-for-TV movies like *The Ron Clark Story* (Brockway et al., 2006), if you're a man and you teach in an inner-city school, you have to fight; the trick is to win over a member of one gang and take on the other gangs' "shot-caller." If you're a woman, the job will cost everything you held dear as a member of the middle class. Everybody in the school self-segregates by race, owning crucial parts of the building. The entire system is in decline, and the staff is fighting a precarious battle for what little is left under its control. Many of the students can be redeemed, however, and technologies exist that can engage students' appetite for learning. Once the bad apples have been rooted out, the teacher is in business. An audiovisual display, a well-timed connection between the curriculum and the students' lives, and students come alive to the opportunities afforded them by the dedicated teacher standing before them. The lessons they learn in the classroom carry over into their families and their relationships, and they are forever transformed, their futures burgeoning with opportunity, their entire past way of seeing the world indelibly transformed.

Robert Bulman (2002) sees the film *Freedom Writers* (DeVito & LavGranvenese, 2007) as a classic exemplar of the "middle-class fantasy" of the "teacher in the 'hood." It is only the latest in a lineage of inner-city teacher movies that promises a spectacularly meaningful and effective career if only a dedicated young White woman will make the commitment to the "underserved." *MADtv* (Bahr & Small, 2007), for example, produced a sketch called "Nice White Lady," a mock-trailer for a teacher movie about a White woman who tames a class of stereotypical gangsters. After having her efforts challenged by a colleague, the teacher declares, "With all due respect, I'm a nice White lady: I can do anything." To many of my preservice teachers, however, to turn a critical lens on such teachers is unwelcome, akin to an act of treachery, as I found when first introducing *Freedom Writers*. Even though I knew the film drew some of my students to the profession, and even with what I thought was some respectful prefacing, I wasn't prepared for the backlash when I led a discussion with my nearly all-White, all-female classes of students. Some preservice teachers dream of taking on the savior role, but fail to realize that the films from which they draw their inspiration often reinforce prior assumptions that are racist, culturally tone-deaf and reductive. Other people in these films lack the skill and interest to raise or teach these students effectively and, thus, the White teachers must deliver them into a better life, which conveniently looks more like their own (Grant, 2002).

Like the other films in this subgenre, *Stand and Deliver* (Labunka, Law, Musca & Menendez, 1988) could easily be cross-listed in the inspirational teacher genre. It starts as most of these films do, with a teacher physically confronting students and finding ways to lure in the most teachable. Mr. Escalante speaks Spanish but, unlike his students, he is South American, skilled, educated and middle-class; he doesn't live in the neighborhood, which makes him part insider/part outsider savior. He establishes credibility with a work ethic that nearly kills him, resulting in his students achieving success on an AP exam the hard way: by study sessions and sacrifice, not through gimmicks. He has unrelentingly high expectations and has little tolerance for absenteeism, in particular. My preservice teachers are quick to notice that the other teachers portrayed in these films lack high expectations and ambition; following that logic, these schools seem poised for a special individual, a game changer. They also recognize that, to get Mr. Escalante's results, you might have to do more than follow his script.

The Solution/School Reform Movies

The last decade has seen a proliferation of films meant to influence policy and public perception of the educational system in the United States. This subgenre is best characterized by the documentary *Waiting for Superman* (Birtel & Guggenheim, 2010). Critics have called the film "slick and manipulative" (Barbieri, 2011). Others point to the film's rampant factual errors (Barbieri, 2011) and its agenda of maligning the public schools and teacher unions while hyping cherry-picked charter schools (Ravitch, 2010; Strauss, 2010). In a perverse reversal of cause and effect, films of this genre represent the public schools as the source of such societal phenomena as high-poverty inner cities and social stratification. The films typically include seemingly obligatory animated sequences of students being conveyed hither and thither on conveyer belts, tearful lottery drawings and rooms of unfireable deadbeat teachers coasting on union protections. My students explore the credibility gap that opens in one such film, *The Lottery* (Ashman et al., 2010), which proposes as an alternative to public education a handful of freakishly well-funded charter schools. While doing little to reform education, the film succeeds in disparaging the professional credibility and reducing the labor conditions of the few and shrinking number of teachers willing to commit long-term to careers in public schools.

The constant refrain of Solution/School Reform Movies is that the schools are failing, which has become a sort of throwaway line, a mandatory and lazy talking point—and one that is believed. Most of the preservice teachers in my class admit to being disgusted with teachers and unions and the state of public education after seeing *Waiting for Superman*. They then speak fondly of their own public school educations, which, as Diane Ravitch (2010) points out, is how three out of four of Americans feel about public education in general:

> The annual Gallup poll about education shows that Americans are overwhelmingly dissatisfied with the quality of the nation's schools, but 77 percent of public school parents award their own child's public school a grade of A or B, the highest level of approval since the question was first asked in 1985.
>
> *(pp. 1–2)*

A notable bright spot that speaks back to the misguided reform movement is *Hard Times at Douglass High: A No Child Left Behind Report* (Raymond & Raymond, 2008), which documents a year in a failing (as categorized by No Child Left Behind) high-poverty inner-city Baltimore school. In many ways, the film offers a corrective to the Inner-City School and Student From Hell subgenres. More than the other films, this documentary shows that teaching is hard, yet even within that context, wonderful students and teachers abound. It is a film that showcases the complexity of education and uses the story of the teachers and administrators who soldier on, despite multiple constraints, to create high-quality instruction, which in turn shows the value of the school.

With that, the survey of teacher movies concludes, with preservice teachers having examined the role and image of teachers, real or imagined, and the constraints under which they operate. By the end of the course, they have considered how teachers navigate complex race, class and gender dynamics. They have held multiple discussions on the achievement gap. They have evaluated innovative teaching practices. They have developed a sense of the work they will soon be doing with eyes open wider to the complexities of the educational field. Perhaps more than anything, they now understand what is meant by the profession of teaching, real instead of imagined.

References

Akel, L., Akel, M., Alvarez, A., Amodei, J., Darbyshire, C. C., . . . Spurlock, M. (Producers), & Akel, M. (Director). (2006). *Chalk* [Motion picture]. United States: Virgil Films and Entertainment.

Ashman, B., Bartels, T., Lanuti, E., Lawler, J., Sackler, M., Schellpfeffer, B. (Producer), & Sackler (Director). (2010). *The lottery* [Motion picture]. United States: Variance Films.

Azoff, I., Erickson, C. O., Linson, A. (Producers), & Heckerling, A. (Director). (1982). *Fast times at Ridgemont High* [Motion picture]. United States: Universal Pictures.

Bahr, F., & Small, A. (2007). Episode #1215. *MADtv*. Retrieved from http://www.tv.com/shows/madtv/episode-1215–982918/

Barbieri, M. (2011, May 25). A teacher reviews *Waiting for Superman*. *The Stenhouse Blog.* Retrieved from http://blog.stenhouse.com/archives/2011/05/25/a-teacher-reviews-waiting-for-superman/

Berger, A., Burke, J., Gale, D., Rose, J., Samples, K., . . . Yerxa, R. (Producers), & Payne, A. (Director). (1999). *Election* [Motion picture]. United States: Paramount Pictures.

Berman, P. S. (Producer), & Brooks, R. (Director). (1955). *Blackboard jungle* [Motion picture]. United States: Metro-Goldwyn-Mayer.

Birtel, M. (Producer), & Guggenheim, D. (Director). (2010). *Waiting for Superman* [Motion picture]. United States: Paramount Pictures.

Bordwell, D., & Thompson, P. (2008). *Film art: An introduction* (8th ed.). Boston, MA: McGraw-Hill.

Britzman, D. P. (2007). Teacher education as uneven development: Toward a psychology of uncertainty. *International Journal of Leadership in Education, 10*(1), 1–12.

Brockway, J., Burkons, H., Cox, T., Friend, B., Gilad, A., . . . Randall, J. (Producer), & Haines, R. (Director). (2006). *The Ron Clark story* [Motion picture]. United States: Turner Network Television.

Brodek, T. H. (Producer), & Cain, C. (Director). (1987). *The principal* [Motion picture]. United States: Tristar Pictures.

Buchmann, M., & Schwille, J. (1983). Education: The overcoming of experience. *American Journal of Education, 92*(1), 30–51.

Bulman, R. (2002). Teachers in the 'Hood: Hollywood's middle-class fantasy. *The Urban Review, 34*(3), 251–276.

Burah, R., Lalou, S., Sandoz, G. (Producer), & Philibert, N. (Director). (2002). *To be and to have* [Motion picture]. United States: New Yorker Films.

Chinich, M. (Producer), & Hughes, J. (Director). (1986). *Ferris Bueller's day off* [Motion picture]. United States: Paramount Pictures.

Clark., B., Dupont, R., Goch, G. (Producer), & Clark, B. (Director). (1983). *A Christmas story* [Motion picture]. United States: Metro-Goldwyn-Mayer.

Clavell, J., Sloan, J. R. (Producers), & Clavell, J. (Director). (1967). *To Sir, with love* [Motion picture]. United States: Columbia Pictures.

Cochran-Smith, M. (2006). *Policy, practice, and politics in teacher education: Editorials from the Journal of Teacher Education.* Thousand Oaks, CA: Corwin Press.

Cort, R. W., Duncan, P. S., Field, T., James, J., Kroopf, S., . . . Teitler, W. (Producer), & Herek, S. (Director). (1995). *Mr. Holland's opus* [Motion picture]. United States: Buena Vista Pictures.

Debray, E. (2006). *Politics, ideology and education: Federal policy during the Clinton and Bush administration.* New York, NY: Teachers College Press.

Delpit, L. D. (1988). The silenced dialogue: Power and pedagogy in educating other people's children. *Harvard Educational Review, 58*(3), 280–298.

DeVito, D. (Producer), & LavGranvenese, G. (Director). (2007). *Freedom writers* [Motion picture]. United States: Paramount Pictures.

Dietrich, C., Eisenbert, L., Householter, D. B., Kacandes, G., Kasdan, J., . . . Stupnitsky, G. (Producers), & Kasdan, J. (Director). (2011). *Bad teacher* [Motion picture]. United States: Columbia Pictures.

Fontaine, H. (2010). An interdisciplinary proposal for employing film to release the imaginations of preservice teachers. *Journal of Aesthetic Education, 44*(1), 58–69.

Gee, J. P. (2008). *Social linguistics and literacies: Ideology in discourses* (3rd ed.). New York, NY: Routledge.

Giroux, H. A. (1983). *Theory and resistance in education: A pedagogy for the opposition.* South Hadley, MA: Bergin & Garvey.

Grant, P. A. (2002). Using popular films to challenge preservice teachers' beliefs about teaching in urban schools. *Urban Education, 37*(1), 77–95.

Haft, S., Henderson, D., Witt, P. J., Thomas, T. (Producers), & Weir, P. (Director). (1989). *Dead poets society* [Motion picture]. United States: Touchstone Pictures.

Kent, A., Lester, M. L., Ross, M. L. (Producer), & Lester, M. L. (Director). (1982). *Class of 1984* [Motion picture]. United States: United Film Distribution.

Key, K-M., & Peele, J. (2012). I'm retired. *Key and Peele.* Retrieved from http://www.tv.com/shows/key-and-peele/im-retired-2593082/

Key, K-M., & Peele, J. (2015). Substitute teacher. *Key and Peele.* Retrieved from http://www.cc.com/video-clips/w5hxki/key-and-peele-substitute-teacher-pt—1

Labunka, I., Law, L., Musca, T. (Producers), & Menéndez, R. (Director). (1988). *Stand and deliver* [Motion picture]. United States: Warner Bros.

MacArthur, J. (2012). Virtuous mess and wicked clarity: Struggle in higher education research. *Routledge Journals, 31*(3), 419–430.

National Council of Teachers of English. (2008). *The NCTE definition of 21st century literacies.* Urbana, IL: National Council of Teachers of English.

New London Group. (1996). A pedagogy of multiliteracies: Designing social futures. *Harvard Educational Review, 66*(1), 60–92.

Ravitch, D. (2010, November 11). The myth of charter schools. *The New York Review of Books.* Retrieved from http://www.nybooks.com/articles/archives/2010/nov/11/myth-charter-schools/

Raymond, A., & Raymond, S. (Producers & Directors). (2008). *Hard times at Douglass High: A No Child Left Behind report card* [Motion picture]. United States: HBO.

Sandholtz, J. H. (2011). Preservice teachers' conceptions of effective and ineffective teaching practices. *Teacher Education Quarterly, 38*(3), 27–47.

Spade, D. (2015). David Spade uses classroom management! *SNL.* Retrieved from https://www.youtube.com/watch?v=0WXhtyVs9Gk&feature=youtube_gdata_player

Strauss, V. (2010, September 27). What 'Superman' got wrong, point by point. *The Washington Post* [Review of motion picture]. Retrieved from http://voices.washingtonpost.com/answer-sheet/guest-bloggers/what-superman-got-wrong-point.html

Swenson, J., Young, C. A., McGrail, E., Rozema, R., & Whitin, P. (2006). Extending the conversation: New technologies, new literacies, and English education. *English Education, 38*(4), 351–369.

Takahashi, M. (1996). *Multicultural teacher preservice education* [Dissertation]. McGill University, Montreal, Canada.

Tikly, L. (2004). Education and the new imperialism. *Comparative Education, 40*, 173–198.

Trier, J. (2006). Reconceptualizing literacy through a discourses perspective by analyzing literacy events represented in films about schools. *Journal of Adolescent & Adult Literacy, 49*(6), 510–523.

Walsh, E. (1995). *Schoolmarms: Women in America's schools*. San Francisco, CA: Caddo Gap Press.

Wood, S., & Franklin, S. (Directors). (1939). *Goodbye, Mr. Chips* [Motion picture]. United Kingdom: Metro-Goldwyn-Mayer.

4

COMING OF AGE IN THE CLASSROOM

Representations of Teachers in the Short Fiction of Toni Cade Bambara and Sandra Cisneros

Rodrigo Joseph Rodríguez

> There are also other kinds of teachers: those without a sense of agency, those who impose inarticulateness on students who seem alien and whose voices the teachers prefer not to hear. Yet the eager teachers do appear and reappear— teachers who provoke learners to pose their own questions, to teach themselves, to go at their own pace, to name their worlds. Young learners have to be noticed, it is now being realized; they have to be consulted, they have to question why.
>
> (Greene, 2000, p. 11)

Coming of Age

As a teacher develops a sense of identity and comes of age among students, students themselves come of age in their teacher's presence during that identity formation. A teacher's identity can impact students in varied ways, including the study of literature. For young people, our schools can be places filled with joy and tenderness or, for our most vulnerable learners, fraught with fear and tribulation; "to be noticed," as Greene (2000) reminds us, supports self-awareness and growth in both students and teachers. Recent ethnographic research studies on children's coming of age reveal some of the most supportive, as well as difficult, schooling and residential environments (Jiménez, 2008; Kirkland, 2014; López & López, 2010; Vilson, 2014). Literary criticism on traumatic experience and familiar affinities reveals testimonies of struggle, perseverance and survival in the African American literary canon, among others (Griffiths, 2010; Morris, 2014; Royster, 2000).

This chapter is informed by Olsen's (2008) definition of and perspectives about teacher identity, which

> highlight the power of context in teacher learning. And many stress critical examinations of race, culture, power, and history in teacher education.

Aligned with these perspectives and practices, teacher identity as analytic frame draws attention to the holistic, dynamic, situated nature of teacher development.

(p. 5)

More specifically, school-based narratives frequently address teachers' use of language, which can communicate how the student is made to feel and, if an instructional lesson is involved, how the student comes to understanding and learning through words, actions and interactions (Kirkland, 2014; Valenzuela, 1999; Vilson, 2014).

As Denton (2014) acknowledges, "Our words and tone of voice play a critical role in establishing the nature of our relationships with students and also can influence students' relationships with each other" (p. 6). These caring relationships with students and intentional uses of language are significant for advancing learning in our classrooms, establishing mutual trust and supporting the essential practices for teaching and learning. Representations of teachers and their use of language are often reflective of teacher identity; they also reflect how communication and trust shape interactions with students. A caring, reflective teacher adopts practices that Paris (2012) advocates through culturally sustaining pedagogy, which "seeks to perpetuate and foster—to sustain—linguistic, literate, and cultural pluralism as part of the democratic project of schooling" (p. 95). Such practices are, in turn, connected to the interconnections of social justice: literacy, power, identity formation and affirmation (Selvester & Summers, 2012).

So, what is the characterization of teachers in literature? More specifically, how do teachers and children gain visibility in short fiction? In popular culture, the classroom teacher can be represented as possessing messiah-like abilities for students and their families (i.e., a savior), collecting an undeserved salary with hardly any influence upon society (i.e., a scapegoat) or being indifferent to the students' interests and needs (i.e., a schoolmarm). Young adult literature, such as Anderson's (2011) *Speak*, Alexie's (2009) *The Absolutely True Diary of a Part-Time Indian*, Medina's (2013) *Yaqui Delgado Wants to Kick Your Ass*, Quintero's (2014) *Gabi, a Girl in Pieces* and Anderson's (2015) *Zack Delacruz: Me and My Big Mouth*, includes teachers as characters who fit or challenge these representations. Anthologized short stories, such as Bradbury's (2010) "All Summer in a Day," Jackson's (2010) "Charles" and Maxwell's (1994) "Love," often feature similar representations of teachers and classroom settings. Admittedly, (mis)representations of teachers can limit perceptions and (mis)shape realities teachers face in the profession; these (mis)representations can, in turn, inform and advance teacher identity development, drawing on what occurs in the classroom as well as the realities that extend beyond schooling and school. As such, representations of teachers can both help and hinder the teaching lives of beginning teachers who are in formative, coming-of-age stages within the profession.

In short, what the general public views about the classroom teacher can distort— or, at best, mislead—perceptions of public education and the teaching profession unless counternarratives challenge the "single story" that Adichie (2009) notes leads to critical misunderstanding and disenfranchisement if it goes unchallenged; rather, we must question and oppose taken-for-granted assumptions to provide the complexity of narratives and intersections of diverse realities. This chapter will examine two short stories widely read in middle school grades that reflect competing representations of the teacher: Toni Cade Bambara's (2003) "Geraldine Moore the Poet" and Sandra Cisneros's (2004) "Eleven." The teachers and youth characters the authors create come alive and come of age in these two distinct short fiction works. Through these stories, preservice teachers can learn about the competing and contradictory representations of the classroom teacher and consider a teacher identity that advocates for students' diverse abilities, backgrounds, cultures, interests and needs through social action and justice. I analyze these short stories to provide windows to and mirrors of teacher identity in short fiction and how these lenses can be instructive in teacher education.

Classroom Teachers in Short Fiction

With meticulous insights, Bambara and Cisneros use their short stories to introduce the main characters' families and their neighborhood lives, revealing caring relationships and emotions as significant pillars for learning, teaching and growing. In their writing, Bambara and Cisneros often adopt the child voice—in particular, that of the young female—to communicate how a child perceives, navigates and confronts an indifferent world that can be filled with hurt and surprise. Adults are frequently presented as indifferent to children's perceptions and feelings, which are essential to understand, create and maintain relationships in the presence of peers and other adults. In these short stories, two female protagonists are led into two distinct classrooms that reveal how teachers notice and respond to children's curiosities, circumstances and needs.

Bambara's "Geraldine Moore the Poet"

In the presence of her classmates and their English language arts teacher, Mrs. Scott, Geraldine Moore discovers her talent as a young poet, despite the problems and hurdles she faces daily at home, on her walk to school and in the classroom. The story opens with her frustration. Geraldine's home life is stretched thin; she does not have daily essentials and resources, such as clothing and food; her family faces eviction from their apartment. Her home life appears irrelevant to and unrecognized in her public schooling, however, which does not take into consideration the personal hardships she endures as a young girl and student coming of age. As a result, she is forced to mask her internal and external conflicts and ongoing struggles for survival in the face of her poverty. This exacerbates her attention span, learning interests and classroom behavior. Through snapshots of her school day, Geraldine reveals how teachers in subjects such as geometry, health and English make learning demands that are disconnected from her everyday struggle for survival, her self-awareness and her outlook on life. Despite this indifference, Geraldine is forced to make sense of these realities in her quest to make a life both at home and at school.

As the short story unfolds, Geraldine's teachers and schooling appear consistently as culturally irrelevant and unresponsive to her struggles and needs. In one example, Mr. Stern, Geraldine's geometry teacher, explains how to solve problems using theorems: "For your homework, set up your problems this way" (pp. 311–312). Geraldine is disconnected from the "cubes and cylinders in the room" as she "sat at her desk adding up a column of figures in her notebook—the rent, the light and gas bills, a new gym suit, some socks" (p. 311). With hope, we learn, "Maybe they would move somewhere else, and she could have her own room. Geraldine turned the squares and triangles [she drew] into little houses in the country."

In his teaching, Mr. Stern's use of language is direct and methodical. Despite his use of direct language, Geraldine remains perplexed by the formula that includes "TO FIND" and "GIVEN" as the two headers that require solving. In fact, Geraldine wants to problem solve: "Geraldine started to raise her hand to ask what all these square and angles had to do with solving real problems, like the ones she had" (p. 312). In a metacognitive voice that becomes audible through Bambara's narrator, however, we hear, "*Better not. Your big mouth got you in trouble last term.*" Furthering Mr. Stern's approach and instruction, Mrs. Potter, the health teacher, declares, "Right now your body is manufacturing all the proteins and tissues and energy you will need to get through tomorrow." Geraldine is left to wonder about the significance through a self-assessment: "*How? How does my body know what it will need, when I don't even know what I'll need to get through tomorrow?*"

Mrs. Scott, Geraldine's English language arts teacher, is different; she is described as having a "silk scarf around her neck" as she asks students to share their homework. Their assignment was to have written a poem of their own. Mrs. Scott adjusts her instruction and says, "So for those who haven't done their homework, try it now. Try expressing what it is to be . . . to be alive in this . . . this glorious world" (p. 313); "Oh, brother," mutters Geraldine quietly. Mrs. Scott's use of language reveals that she wants to be considerate of her students' lives; she allows them to be part of the lesson by offering the homework assignment again in class.

In her English class, however, Geraldine experiences a moment of catharsis and explains to Mrs. Scott and her classmates why she could not complete her homework. Geraldine reveals her dilemmas at home and in school by conceding, "I can't write a poem, Mrs. Scott, because nothing lovely's been happening in my life" (p. 313). Mrs. Scott affirms Geraldine's intellect, creativity and imagination by addressing Geraldine and the class, saying, "You have just said the most . . . the most poetic thing, Geraldine Moore. Class, you have just heard the best poem you will ever hear. I'd like you to copy it down" (p. 314). Mrs. Scott writes the poem on the board, and the students copy it, "bad grammar and all":

Nothing lovely's been happening in my life.
I haven't seen a flower since Mother's Day.

And the sun don't even shine on my side of the street.
No robins come sing on my window sill.
Just the rain comes, and the bills come,
And the men to move out our furniture.
I'm sorry, but I can't write no pretty poem.

Geraldine is affirmed after the bell rings, as "everyone came over to smile at Geraldine or to tap her on the shoulder or to kid her about being the school poet" (p. 314). As the short story comes to an end, Geraldine gathers her personal belongings and waits for Mrs. Scott to turn from the chalkboard and face her, but she does not. Instead, as she exits Mrs. Scott's classroom, Geraldine "thought she heard a whimper—the way Mrs. Watson's dog whimpered sometimes—and she saw Mrs. Scott's shoulders shake a little" (p. 314).

Geraldine, her classmates and the reader learn through Mrs. Scott's words and actions that Geraldine is, indeed, a poet, as her words become lines and stanzas of poetry on the chalkboard for all to read and copy. In this way, Mrs. Scott represents the "eager teacher" that Greene (2000) describes as "provok[ing] learners to pose their own questions, to teach themselves, to go at their own pace, to name their worlds" (p. 11). In Mrs. Scott, Geraldine finds a caring, responsive adult and teacher who listens and adjusts her teaching for learning.

Greene (2000) urges us to reflect on what our teaching does and does not allow in the development and growth of young people. She advocates for an environment that values young people's voices and a space that cultivates imagination and the arts. In the process, students build agency and identity while gaining self-awareness and connections to concepts under study and in the larger world. Similarly, Nieto (2013) envisions a more humane teacher identity and practice with a social justice component that support Paris's (2012) vision of a "democratic project": "Teachers cannot negate their own identity and power when interacting with students, but they *can* attempt to understand their identity as intertwined with those of the students they teach" (p. 126). Nieto's argument is a model and inspiration for how we might infuse humane and democratic values and daily struggles for survival into our classrooms and how we can build and strengthen our identities as teachers among our very own students.

Cisneros's "Eleven"

With her birthday falling on a school day, Rachel faces a difficult circumstance on the day she turns 11. Even at 11, Rachel has convictions about her coming of age, explaining, "[S]ome days you might say something stupid, and that's the part of you that's still ten. Or maybe some days you might need to sit on your mama's lap because you're scared, and that's the part of you that's five" (p. 6). Rachel's interpretations reveal how she has already begun to conceptualize her own sense of self—her identity formation, as it were—which speaks to social and developmental needs as well as consequences.

Rachel's understanding about growing up and gaining an identity that matches one's numeric age is helpful when Mrs. Price, her teacher, finds an ugly, old, unwashed red sweater left behind in the coatroom. Mrs. Price believes the sweater belongs to Rachel and commands her to own a sweater that is not hers. When Rachel attempts to explain to Mrs. Price that the sweater does not belong to her, the teacher dismisses her words and puts the sweater on Rachel's desk. The teacher is presented as indifferent to a child and thus becomes a symbol of what children face as they are developing their own identity among adults with an authoritarian presence.

The conflict is further escalated when a classmate, Sylvia Saldívar, suggests to Mrs. Price that the sweater does belong to Rachel; Mrs. Price then misremembers: "Of course it's yours. I remember you wearing it once" (p. 7). This coconspiratorial agreement between a child and adult against a classmate further intensifies the breach of trust in the classroom. Although Rachel pushes the sweater to the corner of her desk, it still torments her. She avoids following the instructions because she is not being heard, much less cared for, by her teacher. Rachel's dilemma is summed up in her own words as she surrenders to Mrs. Price's authoritative voice: "Because she's older and the teacher, she's right and I'm not" (p. 8). For a child to interpret the situation as such and determine that she must acquiesce further confirms development of an identity that includes maturity as well as distrust about how schooling functions.

With impatience and anger, Mrs. Price commands, "Rachel, you put that sweater on right now and no more nonsense. Now!" (p. 8). Rachel feels she cannot do anything but acquiesce to an adult's demands, although she feels unheard, sad and lonely on her birthday. In a symbolic overtone that mirrors her external and internal conflicts, Rachel cries into her own arms before her classmates and teacher. Cisneros vividly appeals to our senses when she describes Rachel: "My face all hot and spit coming out of my mouth because I can't stop the little animal noises coming out of me, until there aren't any more tears left in my eyes, and it's just my body shaking like when you have the hiccups" (p. 9). Shortly before the bell rings for lunch, Rachel's classmate, "stupid Phyllis López, who is even dumber that Sylvia Saldívar, says she remembers the red sweater is hers! I take it off right away and give it to her, only Mrs. Price pretends like everything is okay" (p. 9). Even after her classmate Phyllis admits her error, the teacher expresses neither regret nor apology for her actions, which could open communications between child and adult. Instead, Mrs. Price proceeds with school business as usual.

In this story about schooling and the loss of innocence in the face of authority, Rachel becomes acquainted with the literacies of injustice and indifference at the hands of her teacher and classmates. Both teacher and youth identities are tested, informed and formed through hardship and unfairness in the classroom. In keeping with her coming-of-age wisdom, Rachel wishes she were much older, unseen to the naked eye and far away from this world she must inhabit:

> I'm eleven today. I'm eleven, ten, nine, eight, seven, six, five, four, three, two, and one, but I wish I was one hundred and two. I wish I was anything but

eleven, because I want today to be far away already, far away like a runaway balloon, like a tiny *o* in the sky, so tiny-tiny you have to close your eyes to see it.

(p. 9)

This short story confirms Greene's (2000) assessment about the kind of teacher who "impose[s] inarticulateness on students who seem alien and whose voices the teachers prefer not to hear" (p. 11). Rachel's interactions at school reveal hostile conditions for learning and socialization in the classroom; the child's voice remains unheard and underdeveloped due to a teacher's coercive authority and direct language use, while her female classmates disregard her emotions and logic. As young female characters in the two short stories, both Rachel and Geraldine come of age by discerning power, authority and voicelessness in a school setting that should be governed by fairness, care and a sense of justice.

Teacher Identity and Education

As illustrated in the short fiction by Bambara and Cisneros, young people's observations can be instructive to adults and schooling practices. Bambara and Cisneros voice the turbulent emotions that youth feel while growing up, facing injustice, experiencing disappointment and figuring out uncertainty in the presence of authoritarian teachers as they, too, form and shape their identities that should include care, empathy and regard for young people. Examining a teacher without agency and care (Mrs. Price) and a teacher eager to notice and colearn with her students (Mrs. Scott) establishes key insights into how teachers can reflect on and examine their intentions, practices and interactions (Greene, 2000). It is not enough to simply teach; rather, teachers must engage deliberately with young people and connect with them through socially responsible literacies and just approaches that value the adolescents they are entrusted to guide in the turbulent world they inhabit and must soon contribute to for social action and justice.

In Bambara's story, Mrs. Scott's teacher identity is attentive to and flexible with students, as when she explains, "So for those who haven't done their homework, try it now" (p. 313). Mrs. Scott shows Geraldine that her life outside the classroom possesses value and meaning; more importantly, there is also value in putting words to these worlds she inhabits, navigates and survives. She explains, "Sometimes an idea [for a poem] takes the form of a picture—an image" (p. 313). By including Geraldine's everyday world in the classroom, the teacher reveals an identity that accepts her student's socioeconomic realities having a place in school. Here, Olsen's (2008) definition of teacher identity reminds us about the "holistic, dynamic, situated nature of teacher development" (p. 5). Bambara's short story ends with Mrs. Scott unable to look at Geraldine; in becoming acquainted with her student's life, her identity as a teacher alters as she teaches among and learns from her own students.

In Cisneros's story, Mrs. Price ignores Rachel's voice and the concerns she raises about the sweater's owner. Rachel speaks up, but her own voice does not match her teacher's in any way. She begins, "That's not, I don't, you're not ... Not mine. [. . .] Not mine, not mine, not mine" (pp. 7–8). Rachel experiences aliena-tion, loneliness and abandonment in the classroom on her birthday, which informs her identity and sense of self; she is made to feel small and insignificant, even though she possesses imagination, joy and zest for learning. Rachel's identity is influenced by Mrs. Price's lack of empathy and care, while Mrs. Price's identity is revealed as authoritative, indifferent and hostile to her students. In the end, Rachel favors invisibility as an identity in the presence of a teacher. Only through invis-ibility, she believes, can her full self emerge and exist in the presence of a teacher identity that assumes authority and exhibits unfairness.

Bambara's and Cisneros's stories are guided by cathartic moments that involve witnessing and transformation for the young characters. The characters' experi-ences are made visible for the reader, and, in turn, the reader can reflect on a student's journey filled with moments of alienation, transition, maturation and responsibility in and out of the school setting. The short stories teach us, as well, that teachers, like students, may struggle to make sense of the world; the mani-festations and ramifications of making sense form their identity and inform their schooling and teaching journey. As Jenlink (2014) argues,

> We [teachers] struggle for identity and recognition each day, we are invisible to many, made so not by our choice but by the social, cultural, and political tensions in our society. The teacher entering a classroom feels this invisibil-ity, both for him- or herself and for the students.
>
> *(p. xiii)*

The struggle Jenlink describes can be alienating and overwhelming for preservice teachers or it can become empowering as more teachers adopt culturally sustaining and socially just pedagogies in their student-teacher connections and relationships for learning.

In an era of teaching and learning accountability, teachers must maintain an aware-ness of the emotional, social, political and pedagogical realities that face our profes-sion and our students' lives, within and beyond the classroom and school. Sherman (2013) challenges us to remain relevant and responsive in our teaching, observing, "Responsiveness in teaching beckons individuals who are energized and inspired by the prospect of engaging in challenging intellectual work with deep moral roots, individuals who are not daunted, and may even be energized, by uncertainty" (p. 10). The uncertainty that Sherman references drives both short stories. Bambara illustrates how a teacher can connect to the lives of her students to sustain them, while Cisneros reminds us that a teacher must be helpful—not hurtful—in young people's lives.

References

Adichie, C. A. (2009, October 7). The danger of a single story. *TED Talks* [Video podcast]. Retrieved from https://www.youtube.com/watch?v=D9Ihs241zeg

Alexie, S. (2009). *The absolutely true diary of a part-time Indian*. New York, NY: Little, Brown Books for Young Readers. (Original work published 2007)

Anderson, J. (2015). *Zack DelaCruz: Me and my big mouth*. New York, NY: Sterling Children's Books.

Anderson, L. H. (2011). *Speak*. New York, NY: Square Fish. (Original work published 1999)

Bambara, T. C. (2003). Geraldine Moore the poet. In *Multicultural America: A Nextext anthology* (pp. 309–314). Evanston, IL: McDougal Littell, Houghton Mifflin.

Bradbury, R. (2010). *The stories of Ray Bradbury*. New York, NY: Everyman's Library.

Cisneros, S. (2004). Eleven. In *Woman Hollering Creek and other stories* (pp. 6–9). London, UK: Bloomsbury. (Original work published 1991)

Denton, P. (2014). *The power of our words: Teacher language that helps children learn* (2nd ed.). Turners Fall, MA: Northeast Foundation for Children.

Greene, M. (2000). *Releasing the imagination: Essays on education, the arts, and social change*. San Francisco, CA: Jossey-Bass, Wiley.

Griffiths, J. L. (2010). *Traumatic possessions: The body and memory in African American women's writing and performance*. Charlottesville: University of Virginia Press.

Jackson, S. (2010). Charles. In J. C. Oates (Ed.), *Shirley Jackson: Novels and stories* (pp. 73–77). New York, NY: The Library of America.

Jenlink, P. M. (Ed.). (2014). *Teacher identity and the struggle for recognition: Meeting the challenges of a diverse society*. Lanham, MD: Rowman & Littlefield Education.

Jiménez, F. (2008). *Reaching out*. Boston, MA: Houghton Mifflin.

Kirkland, D. (2014). *A search past silence: The literacy of young Black men*. New York, NY: Teachers College Press.

López, M. P., & López, G. R. (2010). *Persistent inequality: Contemporary realities in the education of undocumented Latina/o students*. New York, NY: Routledge.

Maxwell, W. (1994). *All the days and nights: The collected stories*. New York, NY: Alfred A. Knopf.

Medina, M. (2013). *Yaqui Delgado wants to kick your ass*. Somerville, MA: Candlewick Press.

Morris, S. M. (2014). *Close kin and distant relatives: The paradox of respectability in Black women's literature*. Charlottesville: University of Virginia Press.

Nieto, S. (2013). *Finding joy in teaching students of diverse backgrounds: Culturally responsive and socially just practices in U.S. classrooms*. Portsmouth, NH: Heinemann.

Olsen, B. (2008). Introducing teacher identity and this volume. *Teacher Education Quarterly*, *35*(3), 3–6.

Paris, D. (2012). Culturally sustaining pedagogy: A needed change in stance, terminology, and practice. *Educational Researcher*, *41*(3), 93–97.

Quintero, I. (2014). *Gabi, a girl in pieces*. El Paso, TX: Cinco Puntos Press.

Royster, J. J. (2000). *Traces of a stream: Literacy and social change among African American women*. Pittsburgh, PA: University of Pittsburgh Press.

Selvester, P. M., & Summers, D. G. (2012). *Socially responsible literacy: Teaching adolescents for purpose and power*. New York, NY: Teachers College Press.

Sherman, S. C. (2013). *Teacher preparation as an inspirational practice: Building capacities for responsiveness*. New York, NY: Routledge.

Valenzuela, A. (1999). *Subtractive schooling: U.S.–Mexican youth and the politics of caring*. Albany: State University Press of New York.

Vilson, J. L. (2014). *This is not a test: A new narrative on race, class, and education*. Chicago, IL: Haymarket Books.

5

FROM CONTENT LITERATE TO PEDAGOGICALLY CONTENT LITERATE

Teachers as Tools for Social Justice

Nalova Westbrook

How does one begin to compare the teaching of a Latino calculus teacher at a high school in East Los Angeles to the teaching of a White French teacher teaching French language and literature at a secondary institution in urban Paris? Moreover, how might analyzing the teaching of a computer scientist and of a French connoisseur help us understand the process of being content literate to becoming pedagogically content literate? Finally, how might the process of becoming pedagogically content literate be a matter of teaching for social justice? These are some of the questions that foreground my reading/literacy in the content area course for preservice secondary candidates.

I show the films *Stand and Deliver* (Labunka, Law, Musca & Menendez, 1988) and *The Class/Entre les Murs* (Arnal, Benjo, Letellier, Scotta & Cantet, 2008) as part of a move to help candidates see the "real-world" utility of what we're learning in action. *Stand and Deliver* depicts Mr. Escalante as the savior of Latino students learning calculus to escape their impoverished surroundings. By contrast, *The Class/Entre les Murs* portrays Mr. Marin as the scapegoat of ethnically diverse middle school students learning French. Although both teachers are very content literate, functionalist literacy education is not enough to meet the needs of their learners.

As my earlier questions indicate, considering literacy pedagogy for secondary learners supports discussion of the implications of secondary teachers' sociocultural backgrounds. We observe that teaching one's content—whether it be math or French—cannot be separated from the culture of the teacher, the learners and the schooling institution. In fact, one may observe that for Mr. Escalante and Mr. Marin to be pedagogically content literate in math and French—particularly within their unique school settings—they must use tools of literacy education in ways that help them to teach for social justice. From these two films, along with other activities in the course, preservice secondary candidates come to see that the process of moving from content to pedagogical content literacy is, in part, an issue of social justice.

Content Literacy and Pedagogical Content Literacy

This chapter explores the understanding of secondary preservice teacher candidates as it moves from being content literate to becoming pedagogically content literate. By content literate, I draw on Bean, Readence and Baldwin's (2011) notion of content area literacy:

> the level of reading and writing skill necessary to read, comprehend, and react to appropriate instructional level materials in a given subject area . . . [the ability] to communicate knowledge and strategies . . . to help . . . students become literate in . . . [a] subject area, with particular attention to its nuances in terms of how knowledge is structured and acquired.
>
> *(p. 5)*

Content area literacy, in this sense, is the point at which an educator possesses expertise of content areas, such as math, French, science and history, with a particular advanced epistemological foundation of the subject itself. Content area literacy combines content and literacy to the point where the content expert is knowledgeable in comprehension, vocabulary, fluency and decoding of the content area. To move from content literate to pedagogically content literate, an educator must not only be content literate, as conceptualized by Bean et al., but also possess a "unique amalgam of content and pedagogy" (Shulman, 1987). Being pedagogically content literate combines content, literacy and pedagogy. In other words, the content educator is able to develop reflexive practice in a way that displays literate knowledge of content for all learners in the secondary learning environment.

Lastly, this chapter recalls the work of Paulo Freire (1970) to create a concept of social justice that is transformative for teachers and learners alike. Teaching for social justice (Merkel, 2009; Nieto, 2010) signifies that there is an element of injustice to oppose, such as classism, racism/ethnocentrism, linguistic chauvinism or intellectual superiority. For Freire, part of social justice is *conscientizagao*: an oppressed group becoming aware of the conditions under which they are oppressed in order to overcome those conditions. Social justice is fully achieved when learners from an oppressed group not only realize their full humanity but also, in fact, are treated in fully humanizing ways among themselves, by their teachers and the broader society. Freire and others (Aronowitz, 2009; Heath, 1983; Gee, 2001; Giroux, 2009 Lankshear & McLaren, 1993; Shor, 1999; Vasquez, 2014) observe that the process of realizing one's humanity occurs with the process of becoming literate. When learners make the leap from reading the world to reading the word (Freire, 1983), they can reimagine or transform oppressive worlds in ways that empower them as active agents in the learning of particular content areas. Accordingly, transformative social justice is intimately tied to literacy education—or, from another angle, literacy education is a matter of social justice.

The importance of these concepts to secondary preservice teacher education is clear. Teaching any subject, whether math, French, music or kinesiology, to adolescent learners requires nuanced knowledge in how the content area is structured and produced, but, as Lee Shulman (1987) reminds us, knowing one's content and teaching it are two different, albeit related, things. When preservice secondary teachers become in-service secondary teachers, they will have to enact their knowledge of the education process and include knowledge of learners and the learning process. As a result, in-service teachers must be aware of their own social position in relation to their learners, as well as their learners' social backgrounds, race/ethnicity, class, gender, language heritage and more, to enact social justice. By knowing the various social dispositions of learners, as well as acknowledging their own, secondary content teachers will be pedagogically content literate by teaching their content in ways that are relevant and humanistic. In tandem, humanistic content literacy pedagogy then is culturally relevant. By culturally relevant pedagogy, I draw from Gloria Ladson-Billings's (1995) definition by maintaining that educators need to recognize the home life of learners and use such home culture as a scaffold for content learning in the classroom.

Literacy Education in *Stand and Deliver* and *The Class*

My content area literacy course is a requirement of the state and teacher education program for certification and degree conferral for all secondary students at my home institution. In the course, I show the two films *Stand and Deliver* (1988) and *The Class* (2008). Preservice candidates watch *Stand and Deliver* in order to see how a core content area subject such as math—one that candidates perceive has no connection to literacy education—is taught by putting into practice explicit literacy education strategies. They view *The Class*, by contrast, to discuss classroom management and cultural diversity issues in a subject where the secondary teacher is very content literate.

To the surprise of my students, Mr. Escalante in *Stand and Deliver* employs a host of literacy strategies, albeit unknowingly, to teach math. First, Mr. Escalante decodes parentheses, in a lesson on multiplying negative and positive numbers, by merely writing (encoding) them on the chalkboard and pointing to the symbolic notation. Immediately afterwards, Mr. Escalante moves to a fluency exercise by having his students repeat, "A negative times a negative is a positive" several times. He completes the lesson on multiplication of positive and negative numbers by posing the text-implicit comprehension question "Why?" In this way, Mr. Escalante induces students to move beyond mere memorization of the formula to a deep conceptual knowledge of it. In a different lesson on algebraic word problems, Mr. Escalante employs a new literacies framework by using his students' out-of-school social worlds to make the problems relevant: use of names such as Juan, Juan's number of girlfriends and gigolos help his learners to connect to the material in a way that immediately answers the "so what" (Tovani, 2004). In short, by using examples from his learners' social worlds, Mr. Escalante shows that he is knowledgeable of and cares about how his learners can use math to address issues in their lives.

One would think, in a French language and literature course, that the teacher would employ a range of literacy strategies, but it is difficult for Mr. Marin to explicitly do so when he is tending to classroom management issues most of the time. Mr. Marin does ask, in a lesson on the subjunctive, text-explicit/decoding questions and text-implicit questions on use of the verb *falloir* (it is necessary). However, he overlooks the use of a critical literacy approach to the teaching of such grammar when engaging in a discussion with his students on the use the subjunctive. Several students of color, in particular two female students of Arab and African descent, want to know why one would use such archaic terms. Mr. Marin does not seize the opportunity to draw from examples that resonate with the social backgrounds of his students and, therefore, fails to help them understand where, why and how they might use such French terms in a way that would have meaning for these students. In this sense, Mr. Marin fails to enact a critical literacy that would help both him and his students see the use of past participle forms of the French verb *falloir*.

Social Justice

Stand and Deliver and *The Class* are films that remind us of the importance of social justice in all secondary content classrooms. It is overwhelmingly clear that Mr. Escalante is able to convince his learners that they could do calculus not only with his knowledge of and professional experience with computer science but also by showing that he understands them socially: who the students are in Garfield High beyond classroom walls, what their family lives are like at home, who their friends are at school. By contrast, it is clear that Mr. Marin is able to convince his learners that he believes they could not master French grammar, such as the imperfect and the subjunctive, by showing that he does not want to understand them socially. Who they are beyond the secondary school in the 20th arrondissement— including their cultural identities—is beyond the scope of being able to learn French language rules.

The use of critical literacy is an issue of social justice that Mr. Escalante is successful in employing. It is clear from the beginning of the film that Mr. Escalante is aware of the perspective of his students—even though he comes from a different class background than that of his students—and is intent on using such a perspective as a means to promote the learning of math. For example, Mr. Escalante uses

Spanish frequently in his class to communicate with his learners and uses Latino names, as mentioned earlier, in word problems. Mr. Escalante also has high expectations of his students, believing in their ability to go from not reading fractions to being able to read derivatives.

In contrast, Mr. Marin has low expectations of his students. When a colleague asks him about the ability of his students to read certain French classics, Mr. Marin laments that such reading is above their level. Unlike Mr. Escalante, he upholds the classist position so commonly associated with knowledge of French language and literature by implicitly believing his students cannot overcome the barrier between the subject matter and themselves.

Preservice Candidates' Literacy Understandings

While I intersperse viewing the films with discussion of content literacy and pedagogical content literate practice, preservice candidates best demonstrate their knowledge of content and pedagogical content literacy in their midterm responses. By the time secondary candidates take the midterm, they see roughly two thirds of each film. From the study guide for the exam, students know the exam may include questions about the pedagogy of Mr. Escalante and Mr. Marin, although they did not know what form the questions on the exam might take. On the day of the midterm, they respond to one essay prompt asking them to compare the literacy pedagogy of Mr. Escalante and Mr. Marin:

> Compare and contrast the content literacy pedagogy of Mr. Marin and Mr. Escalante. Despite teaching different content and different secondary populations, both teachers have some striking similarities in terms of level of content literacy and pedagogy. What are some of these similarities? First, address the question of the extent to which each of these teachers are content literate, citing at least two specific reasons for your argument. Then, address the extent to which each of these teachers is pedagogically content literate. At what point do you believe that each of these teachers will make/ has made the transition from being content literate to being pedagogically content literate? What will they do/have they done to demonstrate being pedagogically content literate? Offer at least two more points to support your position on these latter questions.

Content Literate and Pedagogically Content Literate

What stands out in secondary candidate responses is recognition of the ways in which Mr. Escalante and Mr. Marin demonstrate content literacy pedagogy. Secondary candidates note that Mr. Escalante and Mr. Marin are both skilled in use of the terms and discipline-specific vocabulary that marks a strong content knowledge base. One candidate reasoned that Mr. Escalante's content knowledge is evident from the fact that he is a trained computer scientist coming to teach secondary math. Another secondary student remarked in his essay that Mr. Marin employs "many words and difficult grammatical structures" of the French language. In general, essay responses were consistent with the idea that "through the words and vocabulary they both chose to use"—and the fluent ease with which they use them—Mr. Escalante and Mr. Marin are literate in math and French. In other words, candidates' essay responses suggest that Mr. Escalante and Mr. Marin are highly content literate because they are able to act, think and speak like a mathematician and French literary scholar, respectively.

Candidates' essay responses are also consistent with the position that Mr. Escalante and Mr. Marin differ in the ways in which each teacher is *pedagogically* content literate. Quite unanimously, they opine that Mr. Escalante displays a kind of pedagogical content literacy grounded in hands-on examples. One essay response captured the ethos of candidates' observations of Mr. Escalante's pedagogy: "Mr. E was also pedagogically content literate. The activity where he sliced apples and gave them to the class is a great example. Also, the activity where he made the students repeat 'a negative × a negative equals a +.' He was instilling *automaticity* into the kids." Another candidate reaffirmed the significance of the apples to teach fractions: "He used the *pre-reading* strategy with the apples." More than this, essay responses also revealed that Mr. Escalante develops a kind of pedagogical content literacy grounded in use of "real-world" examples to demonstrate application of math content. Dressing up as a cook and slicing apples to teach percentages and fractions makes the content come alive; it is more easily digested than simply writing equations on a chalkboard and having students do worksheets. Essay responses showed that Mr. Escalante also asks the "why?" question. By asking why a negative times a negative equals a positive, Mr. Escalante poses a higher-order question that asks learners to explain what they know. This sort of questioning, coupled with the hands-on examples, offers secondary learners tangible learning that they can synthesize.

Content Literacy Pedagogy as Social Justice

Unlike Mr. Escalante, Mr. Marin displays a kind of content literacy pedagogy void of social justice. Essay responses revealed that Mr. Marin's pedagogical content literacy overlooks building social relationships or building community. One secondary candidate lamented, "Mr. Marin is not very pedagogically content literate. He doesn't understand his students. He has terrible classroom management." Other candidates observed, "He used language that was above the grade level he was teaching," and "I think he will become pedagogically content literate when he respects where his students come from . . . and adapts his lessons accordingly." Still, another candidate wrote, "He used Bob and cheeseburger, which were American terms to teach [a] French [lesson on the subjunctive]" in a middle school class in

Paris full of Africans, Arabs, Asians and more. These comments offered analysis, showing how little Mr. Marin connects the content of French language and literature to the social worlds of his secondary students. From secondary students' points of view, the paucity of pedagogical content literacy in Mr. Marin's classroom is directly tied to his "other-world" as opposed to "real-world" examples. He fails to manage his class, which is in part a matter of failing to connect with and understand his students in ways that resonate with *their* language and experiences.

One secondary candidate conveyed Mr. Marin's pedagogically content literate shortcomings using literacy education discourse that summed up well the essay responses of her secondary colleagues:

> Mr. Marin is less pedagogically content literate because he struggles to convey the material he understands in a clear, socially relevant way to his students. He lacks an understanding of new literacies, as well as some aspects of critical literacies, because he still insists on teaching students old-fashioned, highly formal ways of saying things.

Implicit in her essay response is the view that Mr. Marin would become pedagogically content literate when his teaching of French involves relationship-building. In this sense, pedagogical content literacy is an issue of the extent to which Mr. Marin enacts culturally relevant pedagogy. How can a White French teacher connect the teaching of a seemingly other-world subject, such as French, to the lives of urban French kids of color? What would such French language and literature pedagogy look like?

Clearly, if Mr. Marin takes a new literacies approach, he will have to become aware of the out-of-school literacy practices of his students and directly tie those into his lessons on "falloir." Would it be too much for him to ask his students what video games they play at home or other leisure activities in which they partake with friends? Where do they go shopping for the clothes they wear? How might they use the verb *falloir* in a sentence to communicate to a boyfriend or girlfriend? These are some of the new literacies approaches Mr. Marin overlooks in his French language teaching, which keeps him from connecting with his students, and hence, evidencing pedagogical content literacy. Mr. Marin is a scapegoat of his students' failed French language and literature learning because he overlooks new literacies ways of teaching them.

As the candidate responses showed, Mr. Marin teaches in a way that lends itself to a structure that is far removed from the literate lives of his students. In many of the essay responses, secondary candidates opined that Mr. Marin is not pedagogically content literate because "he does not respect his students." He does not respect what they know about the French language and does not use their cultural knowledge in any way as a scaffold for learning the language itself. What would it mean for Mr. Marin to record on the board the colloquial language—that is, to engage in a language experience (Allen, 1976) through a pedagogical approach—of his students and compare it with the language of Beaudelaire, Voltaire or Ronsard? What would such a pedagogical move mean for his students, for him, for the class's learning environment? Doing so might celebrate the backgrounds of his students whose language backgrounds are supposedly so seemingly different from 18th-century French poetry and provide a foundation that empowers his learners and him, as well. In essence, for Mr. Marin to nurture meaningful pedagogical content literacy, he will have to embrace the attitude that different is not deficient. Mr. Marin will be pedagogically content literate, in a manner similar to his colleague Mr. Escalante, when he teaches French for social justice.

Conclusion

Why are the viewings of *Stand and Deliver* and *The Class* beneficial for secondary preservice teachers? What do they gain from this work? How does it benefit their development as teachers of both content and literacy? Why is this a useful exercise for other teacher educators to adopt? *Stand and Deliver* and *The Class* remind teacher educators that true content learning will occur only when teachers move beyond a strong content knowledge base to teach content via genuine relationships with their learners. There is no question that Mr. Escalante and Mr. Marin know their content but that is not enough. Mr. Escalante visits the family restaurant where one of his brightest students works in order to convince her father that she should return to school in lieu of being a waitress. Mr. Escalante rides in a car with another student in order to convince him that knowing math could not only help him know the mechanical design of the car but also teach him a lesson about what happens when one is driving and takes a certain path leading to a positive or negative life ahead. Mr. Escalante even allows one of his students entry to his house with his grandmother to discuss the student's home life situation after he has another unexcused absence from school. On the other hand, Mr. Marin spends class time arguing with students over his own sexual identity, whether he degraded a female student and how the cultures in the classroom are just too many for him to use as examples to teach French grammar. As a result, the learning that actually takes place in these urban settings is very different, with Mr. Escalante on an upward and Mr. Marin on a downward trajectory, despite them both being very content literate.

Good content literacy pedagogy begins with a teacher stance that all learners are human beings first. Each learner has a name, a home culture, a family, a language, a heritage, friends and adolescent/teenage interests that may be different from and even unsettling to the secondary content area teacher. However, for true content literacy pedagogy to result in the teacher reaching her learning goals, educators will have to teach in ways that are equitable for the classroom community. What *Stand and Deliver* and *The Class* remind us is that secondary teacher educators should enter their content classrooms prepared to use the social identities of their students as an integral part of the content area literacy lesson. Prereading, during-reading or postreading with examples and literacy strategies that honor who students are nurtures social justice–based pedagogical content literacy. No matter the content, grade level and school setting, what matters most is creating a community in a classroom where learners feel socially on par with each other and with their teacher and engage with the larger community in which the school is situated. Moving from being math and French literate to being pedagogically math and French literate starts, continues and ends with being a teacher for social justice.

References

Allen, R. V. (1976). *Language experiences in communication*. Boston, MA: Houghton Mifflin.

Arnal, S., Benjo, C., Letellier, B., Scotta, C. (Producers), & Cantet, L. (Director). (2008). *The class* [Motion picture]. France: Haut et Court.

Aronowitz, S. (2009). Foreword. In S. L. Macrine (Ed.), *Critical pedagogy in uncertain times: Hope and possibilities* (pp. ix–xi). New York, NY: Palgrave Macmillan.

Bean, T., Readence, J., & Baldwin, R. S. (2011). *Content area literacy: An integrated approach*. Dubuque, IA: Kendall Hunt.

Freire, P. (1970). *Pedagogy of the oppressed*. New York, NY: Penguin.

Freire, P. (1983). The importance of the act of reading. *Journal of Education, 165*(1), 5–11.

Gee, J. P. (2001). Critical literacy/socially perceptive literacy: A study of language in action. In H. Fehring & P. Green (Eds.), *Critical literacy: A collection of articles from the Australian Literacy Educators' Association* (pp. 15–39). Newark, DE: International Reading Association.

Giroux, H. (2009). The attack on higher education and the necessity of critical pedagogy. In S. L. Macrine (Ed.), *Critical pedagogy in uncertain times: Hopes and possibilities* (pp. 11–26). New York, NY: Palgrave Macmillan.

Heath, S. B. (1983). *Ways with words: Language, life, and work in communities and classrooms*. New York, NY: Cambridge University Press.

Labunka, I., Law, L., Musca, T. (Producer), & Menéndez, R. (Director). (1988). *Stand and deliver* [Motion picture]. United States: Warner Bros.

Ladson-Billings, G. (1995). Toward a theory of culturally relevant pedagogy. *American Educational Research Journal, 32*(3), 465–491.

Lankshear, C., & McLaren, P. (1993). *Critical literacy: Politics, praxis, and the postmodern*. SUNY series, Teacher empowerment and school reform. Albany: State University of New York Press.

Merkel, W. (2009). Towards a renewed concept of social justice. In O. Cramme & P. Diamond (Eds.), *Social justice in the global age* (pp. 38–58). Cambridge: Polity Press.

Nieto, S. (2010). Foreword. In T. K. Chapman & N. Hobbel (Eds.), *Social justice pedagogy across the curriculum: The practice of freedom* (pp. ix–x). New York, NY: Routledge.

Shor, I. (1999). What is critical literacy? In I. Shor & C. Pari (Eds.), *Critical literacy in action* (pp. 1–30). Portsmouth, NH: Boynton/Cook.

Shulman, L. S. (1987). Knowledge and teaching: Foundations of the New Reform. *Harvard Educational Review, 57*(1), 1–22.

Tovani, C. (2004). *Do I really have to teach reading? Content comprehension grades 6–12*. Markham, Ontario: Stenhouse.

Vasquez, V. (2014). *Negotiating critical literacies with young children, 10th anniversary edition*. New York, NY: Routledge Press.

6

(RE)IMAGINING LIFE IN THE CLASSROOM

Inciting Dialogue Through an Examination of Teacher–Student Relationships in Film

Mark A. Lewis
Ian Parker Renga

> Common sense can be more dogmatic than any political party, more totalizing than any religious sect—it is insistent in its resistance to contradiction or even complexity.
>
> —William Ayers (2001, p. 209)

Film depictions of teachers as tamers of adolescent aggression persist as common-sensical despite numerous critiques of their stereotypical, racist and classist messages (Ayers, 2001; Barlowe & Cook, 2015; Brown, 2013; Renga, 2015; Trier, 2005). For decades, images of adolescent students locked into stereotypical boxes—the misunderstood introvert, the athlete-bully, the princess, the nerd, the rebel (or all the stock characters from *The Breakfast Club* [Friesen et al., 1985])—have driven plots within "school" films. Mix in the authoritarian principal and these portrayals fit within Western society's traditional expectations of how adults and adolescents should interact in school settings. Essentially, how we see teachers and teenage students interacting in film reflect seemingly intractable assumptions of race, gender, class and age that make it hard to imagine their stories unfolding in any other way.

We would argue that such imagination is possible, but only if we see films as using emotion-laden imagery to engage us in what John Dirkx (2006) refers to as an *imaginative dialogue*. To proactively participate in this dialogue, he suggests that "we take note of our reaction to particular metaphors, symbols, or images—what our attention is drawn to—and our emotional reaction to these images" (p. 25). Such thoughtful participation is crucial for beginning teachers, who enter the profession with certain images of teachers and with assumptions about the form relationships take between teachers and students (Cole & Knowles, 1993). In this chapter, we demonstrate the challenges and imaginative possibilities of dialoguing with film by exploring the adult-adolescent relationships in movies portraying privileged school settings—for example, *The History Boys* (Cusack et al., 2006) and *Dead Poets Society* (Haft, Henderson, Witt, Thomas & Weir, 1989)—and marginalized school settings—for example, *The Class* (Arnal, Benjo, Letellier, Scotta & Cantet, 2008) and *Dangerous Minds* (Bruckheimer et al., 1995). But first we briefly elaborate on imagery and its role in our commonsensical understanding of teenagers and teachers, and the relationships between them, as conveyed through the movies.

Images in Need of Interrogation

The images we hold are powerful because we spend an enormous amount of time imagining the world, both through "desirous daydreaming" and by "remembering past scenes, envisioning future sights, and projecting mental images onto present perceptions" (Brann, 1993, p. 4). This vibrant mental activity may seem superfluous, but Brann contends that the activity we undertake within the "inner visual space" (p. 17) of our imaginations can constitute a form of power as we change the physical, psychological and social world by enacting what we envision. To wield that power, we must see the world we are creating in relation to the raw material that shapes our imagination.

Charles Taylor (2002) observes that our imagination is not bounded by the immediacy of the present. Rather, it draws upon historical and cultural resources that are traceable to key theories of human flourishing that permeate our daily activity. He suggests that these theories, evident in society's stories, myths and popular culture, establish a *modern social imaginary* that shapes our reality. In fact, we are so immersed in this reality that we struggle to see it as a construction in constant formation and renewal. Through this imaginary, our beliefs, routines and social structures become normalized. As Taylor (2002) explains, the social imaginary "incorporates a sense of the normal expectations that we have of one another, the kind of common understanding which enables us to carry out the collective practices that make up our social life" (p. 106). Eventually these practices and the world they establish become commonplace, the scripts and sets largely fixed both in reality and within the actors' imagination.

The expectations established within the public imagination serve an important social function. Taylor (2002) contends that we move through the world with an "implicit map of social space" in mind that delineates "what kinds of people we can associate with, in what ways, and under what circumstances" (p. 107). Because we take these "maps" within the imaginary to be a given, the scope of our creative vision for alternate constructions and new realities is often limited. This limitation has important implications for a medium such as film that presumably offers novel visions of the world. As with most stories and myths, movies may look and sound fresh to new audiences yet still project the same old "map" foretelling how people are supposed to interact and what they are supposed to value, thereby serving to establish certain theories of the world as commonplace. This process can prove especially problematic for how preservice teachers imagine the features of and issues related to historically disadvantaged school environments, particularly in terms of understanding adolescence, youth of color and teacher-student relationships.

A problematic view of adolescence. Scholarship in critical youth studies considers adolescence a construct built as much on social and cultural norms as on the developmentalist paradigms of biology and psychology (e.g., Austin & Willard, 1998; Best, 2007; Lesko, 2012). This perspective helpfully questions whether cultural artifacts, such as school films and young adult literature, reflect the realities of adolescence as a natural, inevitable stage of life or if they work to fabricate "typical" youth within the social imagination. In other words, we might ask if adolescents naturally embody such "confident characterizations" (Lesko, 2012, pp. 2–3) of peer-orientedness, out-of-control hormones and angst or if adolescents take on these characterizations because society has told them they should act and think in these ways. For example, society tends to be comfortable with films like *Project X* (Budnick et al., 2012); it expects adolescent boys to lose control because they are incapacitated by hormones, peer pressures and limited cognitive development. However, when youth characters disrupt such commonsensical perspectives of adolescence, such as in *Juno* (Drake et al., 2007), outrage ensues because adolescents are depicted acting outside of characterizations society has prescribed. Moreover, this outrage expresses an adult worry over the types of messages such fictional stories convey to adolescent audiences who might enact them since they lack critical thought.

Further, developmentalist paradigms can be limiting, if not debilitating, for adolescent-adult relationships because they are rooted in an adult desire to surveil and control adolescent bodies, thoughts and actions (cf. Lewis, Petrone & Sarigianides, 2016; Oppenheim, 2012). For instance, depictions of adolescent sexuality in young adult literature primarily communicate conservative values to its teenage readers (Kokkola, 2013; Lewis & Durand, 2014; Younger, 2003). Often, adolescents who engage in sexual action are severely punished, such as Bella's violent consummation of her relationship with Edward and the ensuing decision to become a vampire (a literal monster) in order to save her unborn child in the *Twilight* series (Kokkola, 2011). These didactic messages are attempts by adult authors and publishers to instruct adolescents how to be "ideal sexual citizens" (Rasmussen, 2012, p. 186). Many school films function similarly as they message how teachers and students *should* act and be to their audiences. As such, they help establish problematic images of adolescence as normative in the social imaginary. Understanding adolescence as a construct informs our exploration of adult-adolescent relationships within school films by providing a foundation for critiquing and imagining alternative interactions among teachers and students.

Competing images of teachers and teaching. The image of the teacher within the public imagination is arguably two images—one real, the other fantasy—held in an uneasy tension. The first more or less "real" image is composed from our actual schooling experience. Teachers in the United States tend to be women, usually White—though increasingly less so—who are likely to leave the classroom sooner rather than later (Ingersoll & Merrill, 2012). In an international survey of written and illustrated images of teachers, the resulting portrait depicted the typical teacher as a modestly dressed woman who "speaks in a clear, loud voice" and is overworked, leading to "strained relations with her pupils" (Kestere, Wolhuter & Lozano, 2013, pp. 101–102). Farber (1991) similarly observes that teacher burnout is a commonly accepted outcome of the profession, which has given rise to the image of the teacher as an exhausted and exasperated functionary trapped within an intractable system. Therefore, it is no surprise that the public imagination craves a second, more desirable image that shows teachers achieving the kind of success worthy of admiration. The film industry has frequently indulged this desire through idealized teachers who get the results eluding most real teachers (Ayers, 2001; Barlowe & Cook, 2015; Bulman, 2002). What they offer, however, depends on the school setting and how the films present qualities and challenges of the students they depict.

Settings of Privilege: The Teacher as Devoted Guide of Students With Potential

The films *The History Boys* (*HB*) (Cusack et al., 2006) and *Dead Poets Society* (*DPS*) (Haft et al., 1989) are both set in all-male academies and feature teachers who are driven, wise and inspiring, with a fondness for poetry and the classics. *DPS* is set in the 1950s at Welton Academy, a school of prestige nestled within an idyllic U.S. landscape of hardwood forests. The new poetry teacher is John Keating, himself a graduate of Welton. Keating invites the boys to think for themselves, be expressive and find their calling. In 1980s Great Britain, Hector in *HB* similarly encourages expression and entreats his middle-class students at the suburban Cutlers' Grammar School to embrace the great works of writing, song and cinema with the hope that it will be useful as an "inoculation" against life's most painful moments and help them get into the highly selective Oxford and Cambridge.

Both films treat their teenage students as emerging adults, with adulthood marked in part by individuation and the achievement of some measure of distinction. In *DPS*, we see Keating asking his students to look upon generations of previous Welton graduates, all "full of hormones" like them, and listen carefully for their message to seize the day ("carpe diem"). He also tells them, "The powerful play goes on, and you may contribute a verse. What will your verse be?" Keating's presumption is that the boys have roles in the "powerful play"—speaking parts that they may author if they take command of their lives. In another scene, Keating reaffirms this message by stating,

> Boys, you must strive to find your own voice because the longer you wait to begin, the less likely you are to find it at all. Thoreau said, "Most men lead lives of quiet desperation." Don't be resigned to that. Break out!

The boys in *HB* are similarly encouraged to stand out and accomplish that which even their teachers have not achieved. Cutlers' headmaster wants them to be "Renaissance men" capable of wowing the country's best history professors. Complementing the abundance of adult encouragement, the physical spaces shown in each film contribute to the sense of possibility available to these boys if they succeed. The relatively small class sizes, spaciousness of the classrooms and imagery of students freely roaming the school grounds suggest expansive horizons and enough elbow room to accommodate an abundance of budding egos.

The image of the student in these privileged settings of mostly White young men is one of energy, capability and potential, where the only danger is the boys not being successful enough. Both films thus adhere to the popular narrative of adolescence as a time of impulsivity and angst but frame it as positive and invigorating for the teachers. There is mischief as the Welton boys sneak off the grounds to a secret cave where they indulge their yearning for self-expression (and women); the Cutlers' boys can hardly contain their lust and one student, Dakin, chases women and men. The transgressions, though dramatic, hardly seem to threaten their lives or futures; their behavior is risqué but not risky. Absent are any scenes of gratuitous sex, drugs or violence; the most violent scene in either film—a student suicide by gunshot, heard rather than seen—is an act clearly meant to implicate the boy's overbearing father. Indeed, it is the adults in the film who are the problem.

On his students' behalf, Keating argues that the boys deserve a chance to author their own lives. "At these boys' age, not on your life," replies the headmaster. "Tradition, John. Discipline. Prepare them for college and the rest will take care of itself." Their adolescence, he suggests, requires careful monitoring and lessons in self-control reflecting the overbearing adult gaze. But Keating sees it differently, as does Hector, and both teachers engage the students in playful exercises aimed at nurturing and unleashing their youthfulness to invigorate the stale rigors of adult life. Both teachers arguably romanticize the youth embodied in their charges and seem to long wistfully for days past and opportunities lost to time. The students are thus presented not as potential burdens but as sources of nourishment, possessing desirable but underappreciated gifts to be channeled by teachers wise enough to see them as such.

Finally, by imagining adolescence as an asset, *DPS* and *HB* enable the teacher-student relationships to be framed as mutually beneficial rather than a one-way street where the teacher comes across as a martyr, giving but rarely receiving. The boys offer a youthful elixir and, in exchange, the teachers groom them as potential peers—torchbearers entrusted to, in Hector's words, "pass it on"—in a relational dynamic reflecting an apprenticeship model. For Hector, whose life is rather disappointing, this exchange is vital. He is enlivened by his role as educator, as is Keating. Both teachers appear to presume their students' academic competency and give them permission to transgress for the sake of personal and professional fulfillment. In a poignant scene from *DPS*, Keating calls out Todd's fear of speaking and forces him to get up and speak in a silly stream of consciousness to powerful effect. He implores the boy to dig deep into his emotional core and let out a "barbaric yawp!" When the boys at Welton uncover the secret society that he founded, Keating tacitly directs them to risk punishment by resurrecting it and its rituals. In *HB*, we learn that Hector's cordial relations with his students involve sexual indiscretions. Both teachers thus cross professional boundaries, but the resilience of youth prevails in the end as the boys in *DPS* and *HB* ultimately forgive and stand up for their teachers.

Marginalized Settings: The Noble Teacher Handling Students With Issues

The "urban school" film paints a different portrait of classroom life: impoverished neighborhoods, graffitied walls, broken traffic signs, drug deals within sight of the school bus. These images are all included in the opening credits of *Dangerous Minds* (*DM*) (Bruckheimer et al., 1995) as students catch their bus in what can only be an attempt to make clear to the audience that this story will be about students turned tough by inner-city streets. The viewer is then dropped into the assistant principal's office moments before she briefly interviews the heroine—LouAnne Johnson— and hires her to become a full-time substitute as an Academy teacher, despite no professional certificate or classroom experience. The setting of *DM* is now complete, with tough students pitted against a substitute teacher who is clearly passionate yet ultimately inexperienced. *The Class* (*TC*) (Arnal et al., 2008) begins in a faculty lounge as teachers and staff introduce themselves, revealing their perspectives on what it means to teach at an inner-city Paris school. One teacher tells his new colleagues that the "students can be tough but they're good kids" and another teacher hopes the new teachers have courage. The scene closes with one teacher reviewing another teacher's roster, labeling each student as "nice" or "not nice," pausing to warn the teacher to "watch" a certain student. Similar to *DM*, viewers of *TC* are positioned to assume that this school is full of difficult-to-teach youth along with well-meaning teachers with uneven experience and skill. Low expectations are the norm, with *TC*'s protagonist, François Marin, admitting to the history teacher that Voltaire would be "too tough" for his French language arts students.

As the stories progress, the viewer is repeatedly exposed to the teachers' negative views of inner-city youth. In *DM*, Johnson sets out to teach these "rejects from hell"; her colleague, Hal Griffith, tells her all she has to do is "get their attention," which she does by opening a lesson teaching karate; Griffith laments that he is teaching "another fucking idiot" while grading papers; the principal tells Johnson to simply "go along with our policies" when she questions the curriculum. In *TC*, the teachers offer negative perspectives about adolescents' thoughts and actions. For example, in one scene, a teacher storms into the lounge, angrily venting about his students:

> I'm sick of these clowns. . . . They're nothing, they know nothing. . . . They can stay in their shit [neighborhood]. I'm not going to help them. . . . Have

you seen them in the yard? It's like they are in heat! They're all over each other like animals.

He has wrapped impoverished settings, intelligence and adolescent sexuality into a set of pejorative descriptors marking his students as unteachable. Later, Marin tells two girls that they acted "like skanks" during a committee meeting, which leads to classroom violence in which one boy, Souleymane, harms another student and storms out. Marin defends himself to his students by saying that a teacher can simply say things that a student cannot. In other words, he demands respect from his students but makes many missteps in showing them how he respects them. The fact that sexual action is at the center of his insult is not by chance. He marks them as sexual creatures and, therefore, as disreputable members of society. These series of scenes set a particular dynamic between adult educators and adolescent students—namely, that youth have deficits and gaps that need to be filled by adult educators.

In most urban school films portraying adolescence, sex and sexuality become a large, if not central, component of the storyline, thus illuminating how society imagines youth as full of out-of-control hormones that overtake their everyday thoughts and actions. In other words, writers and producers of school films seem to feel they must include this topic to maintain authenticity in the public imagination. In marginalized settings, however, the students are stripped of sexual innocence. For instance, in *TC* we see students directly questioning Marin's sexuality by asking him during class if he is a homosexual, implying their concern over whether he is "man enough" to teach them. In *DM*, Emilio aggressively propositions Johnson on her first day. When we juxtapose this scene with Dakin's flirtation with his teacher, the difference is stark—Emilio refers to a sexual encounter, where Dakin refers to a possible relationship—thereby ascribing the former as "adult" knowledge and the latter with "adolescent" curiosity. *DM* also includes a pregnant teenage mother storyline for Callie, portrayed as one of the more gifted Academy students. She is counseled to enroll in an alternative school for teenage mothers because of concerns by the school's administration, embodied in the assistant principal's characterization that "pregnancy is contagious" among adolescents. Through Johnson's passionate investigation, the audience finds out that this move to the alternative school is preference, not policy, illustrating an adult desire to control adolescent bodies by ostracizing any young woman who has clearly acted upon her sexual thoughts.

Violence is also a dominant theme, with the films in marginalized settings characterizing youth of color as lacking the luxury of relative security and innocence afforded the White students in privileged settings. The viewer expects that, in such harsh environments, boys have to stand up to each other to demonstrate their manhood. A disagreement between two of the more prominent male students in *DM*—Raul and Emilio—must end in a fight, despite Johnson's attempts to intercede. The implication stemming from both this scene and Souleymane's violent reaction in *TC* is that violence is inevitable in the lives of youth of color.

This may indeed be true, though rather than offering complex and nuanced perspectives on the systemic forces of racism and poverty undergirding violence, these films tend to treat it as a lapse in individual character.

Finally, rather than a devoted guide, these films show teachers as adults desiring control over their adolescent students. In *TC*, the central pedagogical concern of Marin and his colleagues is how to discipline students and affect behavioral change through punitive means. Most notably, Khoumba wonders why Marin picks on her to read aloud in class when other students have not completed their reading assignment and writes persuasively in a letter to him that she cannot respect him if he does not respect her. It seems she equates the forced reading, or control over her participation, with lack of mutual respect. As well, in the disciplinary hearing for Souleymane after his violent outburst, another teacher tells him directly that since he "can't control what you say or do" then this school might not be the best place for him. Her statement reveals both that she does not believe he has a certain capacity for monitoring his faculties and that his teachers do not have the facility to control his behavior. Since Marin and Johnson—who, for example, uses candy as bribery as a means to maintain her authority—seem to view disciplinary control as so vital to their work, it arguably debilitates and deforms their possible relationships with their students. Indeed, these two teachers are so preoccupied with gaining control over their students that, besides acquiescence, the students come across as having little to offer.

Reimagining the Teacher-Adolescent Dynamic With Preservice Teachers

Though not the whole picture, these films offer insights into how Western society imagines the typical adolescent-teacher relationship and the role of schools. For settings of privilege populated mostly by White males, we are led to believe that school should be a place for youth to establish their identity, facilitated by devoted teachers, as they prepare to enter society as full-fledged adults. It is a different story for students in marginalized settings, where schools are portrayed as rigid spaces in which gutsy teachers goad and coerce youth of color onto more productive paths. It is important to note that the overarching view of adolescence shown in both sets of films is largely the same: a time of hormonally induced angst and sexuality. It is treated differently, however, as potentially positive in the privileged setting and largely negative in the marginalized setting. This racialized framing of adolescence thus establishes what type of idealized teacher the viewer can expect in these spaces. The teacher in privileged settings is one who will open up opportunities for youth to use their adolescent potential to grow and become an adult. The teacher in marginalized settings is one who will don a disciplinarian mantle in order to constrain and instruct youth to repress their adolescent urges so they can become generative members of society. Indeed, these students are portrayed as inherently broken—socially, culturally, academically—and in need of fixing, as opposed to their privileged peers, who are presented as whole but unrefined beings just waiting to be unleashed.

To reimagine the teacher-adolescent dynamic, we recommend that preservice teachers question both their view of adolescence and the idealized images of teachers they hold in their imaginations. As we have shown, these images are intertwined along with common understandings of race and class; many school films show what viewers expect to see. Preservice secondary teachers deserve and benefit (cf. Bach & Weinstein, 2014) from a space in their teacher education programs to question and resist these problematic images for the sake of the adolescent students they will eventually teach. We think it is a fair assumption that many preservice teachers have been passively accepting the images of teachers and students we described in this chapter and may have chosen to enter the education field based upon these images, either consciously or subconsciously. Therefore, viewing and discussing these films in a teacher education setting can provide preservice teachers with an opportunity to interrogate their participation within the damaging social imaginary that shapes U.S. schooling. Such discussions can help them more proactively engage their imaginations with the aim of revoicing their perspectives on commonly accepted views of teacher-student relationships.

Teacher educators interested in facilitating such a discussion might begin by asking preservice teachers to identify and document how adolescents and adolescence are characterized in contrasting school films, like the ones we have discussed. Next, we recommend posing reflective questions, such as: How did the characterization of adolescents and teachers compare in the films? Were there images of teachers and adolescents that bothered you? Why? What images of adolescents and teachers seem to be lacking in those films and how can you explain this absence?

Finally, we suggest encouraging preservice teachers to consider the possible implications that these representations have for real-world adult-adolescent relationships, with opportunities to explore their affective reactions to particular images of teachers, students and the settings they inhabit. The goal of this analysis and discussion would be for preservice teachers to use film to imagine other stories that could be told about students, teachers, adults and youth set within diverse school contexts. In other words, by dialoguing with such disparate film portrayals of teacher-student, adolescent-adult relationships, preservice teachers can complicate seemingly commonsense visions of teaching, both in their lived classrooms and in the movies.

References

Arnal, S., Benjo, C., Letellier, B., Scotta, C. (Producers), & Cantet, L. (Director). (2008). *The class* [Motion picture]. France: Haut et Court.

Austin, J., & Willard, M. N. (1998). *Generations of youth: Youth cultures and history in twentieth-century America.* New York: New York University Press.

Ayers, W. (2001). A teacher ain't nothin' but a hero: Teachers and teaching in film. In P. B. Joseph & G. E. Burnaford (Eds.), *Images of schoolteachers in America* (2nd ed., pp. 201–209). Mahwah, NJ: Lawrence Erlbaum.

Bach, J., & Weinstein, S. (2014). Who's the teacher? What Tony Danza taught us about English education. *English Education, 46,* 300–326.

Barlowe, A., & Cook, A. (2015). From blackboard to smartboard: Hollywood's perennially misleading teacher heroes. In D. P. Liston & I. P. Renga (Eds.), *Teaching, learning, and schooling in film: Reel education* (pp. 25–40). New York, NY: Routledge.

Best, A. (2007). *Representing youth: Methodological issues in critical youth studies.* New York: New York University Press.

Brann, E. T. (1993). *The world of the imagination: Sum and substance.* Lanham, MD: Rowman & Littlefield.

Brown, A. (2013). Waiting for superwoman: White female teachers and the construction of the "neoliberal savior" in a New York City public school. *Journal for Critical Education Policy Studies, 11*(2), 123–164.

Bruckheimer, J., Foster, L., Guinzburg, K., Rabins, S., Simpson, D. (Producers), & Smith, J. N. (Director). (1995). *Dangerous minds* [Motion picture]. United States: Hollywood Pictures.

Budnick, S., Ewing, M. P., Heineman, A., Phillips, T., Richards, S. . . . Silver, J. (Producers), & Nourizadeh, N. (Director). (2012). *Project X* [Motion picture]. United States: Warner Bros.

Bulman, R. C. (2002). Teachers in the 'hood: Hollywood's middle-class fantasy. *The Urban Review, 34,* 251–276.

Cole, A. L., & Knowles, J. G. (1993). Shattered images: Understanding expectations and realities of field experiences. *Teaching & Teacher Education, 9,* 457–471.

Cusack, P., Hytner, N., Jones, D., Ketley, M., Loader, K., . . . Macdonald, A. (Producers), & Hytner, N. (Director). (2006). *The history boys* [Motion picture]. London, UK: 20th Century Fox.

Dirkx, J. M. (2006). Authenticity and imagination. *New Directions for Adult & Continuing Education, 111,* 27–39.

Drake, J., Dubiecki, D., Halfon, L., Kahane, N., Konop, K., . . . Malkovich, J. (Producers), & Reitman, J. (Director). (2007). *Juno* [Motion picture]. United States: Fox Searchlight Pictures.

Farber, B. A. (1991). *Crisis in education: Stress and burnout in the American teacher.* San Francisco, CA: Jossey-Bass.

Friesen, G., Hughes, J., Manning, M., Meyer, A., Tanen, N. (Producers), & Hughes, J. (Director). (1985). *The breakfast club* [Motion picture]. United States: Universal Pictures.

Haft, S., Henderson, D., Witt, P. J., Thomas, T. (Producers), & Weir, P. (Director). (1989). *Dead poets society* [Motion picture]. United States: Touchstone Pictures.

Ingersoll, R., & Merrill, L. (2012). Seven trends: The transformation of the teaching force. Retrieved from http://repository.upenn.edu/gse_pubs/241

Kestere, I., Wolhuter, C., & Lozano, R. (2013). The visual image of the teacher: A comparative study. *Acta Paedagogica Vilnensia, 30,* 92–103.

Kokkola, L. (2011). Virtuous vampires and voluptuous vamps: Romance conventions reconsidered in Stephanie Meyer's "Twilight" series. *Children's Literature in Education, 42,* 165–179.

Kokkola, L. (2013). *Fictions of adolescent carnality: Sexy sinners and delinquent deviants.* Philadelphia, PA: John Benjamins.

Lesko, N. (2012). *Act your age!: A cultural construction of adolescence* (2nd ed.). New York, NY: Routledge.

Lewis, M. A., & Durand, E. S. (2014). Sexuality as risk and resistance in young adult literature. In C. Hill (Ed.), *The critical merits of young adult literature: Coming of age* (pp. 38–54). New York, NY: Routledge.

Lewis, M. A., Petrone, R., & Sarigianides, S. T. (2016). Acting adolescent?: Critical examinations of the youth-adult binary in *Feed* and *Looking for Alaska*. *The ALAN Review, 43,* 43–50.

Oppenheim, R. (2012). Surveillance. In N. Lesko & S. Talburt (Eds.), *Keywords in youth studies: Tracing affects, movements, knowledges* (pp. 54–58). New York, NY: Routledge.

Rasmussen, M. L. (2012). Sex education. In N. Lesko & S. Talburt (Eds.), *Keywords in youth studies: Tracing affects, movements, knowledges* (pp. 185–189). New York, NY: Routledge.

Renga, I. P. (2015). Exploring the heroic teacher narrative with help from the trickster. In D. P. Liston & I. P. Renga (Eds.), *Teaching, learning, and schooling in film: Reel education* (pp. 41–55). New York, NY: Routledge.

Taylor, C. (2002). Modern social imaginaries. *Public Culture, 14*(1), 91–124.

Trier, J. (2005). "Sordid fantasies": Reading popular "inner-city" school films as racialized texts with pre-service teachers. *Race, Ethnicity and Education, 8,* 171–189.

Younger, B. (2003). Pleasure, pain, and the power of being thin: Female sexuality in young adult literature. *NWSA Journal, 15*(2), 45–56.

PART II

Constructing the Teacher With Content

I have read like a man on fire my whole life because the genius of English teachers touched me with the dazzling beauty of language.

—Pat Conroy

My physics teacher, Thomas Miner, was particularly gifted. To this day, I remember how he introduced the subject of physics. He told us we were going to learn how to deal with very simple questions such as how a body falls due to the acceleration of gravity.

—Steven Chu

Tough guys don't do math. Tough guys fry chicken.

—Jaime Escalante

7

TEACHER IMAGES IN YOUNG ADULT LITERATURE

Pedagogical Implications for English Preservice Teachers

Benjamin Boche

Preservice English teachers often enter into teacher preparation programs with simplified conceptions of and uninformed concerns about the work of teachers (McCann, Johannessen & Ricca, 2005; Rust, 1994). Many of these concerns revolve around developing their teacher persona: that is, adopting the characteristics they believe create a successful teacher, such as creating an effective learning environment, developing relationships with students, managing time effectively, having minimal discipline issues and adopting certain physical and personal "teacher" characteristics (McCann et al., 2005; Shoffner, 2011; Walls, Nardi, von Minde & Hoffman, 2002). Preservice English teachers may struggle with this work, however, as they begin to understand the complexities of "preparing students, at any age, in the effective production and reception of the range of possible textual representations of human experience—in short, to become sophisticated writers and readers, broadly speaking" (CEE, 2008, paragraph 3).

Since preservice teachers come to teacher preparation with prior beliefs about effective teachers and teaching, teacher educators must reveal the factors underlying the complexity of classroom teaching (Grossman, Hammerness & McDonald, 2009; Walls et al., 2002) and find connections between the theory and practice of teaching to develop the necessary praxis preservice teachers need to be successful in the classroom (Conway & Clark, 2003; Dickson et al., 2006). One way to develop such understandings is by studying the presentation of teachers in literary texts to allow preservice teachers "to experience situations vicariously and . . . [engage] in examining their assumptions, beliefs, and knowledge about a range of educational issues" (Trier, 2001, p. 129). These presentations provide opportunities to develop preservice English teachers' understandings of pedagogy and practice as outlined by the National Council of Teachers of English (NCTE) and the Council for Accreditation of Educator Preparation (CAEP) standards for initial preparation of teachers of secondary English language arts (ELA).

Using young adult (YA) literature in English teacher education programs provides English preservice teachers the opportunity to "build connections between the theories and the gap in their experiences" (Stanulis, 1999, p. 36) and make connections to their future students, their future classrooms and their future teacher selves. In this chapter, I examine English teachers in three YA novels against the standards used to prepare secondary ELA teachers to explore how these fictional teachers enact their pedagogical understanding in the classroom, what it looks like to the adolescent protagonists, how well these teachers meet the ideal standards and how this examination can help preservice teachers better understand the complexities of English teaching.

Cumulative Cultural Text of Teacher

In her transactional theory of reader response, Rosenblatt (1938/1978) argued that readers are active participants in literacy experiences. Rosenblatt (1938) viewed reading as "an individual and unique occurrence involving the mind and emotions of some particular reader" (p. 32). Readers, therefore, influence the literary experience with their own images, feelings and attitudes. They "bring to the work personality traits, memories of past events, present needs and preoccupations, a particular mood of the moment, and a particular physical condition" (p. 37). At the same time, the author of a text "attempts to bring into the reader's consciousness certain concepts, certain sensuous experiences, certain images of things, people, actions, and scenes" (p. 37). While reading YA literature, preservice teachers draw on prior life experiences while reading as well as living vicariously and thinking about their future lives as teachers (Pytash, 2013). These lived experiences and thoughts then come into contact with the cumulative cultural text of teachers (Weber & Mitchell, 1995) as presented in YA literature.

Society has put forth cultural constructs of what a teacher is and is not in a variety of artifacts: movies, comic books, TV shows, novels, media. Constructs can be everything from the young, new teacher coming in to change the lives of down-and-out urban teens to the grey-haired old teacher who walks around yielding a giant stick to slap the hands of misbehaving children. These cultural constructs, or texts, "[extend] beyond the notion of written and oral texts to include artifacts, social activities, and people—all of which can be interpreted or 'read'" (Mitchell & Weber, 2003, p. 166) while the term cumulative cultural text describes the longevity and influence of such texts. Mitchell and Weber (2003) argue the cumulative cultural text of teacher influences how preservice teachers construct their own teacher persona, knowingly or not, as they insert or separate themselves from the variety of teacher images present.

Using the cumulative cultural text of teacher in teacher education can serve as a curriculum for preservice teachers, exposing them to a wide variety of pedagogies and teaching styles that may influence them to be agents of change or of subversion (Mitchell & Weber, 2003). They can gain new insight into being a teacher through examination of these cumulative cultural texts for "it is in the process of interrogating the text that readers find its meanings" (Dalton, 2010, p. 5):

> The implausibility of some images and the juxtaposition of contradictory messages within the same image problematize our conceptions of teacher. The cumulative cultural text of competing teacher images forms the background against which we struggle to clarify our professional identities.
>
> *(Mitchell & Weber, 2003, p. 170)*

The cumulative cultural text shapes what preservice teachers bring to the reading process and how they interpret it, as well as what is present in the texts they encounter. By studying teachers found in popular culture—such as the young adult (YA) literature—teacher educators can help preservice teachers gain greater insight into the teaching profession while interrogating the cultural representation of teachers in society.

Why YA?

Young adult literature—literature that addresses situations related to readers from ages 12 to 18—has grown in both popularity and readership in the past 20 years. Cart (2008) argues one of the chief values of YA literature is "its capacity for fostering understanding, empathy, and compassion" (paragraph 11), and therefore invites readers to understand humanity better. In this way, YA literature offers preservice teachers "the opportunity to reflect, gain insight, and develop introspective and empathetic points of view concerning their future students" (Pytash, 2013, p. 476). Teacher educators have used YA literature to develop preservice teachers' empathy, understanding and professional practice about students with disabilities, diverse cultures, social justice, bullying, suicide, school and adolescence in general (Buck et al., 2011; Glasgow, 2001; Kurtts & Gavigan, 2008; Pytash, Morgan & Batchelor, 2013; Saunders & Ash, 2013). Preservice teachers should also be aware of teacher images present in these texts, as these images may potentially influence their conceptions of good and bad pedagogy and the conceived role of the teacher in students' lives.

In addition to dissecting the images of teachers in YA literature, there is also the opportunity for preservice teachers "to wrestle with issues, to experience up close how words and actions shape and influence main characters and events" (Pytash et al., 2013, p. 15). YA literature can provide preservice teachers with new perspectives and move beyond facts and assumptions about students, schools and teaching (Kurtts & Gavigan, 2008) while offering "vicarious experiences of people and situations beyond the context of their immediate lives" (Laframboise & Griffith, 1997, p. 382). In this regard, YA literature provides a safe forum to dissect difficult issues (Stanulis, 1999), helps preservice teachers make personal connections while examining their own beliefs (Brindley & Laframboise, 2002) and provides a different context "to become conscious of their operating worldview and to examine critically alternative ways of understanding the world and social relations" (Glasgow, 2001, p. 54).

The Standards

The National Council of Teachers of English (NCTE) and the Council for Accreditation of Educator Preparation (CAEP) standards for initial preparation of teachers of secondary English language arts (2012) include seven main standards encompassing five different areas: S1) Content Knowledge, where teacher candidates demonstrate knowledge of English language arts related to literature, multimedia texts, language and writing in relation to adolescents; S2) Content Pedagogy: Planning Literature and Reading Instruction in ELA, where teacher candidates plan instruction and design assessments for reading; S3) Content Pedagogy: Planning Composition Instruction in ELA, where teacher candidates plan instruction and design assessments for writing; S4) Learners and Learning: Implementing ELA Instruction, where teacher candidates plan, implement, assess and reflect on research-based instruction; and S5) Professional Knowledge and Skills, where teacher candidates proficiently demonstrate the knowledge they've learned and continually develop as professional educators through interactions with students and colleagues.

These standards are the foundation for preparation for English teachers and should reflect in teachers' pedagogical practices in the classroom. In teacher education programs, preservice teachers learn these concepts and attempt to use them in their own teaching but may struggle with fully understanding how to successfully implement the standards, especially when the standards do not necessarily match up to classroom teaching. English teachers in the YA novels *Minnie McClary Speaks Her Mind* (Hobbs, 2012), *The Wednesday Wars* (Schmidt, 2007) and *Sleeping Freshmen Never Lie* (Lubar, 2005) are strong characters and make a lasting impression upon the main protagonists. Analyzing these fictional teachers against the standards provides opportunities to interrogate the cumulative cultural text of teacher and may help preservice teachers come to a deeper understanding of English teaching.

The Power of Words

Told from the viewpoint of eleven-and-a-half-year-old Minnie McClary, *Minnie McClary Speaks Her Mind* (Hobbs, 2012) tells the story of Minnie and her transition to a new school. Minnie begins 6th grade with a parade of substitute teachers in her English class, all displaying different pedagogy. The first teacher spends two days on the beauty of verb phrases. The fourth one, a retired engineer, teaches the students to make stealth planes out of notebook paper. The principal spends three days reading *Crime and Punishment* aloud to the students. It is only after Minnie meets Miss Marks, the permanent substitute, that the class settles down and real learning begins.

Miss Marks, a graduate from the University of California, Berkley, with a degree in English, above all believes "in the power of words" (Hobbs, 2012, p. 30). The primary focus of Miss Marks's pedagogy is on writing and reading in the classroom. Miss Marks begins each class with journal writing, with students focusing on questions that bother them or they think about constantly. These informal writing assignments—where Miss Marks tells the students not to "worry about organization or spelling; just write whatever comes to mind" (p. 67)—are later used to compose more focused written pieces, demonstrating that the teacher understands how "writing is a recursive practice" (S2.1). As the journal entries turn more political, Miss Marks enacts her one class rule of respect when students share their entries out loud, demonstrating her ability to plan and implement "English language arts and literacy instruction that promotes social justice and critical engagement with complex issues related to maintaining a diverse, inclusive, equitable society" (S6.1).

When Miss Marks is warned by the administration about her less-than-professional behavior and dress code, she takes the opportunity to teach her students about passive voice in a sentence taken directly from the letter she receives: "It has been determined that due to unforeseen circumstances the teaching position presently being filled will not be available in the 2013–2014 academic year" (p. 135). Not only is Miss Marks using this sentence to teach grammar (S 2.2; S4.3), she also uses the letter as an informal assessment to "demonstrate an understanding of how learners develop and address interpretive, critical and evaluative abilities in reading" (S3.2) as well as modeling "literate and ethical practices in ELA teaching, and engag[ing] in/reflect[ing] on a variety of experiences related to ELA" (S7.1) by having her students reflect on the inappropriateness of the administration's actions instead of directly complaining to them. Miss Marks uses her own life as a learning opportunity, an idea she hopes her students will learn.

In addition to writing, Miss Marks devotes much of her pedagogy to reading in the classroom. When the students study *Animal Farm*, Miss Marks shares that "it was all about power and who gets to make the rules" (p. 72), demonstrating her knowledge of texts and the ability to critique and interpret them (S1.1). After the librarian informs Miss Marks that *Animal Farm* is not approved for the 6th grade reading list, Miss Marks finishes the story by having her students dissect the words "greed" and "injustice." This particular emphasis on words and their meanings follows through to study of the next novel, *Number the Stars*, where the word "stupid" is discussed in class, as well as Miss Marks's belief that words can "hurt like stones . . . or can make us strong . . . Words have the power to change us, and to change our world" (p. 156). As students study all these novels, discuss different words and work in groups, Miss Marks demonstrates her knowledge of how adolescents read texts (S1.2), plans learning experiences utilizing different texts and motivating instructional strategies (S3.1) and enacts instruction responsive to students' identities (S6.2).

Although Miss Marks demonstrates her ability to meet different standards in her classroom instruction, much about her practice remains invisible. The reader has no information about Miss Marks's understanding of theory and research in English language arts in her teaching. The reader does not know whether Miss Marks is designing her instruction and assessment in connection with certain standards or specific knowledge gained through professional development. While it is clear that Miss Marks is passionate about her convictions and uses the English language arts to demonstrate this to her students, readers are not privy to her thought processes as she makes her pedagogical decisions on a daily basis. This confusion only deepens the complexity of English teaching and requires preservice English teachers to further examine the teaching practice.

The Red Felt Pen

Set during the Vietnam War, *The Wednesday Wars* (Schmidt, 2007) occurs during a time when students were released from school early one day a week for religious education; since the main character, Holling Hoodhood, is neither Jewish nor Catholic, he spends his Wednesday afternoons with his English teacher, Mrs. Baker. After months of mindlessly cleaning chalkboards and banging erasers, Holling eventually begins reading Shakespeare's plays at Mrs. Baker's insistence.

Mrs. Baker is a teacher "born behind [her] desk, fully grown with a red pen in [her] hand ready to grade" (Schmidt, 2007, p. 170). Her curriculum comes from the textbook *English for You and Me*; the first instance of any teaching comes in the form of diagramming sentences, indicating her strong understanding of the English language in relation to rhetorical situations and grammar systems (S2.2). Mrs. Baker, though, adjusts her instruction to individual students, giving a new English language learner a very short sentence to diagram, demonstrating her knowledge of utilizing a wide range of instructional strategies "that are motivating and accessible to all students including English language learners" (S3.1). During the novel, there are glimpses of students reading short stories and poems and writing essays, suggesting that she is knowledgeable about texts and writing (S1, S2), but the main focus of Mrs. Baker's pedagogy is on diagramming sentences, which demonstrates her failure to use research-based practices for strong grammar instruction as put forth by the standards.

On Wednesday afternoons, though, readers get a different glimpse into the pedagogical practices of Mrs. Baker as Holling begins to read Shakespeare's plays. During these times, Mrs. Baker engages Holling in discussion about characters and themes of the plays, indicating her ability to design a range of authentic assessments (S3.2). Holling also writes essays about the plays, providing data about his interests, reading proficiencies and reading processes (S3.4) that ultimately inform Mrs. Baker's instruction. Throughout the novel, Mrs. Baker's pedagogy with Holling morphs to encompass out-of-the-classroom contexts. When Holling joins the local Shakespeare Company's Christmas extravaganza, Mrs. Baker helps him practice his lines, which leads to Holling's increased motivation and participation in class (S5.2, 5.3). Mrs. Baker, a former Olympic track runner, helps Holling learn how to run for the school's cross-country team. Mrs. Baker's teaching of such non-ELA subjects, though, cannot be found in the standards for initial preparation of teachers.

Mrs. Baker's instruction with Holling varies quite a bit from her whole-class instruction and thus shows how she differentiates her instruction to support his learning (S5.3). She incorporates much more discussion with Holling; she also strays from the mandated curriculum, even though reading Shakespeare does relate to the English language arts. However, some of Mrs. Baker's strongest teaching moments come from instances not related to English at all: attending Holling's play, supporting her student Mai Thi by teaching the class about Vietnamese culture amidst backlash against the Vietnam War and helping Holling with his running form during cross-country season. These moments capture Mrs. Baker's knowledge of social justice, critical engagement and student identity (S6.1, 6.2), although not within the context of the English language arts.

In her classroom, Mrs. Baker crosses her arms when students act up, rolls her eyes at silly remarks and comes across as the stereotypical crotchety English teacher. Her overemphasis on sentence diagramming and grammar adds to this image of the old schoolmarm. However, her interactions with students, particularly with Holling, reveal her personality and show that she genuinely cares about her students. These contrasting images further complicate the cumulative cultural text of teacher for preservice teachers and deepen the complexity of English teaching.

A Surgeon, Not an Assassin

Scott Hudson makes the transition from middle to high school in *Sleeping Freshmen Never Lie* (Lubar, 2005). While adapting to the social pressures of high school, Scott enjoys the challenge of Honors Freshman English with Mr. Franka. Scott is interested and excited by the various reading assignments he encounters throughout the year. He starts the year by reading the short story "The Lottery," followed by *To Kill a Mockingbird*, "The Gift of the Magi," *The Outsiders, Ender's Game*, a wide variety of poems, Shakespeare's plays, "The Waltz" and comic books before ending the year with the script of the movie *Terminator 2*. Not only do these reading assignments demonstrate Mr. Franka's knowledge of "print and non-print texts, media texts, classic texts and contemporary texts, including young adult" (S1.1); the assignments connected to these texts demonstrate his knowledge of how adolescents read texts and make meaning from them (S1.2). Mr. Franka also demonstrates his knowledge of language and writing (S2) by introducing the concept of the Tom Swifty:

> One of the most popular series from long ago was *Tom Swift*. The key thing about Tom, for our purposes, was that he never just said anything. The

writer was always ramping things up. Tom would "exclaim surprisedly," or "shout vigorously." Tom's speech habits became so well known that people started making fun of them. It turned into a word game.

(Lubar, 2005, p. 34)

Later in the year, Mr. Franka uses Shakespeare to teach mixed metaphors and oxymorons:

> Take arms against a sea of troubles. Anyone troubled by it? It's what we call a mixed metaphor. In Shakespeare's case, he can pull it off. But lesser writers can really drop the ball. Or to use a mixed metaphor, they can fumble the beans . . . In a similar vein, we have oxymorons. Words that seem to contradict each other. Jumbo shrimp is a classic example. Those are words that just don't belong together.
>
> *(p. 118)*

These specific pedagogical examples demonstrate Mr. Franka's knowledge of English language conventions (S2.3), which he can then use to help his students understand as well. In addition, Mr. Franka incorporates different types of formal and informal texts (S2.1), such as stream-of-consciousness writing and the four types of prose for testing purposes to not only motivate his students but also assess their understanding.

Mr. Franka meets Standards 3 and 4 by planning instruction and designing assessments for reading and writing in a variety of ways. Scott answers questions from a textbook at the beginning of the year, takes quizzes over the different short stories, turns in written assignments and essays, reads a wide variety of texts and discusses them in class, all of which fulfill different elements in each of these standards. Although the reader does not see Mr. Franka tie these assessments to standards, theory or research, he demonstrates his proficiency in these standards through his pedagogy and classroom practice.

Most importantly to Scott, at the beginning of the year, he believes after reading "The Lottery" that the story is "creepy enough to give me hope that English would be fun this year" (p. 24). Scott praises Mr. Franka's ability to make English fun, which speaks to his ability to motivate and engage his students while building sustained learning of English language arts (S5). When discussing poetry, Scott notes that Mr. Franka skips around to some of his favorite poets: "Not once during the whole class did Mr. Franka utter those deadly words, 'Now, what does this line mean?' He actually let us enjoy the poems without analyzing them to death" (p. 106). Later, as Mr. Franka teaches the class about viewpoints in fiction, Scott notes how "he enjoyed the way his teacher was able to take a story apart without killing it. Mr. Franka was definitely a surgeon and not an assassin" (p. 205). Throughout the novel, Scott employs the concepts Mr. Franka teaches in class with other areas of his own learning (S5.3), making direct connections between what he does with his school newspaper articles and what he learns in English class about writing.

In somewhat limited ways, Mr. Franka demonstrates his knowledge and skills as a professional educator (S6, 7). Scott reflects on how Mr. Franka is always telling the students to "examine and question everything we hear" (p. 220), which is a way to promote "critical engagement with complex issues related to maintaining a diverse, inclusive, equitable society" (S6.1). Only once do we see Mr. Franka struggle professionally (S7): when Scott overhears Mr. Franka complain about "killing [the teachers] with all this paperwork" (p. 155). In Mr. Franka, then, readers have an English teacher who fulfills nearly all the standards for initial preparation of teachers of secondary English language arts. His pedagogy matches up well against the standards and, interestingly, this alignment results in Scott's excitement and joy in the English classroom.

Pedagogically speaking, these three novels present teachers who are passionate about their subject and employ multiple methods to interest their students in English language arts, providing excellent models in effective pedagogy for preservice teachers. Miss Marks uses free-writing journal entries to give her students agency and voice and takes the time to let them share what they are thinking and struggling with in their lives. With Holling, Mrs. Baker engages in discussion about the larger themes in Shakespeare's works and directs these themes to Holling's personal life, helping him connect what he is learning in school to his everyday life while also teaching him important skills in areas other than English. Mr. Franka provides his students with a wide range of texts and assignments as different entry points into English language arts and appeals to his students' everyday interests through his units on comic books and screenplays of popular movies.

Conclusion

YA literature is written to appeal to its intended audience, so it is perfectly understandable that little insight would be given into the decision-making of teachers in these texts. That does not mean, however, that preservice teachers cannot gain knowledge of the teaching profession or pedagogy through the way these teachers are portrayed. To fully understand the complexity of English teaching, however, preservice English teachers need to move beyond the initial standards for teacher preparation. Fictional portrayals do address authentic teacher education preparation standards, but more importantly, they provide insight into the qualities of good teaching that are not standardized but valued: relationships, care, engagement, democracy and teaching the whole student.

Miss Marks shares her deep concern for political issues concerning equity and diversity and encourages it in her students. Mrs. Baker uses her conversations with Holling about Shakespeare to discuss larger issues in Holling's life, including love, his relationship with his father, friendship and the future as a way to share both her personal life and what she believes is important in life. Mr. Franka takes the time to congratulate Scott on his various activities at school, particularly those related to English, and even expresses his appreciation for Scott as a student at the end of the novel. Would any of this have happened if personal relationships had not been formed between the teacher and the students? By analyzing Miss Marks, Mrs. Baker, Mr. Franka and other fictional representations of teachers against the standards and the cumulative cultural text of teacher, preservice teachers and teacher educators can gain an increased awareness of the teaching practice, learn how formal knowledge, such as standards, connects to teaching and continue to shape the cumulative cultural text of teacher.

References

Brindley, R., & Laframboise, K. L. (2002). The need to do more: Promoting multiple perspectives in pre-service teacher education through children's literature. *Teaching and Teacher Education, 18*(4), 405–420.

Buck, C., Gilrane, C. P., Brown, C., Hendricks, D. A., Rearden, K. T., & Wilson, N. (2011). There's hope in the story: Learning culture through international and intercultural children's and young adult literature. *New England Reading Association Journal, 47*(1), 49–59.

Cart, M. (2008). The value of young adult literature. *Young Adult Library Services Association.* Retrieved from http://www.ala.org/yalsa/guidelines/whitepapers/yalit

CEE. (2008). CEE position statement: *What is English education.* Retrieved from http://www.ncte.org/cee/positions/whatisenglished

Conway, P. F., & Clark, C. M. (2003). The journey inward and outward: A re-examination of Fuller's concerns-based model of teacher development. *Teaching and Teacher Education, 19*(5), 465–482.

Dalton, M. M. (2010). *The Hollywood curriculum: Teachers in the movies* (2nd ed.). New York, NY: Peter Lang.

Dickson, R., Smagorinsky, P., Bush, J., Christenbury, L., Cummings, B., George, M., . . . & Weinstein, S. (2006). Are methods enough? Situating English education programs within the multiple settings of learning to teach. *English Education, 38*(4), 312–328.

Glasgow, J. N. (2001). Teaching social justice through young adult literature. *The English Journal, 90*(6), 54–61.

Grossman, P., Hammerness, K., & McDonald, M. (2009). Redefining teaching, re-imagining teacher education. *Teachers and teaching: Theory and practice, 15*(2), 273–289.

Hobbs, V. (2012). *Minnie McClary speaks her mind.* New York, NY: Farrar Straus Giroux.

Kurtts, S. A., & Gavigan, K. W. (2008). Understanding (dis)abilities through children's literature. *Education Libraries, 31*(1), 23–31.

Laframboise, K. L., & Griffith, P. L. (1997). Using literature cases to examine diversity issues with preservice teachers. *Teaching and Teacher Education, 13*(4), 369–382.

Lubar, D. (2005). *Sleeping freshmen never lie.* New York, NY: Speak.

McCann, T. M., Johannessen, L. R., & Ricca, B. (2005). Responding to new teachers' concerns. *Educational Leadership, 62*(8), 30–34.

Mitchell, C., & Weber, S. (2003). Reel to real: Popular culture and teacher identity. In *Reinventing ourselves as teachers: Beyond nostalgia* (pp. 164–188). Philadelphia, PA: Falmer Press.

NCTE/CAEP. (2012). NCTE/CAEP Standards for initial preparation of teachers of secondary English language arts, grades 7–12. Retrieved from http://www.ncte.org/library/NCTEFiles/Groups/CEE/NCATE/ApprovedStandards_111212.pdf

Pytash, K. E. (2013). Using YA literature to help preservice teachers deal with bullying and suicide. *Journal of Adolescent & Adult Literacy, 56*(6), 470–479.

Pytash, K. E., Morgan, D. N., & Batchelor, K. E. (2013). Recognize the signs: Reading young adult literature to address bullying. *Voices From the Middle, 20*(3), 15–20.

Rosenblatt, L. M. (1938). *Literature as exploration.* New York, NY: D. Appleton-Century.

Rosenblatt, L. M. (1978). *The reader, the text, the poem: The transactional theory of the literary work.* Carbondale: Southern Illinois University Press.

Rust, F.O.C. (1994). The first year of teaching: It's not what they expected. *Teaching and Teacher Education, 10*(2), 205–217.

Saunders, J. M., & Ash, G. E. (2013). Entering the arena: The figured worlds transition of preservice teachers. *Journal of Adolescent & Adult Literacy, 56*(6), 490–499.

Schmidt, G. (2007). *The Wednesday wars.* New York, NY: Scholastic.

Shoffner, M. (2011). Considering the first year: Reflection as a means to address beginning teachers' concerns. *Teachers and Teaching, 17*(4), 417–433.

Stanulis, R. N. (1999). Adolescent literature as virtual experience for training middle school teachers. *Middle School Journal, 31*(1), 36–40.

Trier, J. D. (2001). The cinematic representation of the personal and professional lives of teachers. *Teacher Education Quarterly, 28*(3), 127–142.

Walls, R. T., Nardi, A. H., von Minden, A. M., & Hoffman, N. (2002). The characteristics of effective and ineffective teachers. *Teacher Education Quarterly, 29*(1), 39–48.

Weber, S. J., & Mitchell, C. (1995). *That's funny, you don't look like a teacher!: Interrogating images and identity in popular culture.* New York, NY: Routledge.

8

WHY TEACH MATHEMATICS?

Values Underlying Mathematics Teaching in Feature Films

Amanda Jansen
Charles Hohensee

Despite a widespread (and mistaken) belief that mathematics is value-free, values shape how teachers teach mathematics. For instance, according to Bishop (2001), teachers promote a value for *rationalism* when they teach mathematics by giving students opportunities to develop their understandings through reasoning, arguing, justifying and proving. Teachers demonstrate a value for *mystery* when mathematics is taught through puzzle solving and through encouraging curiosity and wonder about grand abstract concepts, such as infinity. The values that underlie mathematics instruction may remain implicit to teachers; after all, many teachers may not be aware of or have explicitly considered which values they impart when they teach mathematics.

Images of teaching (e.g., instances of teaching that appear in films) can provide a vicarious encounter of teaching practice that affords reflection and critical analysis of mathematics teaching. These images are cases of teaching that provide a removed look at practice from a distance (Putnam & Borko, 2000). Examples of teachers in media carry cultural understandings of good mathematics teaching, both explicitly and inadvertently (Gieger, 2007), because films, as popular texts, "offer constructions of reality that compete with those offered by academic, state, and professional discourses about education" (Fisher, Harris & Jarvis, 2008, p. 2). Given that teachers both carry and mediate values in a classroom (Bishop, 2001), as teacher educators, we are interested in exploring and understanding the values that prospective teachers bring to mathematics teaching. To support future middle school mathematics teachers with developing awareness of their own values about mathematics teaching, we developed a Math Movie Club. During club meetings, prospective teachers watched films that included mathematics teachers as either leading or prominent supporting characters. Through discussing these films in Math Movie Club, we hoped to mediate prospective teachers' developing values about mathematics teaching.

In this chapter, we consider what six contemporary Hollywood films *potentially* communicate about teaching mathematics and the experience of being a mathematics teacher. We then examine what prospective teachers *actually* noticed about mathematics teaching after viewing the films in the Math Movie Club. First, however, we share examples of possible values communicated by various purposes for teaching mathematics.

Possible Values That Underlie Mathematics Teaching

In our experience, future middle school mathematics teachers offer a variety of reasons for wanting to teach math: create more positive experiences with mathematics for their students than they had as learners, decrease mathematics anxiety among students, promote positive connections with the discipline. To provide lenses for a range of additional purposes for teaching mathematics, we offer an integration of three perspectives on mathematics teaching, each approximately 30 years apart (Eisner & Vallance, 1974; Ernest, 2010; Kinney, 1942), that capture enduring views of the purposes of teaching mathematics, considered in light of Labaree's (1997) discussion of three competing visions for schooling in the U.S. educational system. We also had the participants in the Math Movie Club read two of these texts—Ernest (2010) and Kinney (1942)—to stimulate discussion about purposes of teaching mathematics. These integrated perspectives address benefits of teaching mathematics for society at large and for individual learners.

Benefits for Society

Mathematics is often pushed as a core subject in public schools to prepare citizens for the workforce. Kinney (1942) describes this as teaching mathematics to achieve the value of *economic efficiency*, developing both efficient workers and discerning consumers. This focus on training workers (*social efficiency*) is a goal for the education system broadly, not just in mathematics (Labaree, 1997). The current public debate about the need to prepare workers for mathematics- and science-related occupations in the United States has an air of urgency, spawning books such as *Rising Above the Gathering Storm, Revisited: Rapidly Approaching Category 5* (Augustine et al., 2010). This book points to a U.S. crisis in terms of international competitiveness in mathematics and science, and it presents recommendations and implementation action steps for federal policy makers that can promote job growth in science, technology, engineering and mathematics.

Mathematics can also be taught to empower learners to critique society and enact change. This approach addresses a value for *social reconstruction* (Eisner & Vallance, 1974), using mathematics "as an agent for social change" (p. 11). Teaching mathematics is then considered part of a school's civic responsibility (Kinney, 1942) to promote numeracy in order to develop informed and critical voting citizenry. For example, Gutstein (2003) engaged middle school students in learning mathematics content (percentages, fractions and proportional reasoning) to examine wealth distribution in the world and within the United States and supported his students' efforts to critically discuss inequality. Labaree (1997) similarly identified a goal of *democratic equality*, or providing all citizens with the opportunity to flourish, for the education system generally. Teaching mathematics for social reconstruction encourages students to improve society for the *future* by using mathematics, whereas teaching mathematics for economic efficiency addresses preparing students to support society's *current* efforts to thrive financially.

Mathematics can also be taught to preserve cultural practices by promoting the value of *aesthetic appreciation of the discipline*. Mathematical practices have been historically valued and prominently represented in Eastern (Ueno, 2006) and Western (Keitel, 2006) cultures. Therefore, teaching mathematics both preserves cultural traditions (Eisner & Vallance, 1974) and promotes within society an appreciation for the practices involved with doing mathematics and the beauty of the discipline (Ernest, 2010). For example, students exploring the beauty of mathematical patterns that appear in nature, such as the Fibonacci sequence, have the opportunity to understand mathematics from an aesthetic perspective (Miller & Veenstra, 2002).

Benefits for Individuals

When mathematics is taught for a value of *attaining one's full potential*, the goal is for individuals to benefit intellectually from developing mathematics knowledge. In such a mathematics classroom, learners develop general problem-posing and problem-solving skills (Ernest, 2010) and cognitive processes, such as logical thinking (Eisner & Vallance, 1974); they also develop mathematical numeracy to engage as critical citizens and participate in economic practices (Ernest, 2010). Studying mathematics in this way provides experiences that support the development of positive dispositions, such as mathematical confidence (Ernest, 2010). Positive experiences with learning and doing mathematics can also serve as a process of self-realization (Kinney, 1942) or self-actualization (Eisner & Vallance, 1974) if learners come to see themselves as capable of doing mathematics. Interpersonal relationships and communication skills may also be promoted in such mathematics classrooms through group work and discussion (Kinney, 1942).

Individuals can also develop practical, work-related knowledge and advanced specialist knowledge that supports future employment (Ernest, 2010) and encourages *professional aspiration*. Mathematics provides economic empowerment by opening doors to STEM careers; taken further, by providing access to employment opportunities, mathematics also provides access to a better financial future and, ostensibly, a better life. This aligns with a goal for *social mobility*, or preparing individuals to compete for social and economic positions, a goal that applies to the educational system in general (Labaree, 1997).

It is important to note that not all these values and goals are complementary. In particular, Labaree (1997) notes that social mobility has become a more dominant goal over social efficiency and democratic equality in the U.S. educational system; these competing visions can impair the effectiveness of schooling in different ways. When considering the potential values being promoted through mathematics instruction, teacher educators can draw on film to help future teachers develop awareness of and critically consider these values and goals.

Math Movie Club

The Math Movie Club was designed as an opportunity to support preservice mathematics teachers' efforts to notice the different values underlying mathematics teaching, as presented through the films, as well as an opportunity to become aware of their own values. By participating in the club, we hoped preservice teachers would activate and clarify their values, although we were also open to any efforts to identify conflicts between and criticisms of values. To support preservice teachers' awareness of and engagement with their own values, we sought to initiate activities that focused on (a) activating attention to values, (b) clarification of values, (c) conflicts between values and (d) criticisms of values (Bishop, 2001). The club supported the preservice teachers' noticing of values in films by first *attending* to and then *interpreting* the ways in which mathematics teaching was represented (Jacobs, Lamb & Philipp, 2010). We directed preservice teachers' attention to purposes of teaching mathematics prior to the films, provided readings as lenses to support their interpretation of those purposes, conducted discussions following our viewing of the films and asked them to write responses to the films.

We invited all undergraduates enrolled in one section of a pedagogical course focused on teaching middle grades mathematics to participate in our Math Movie Club. This group of students consisted of a cohort of preservice teachers in an elementary teacher education program seeking a second certification in middle grades mathematics. We offered the preservice teachers a one credit-bearing course (pass/fail) that met seven times: first to orient students and then to watch and discuss six films. Three prospective teachers participated in the club: Benjamin, Clara and Jen (the names used are pseudonyms). For the first course meeting, the preservice teachers read Ernest (2010) and Kinney (1942) prior to the session; we then discussed various purposes for teaching mathematics. During the following course meetings, after watching each film, the group engaged in a 15–20-minute discussion about the films, responding to an open prompt (e.g., What did you notice about mathematics teachers and teaching of mathematics in the film?). After each club session, the preservice teachers posted a written response about the film in an online course management system. For their final paper, they responded to the following prompt in a formal essay: "Discuss societal, professional and personal implications of ways in which mathematics teachers are portrayed and represented in the medium of Hollywood films."

Mathematics Teachers and Teaching in Six Films: Teacher Educators' Views

Prior to inviting the preservice teachers to consider mathematics teaching in the films, we conducted our own analysis of each film from the perspectives of mathematics teacher educators. We identified values for teaching mathematics implied by the films and what the films could communicate about mathematics teachers. Our film-by-film summary ahead is meant to illustrate the opportunities presented by these films.

Mathematics teachers were lead characters in three of the six films that we selected (*Stand and Deliver* [Labunka, Law, Musca & Menendez, 1988], *Fever Pitch* [Barrymore et al., 2005] and *Invisible Sign* [Berfield et al., 2010]) and supporting characters in the other three films (*Good Will Hunting* [Armstrong et al., 1997], *21* [Beasley et al., 2008] and *Mean Girls* [Guinier et al., 2004]). Two of the characters were female mathematics teachers (Ms. Norbury in *Mean Girls* and Mona Gray in *Invisible Sign*) while the others were male. For the range of grade levels, there were college mathematics professors (*21* and *Good Will Hunting*), high school mathematics teachers (*Stand and Deliver*, *Mean Girls* and *Fever Pitch*) and an elementary school teacher (*Invisible Sign*). With the exception of *Stand and Deliver*, even when these films featured teachers as characters who were foundational to their plots, the activity of teaching mathematics was not central to the plotlines.

Stand and Deliver (1988)

This film is likely to come to mind for many people when thinking about movies featuring mathematics teachers. It is the story of Jaime Escalante, a charismatic and passionate high school mathematics teacher known for developing a successful Advanced Placement Calculus program at a school in East Los Angeles, California, with a majority of lower-income Hispanic students. The movie takes viewers through Escalante's process of recruiting, coaching and holding students to high expectations, while leading students to success through a highly structured mathematics program.

Stand and Deliver shows mathematics teaching from an insider's perspective. This emotional story has the life and work of a mathematics teacher at its center. We see Mr. Escalante not only conducting mathematics lessons but also talking with his family about teaching over the dinner table, visiting students and their families outside of school and attending faculty meetings. The mathematics teacher is in almost every scene.

Promoting a value for social mobility, *Stand and Deliver* advocates that learning mathematics helps individuals develop practical, work-related knowledge and mathematical dispositions and prepares workers for STEM careers. The film also promotes a value for democratic equality, explicitly addressing the importance of reaching underrepresented students. However, the movie may also send the message that mathematics teaching requires little to no teacher preparation; Mr. Escalante is hired without teaching certification in mathematics. Thus, while this film portrays several important purposes of learning and teaching mathematics, it may also unintentionally trivialize teacher preparation.

Mean Girls (2004)

Tina Fey wrote the screenplay of *Mean Girls* based on a nonfiction book about the concept of relational aggression (Wiseman, 2002) or the use of relationships to harm someone, such as covert social bullying and manipulative behaviors like gossip and exclusion. Tina Fey also acts in the film, playing the supporting role of high school mathematics teacher Ms. Norbury.

This film captures the teacher's role in the work of mathematics teaching in two primary ways. First, Ms. Norbury attempts to promote productive dispositions toward mathematics. She notices that Cady, a newly enrolled girl at the school, has strong mathematical skills and capabilities. However, Cady pretends to need tutoring to get attention from a male classmate. Ms. Norbury encourages Cady to join the "Mathletes" team (considered by peers to be "social suicide") and to take pride in her capabilities. In this way, the work of mathematics teaching enacts the value of promoting the attainment of one's full potential. Secondly, Ms. Norbury supports the development of productive interpersonal relationships outside of the mathematics classroom. She somewhat reluctantly assumes the role of mentor when she confronts several high school girls about their relational aggression toward each other, helping the high school students to develop greater empathy and act in more caring ways toward each other.

It is worth noting that Ms. Norbury's character exhibits a number of somewhat stereotypical characterizations of teachers. She works a second job at a bar and restaurant, presumably to make ends meet, which illustrates teachers' low financial status. Her work as a teacher is infused into her interactions with others, which strain her personal relationships. She pushes people emotionally in her personal life, and, in the classroom, she pushes students to work harder. When she says, "I'm a pusher, I push people!" the implication is that her intensity in personal interactions led to her divorce.

Invisible Sign (2010)

This was the only film we found that features an elementary school teacher teaching mathematics. The premise of the film is that, since childhood, Mona (the teacher) has loved numbers more than people; she is relatively awkward and emotionally distant from others. When she is offered a chance to teach elementary mathematics, her love of math and her social awkwardness collide.

Invisible Sign suggests two purposes for teaching mathematics. One is to foster a value for the aesthetic appreciation of the discipline. In the scenes featuring classroom interactions, Mona promotes the beauty of mathematics by asking students to connect mathematics to their lives. For example, she asks her third grade students to form numbers with their bodies ("Who wants to be the plus sign?"). She also creates an activity called Numbers and Materials, a show-and-tell of numbers in students' lives. The second purpose of teaching mathematics in this film is to foster interpersonal relationships. There are multiple instances within the film in which mathematics connects Mona to the few people in her life. As a child, Mona connected with her math teacher by interpreting what the numbers he wore around his neck indicated about his mood. Later, as an adult, Mona connects with Lisa, a young student whose mother is ill with cancer, through discussions about numbers. Numbers are the common thread in Mona's relationships.

Invisible Sign reinforces stereotypes about people who enjoy mathematics, however, and represents the work of teaching superficially. Mona's characterization as a recluse who does not relate well with people is a familiar portrayal of someone with a passion for mathematics. Her teaching generates little substantive interactions about quantities and mathematical operations and instead focuses on aesthetic appearances of mathematics symbols. Additionally, this is another film with a character who becomes a teacher without teacher preparation. Mona is recruited into teaching because she has a college degree in mathematics and there is a vacancy at the elementary school. Like *Stand and Deliver*, this film may send the message that lack of teacher preparation is not important.

21 (2008)

This film primarily depicts instances in which mathematics abilities are used in ethically questionable ways, promoting the value of social mobility from a different perspective. *21* is a semibiographical film about an M.I.T. mathematics professor, Mickey Rosa, and several mathematically gifted students who work together for personal financial gain by counting cards while playing blackjack in casinos. Furthermore, the movie contains discussions between the mathematics professor and his class about instances in history when mathematicians were suspected of dishonesty (i.e., Isaac Newton's and Augustin Cauchy's suspected thefts of mathematical ideas attributed to them). Mickey, who is part of the casino scam, is highly controlling and authoritarian with his students and the brightest students are given preferential treatment. We concluded that *21* projects potentially negative images about doing mathematics and mathematics teaching.

Good Will Hunting (1997)

This film is about Will, a janitor whose natural genius in mathematics is noticed by an M.I.T. mathematics professor. The professor acts as a mentor for Will and includes him in the professor's research group. On a personal level, Will's intelligence is validated though his interactions with the professor. The professor also connects Will with a therapist, who gives Will the support needed to heal personal wounds. On a professional level, Will is challenged to pursue a more financially lucrative career than his janitorial position. Indeed, Will's natural mathematics abilities promise to be his ticket to a better financial future. This film gives viewers a glimpse into the work of mathematicians and depicts the discipline of mathematics as interesting, challenging and creative. This depiction contrasts the widespread belief that mathematics is "extremely boring and tedious" (Boaler, 1998, p. 45). Learning and doing mathematics are shown as both personally and professionally liberating, promoting values of attaining one's full potential, as well as social mobility. However, this film also delivers negative messages about mathematics and teaching math. It depicts the mathematics professor as self-centered because he tries to use Will's talents to further his own research; like *21*, the mathematics professor appears to use students as much as or more than helping them. Additionally, this film reinforces the mind set (Dweck, 2007) that the ability to be good at mathematics is primarily innate rather than developed through effort.

Fever Pitch (2005)

In *Fever Pitch*, Ben, a mathematics teacher, attempts to balance his passion for baseball with a new romantic relationship. Throughout the film, mathematics teaching is subtly presented as inferior to other professions in terms of prestige and salary. This is conveyed in part during a discussion between Lindsey, a female business executive, and her colleagues as they discuss, with some disdain, the prospect of dating a math teacher. Additionally, mathematics teachers are depicted as not devoted to their profession, while mathematics teaching is portrayed as undemanding. For example, Ben is shown spending extended time on baseball-related activities (e.g., watching games and buying tickets) and little time on teaching. He skips work to attend baseball games and attend spring training in Florida. In contrast, Lindsey wrestles with balancing her significant work responsibilities and participating in Ben's passion for baseball. While this film delivers a number of negative messages about mathematics teaching, it does not directly address the purpose of teaching mathematics.

Mathematics Teachers and Teaching in Six Films: Prospective Teachers' Views

In their final papers for the Math Movie Club, the prospective teachers attended to values in mathematics teaching, such as professional aspiration and social mobility, attaining one's full potential and strengthening interpersonal relationships through teaching mathematics. Most of their interpretations were positive. Only one prospective teacher attended to and interpreted a slightly negative theme, headed toward criticism that some mathematics teachers were represented as outcasts.

Teaching Mathematics to Promote Social Mobility

All three prospective teachers indicated that four of the films (*Good Will Hunting*, *Stand and Deliver*, *Fever Pitch* and *21*) showed teachers who advocated that learning mathematics can have personal economic benefits. Benjamin wrote about how, in *Good Will Hunting*, Lambeau, the mathematics professor, recognized Will's mathematical capabilities and then went out of his way to help Will: "Lambeau gets Hunting multiple job interviews that would be a huge upgrade." In one of Clara's observations about *Stand and Deliver*, she wrote,

> By providing examples of how the students could be designing cars instead of fixing them, or running a restaurant rather than working at one, the film can motivate its viewers to continue their passion for math, or spark an interest in the subject and go on to succeed in their future careers.

In *Fever Pitch*, they noted that this theme was present but less prominent—as Clara reported, "a minor plot line"—and highlighted one situation when Ben, the math teacher, took students on a field trip to see mathematics in a workplace. When considering *21*, they observed that the brightest students were recruited by their professor to count cards and win large sums of money at Las Vegas blackjack tables. Clara wrote, "Although the application of the learned math is not necessarily a career builder, the film still demonstrates how learning a skill, especially in math, can result in great rewards." Benjamin shared that this value for promoting social mobility resonated with how he viewed his work as a teacher, writing, "I want to see the students succeed in the classroom, and maybe more importantly, succeed in life." Clara reported wanting to enact a value for democratic equality, explaining,

> Additionally, knowing that Mr. Escalante is a real teacher, as noted by *Stand and Deliver*, inspires me to strive to be like him even more knowing that it is possible to reach so many students that might have otherwise gotten lost in the education system.

These observations by prospective teachers echo common societal views: Those with more knowledge of mathematics can reap financial rewards and mathematics can provide opportunities to those from underrepresented populations.

Teaching Mathematics to Promote the Attainment of One's Full Potential

Benjamin, Clara and Jen also observed that the mathematics teachers in the films fostered positive dispositions toward mathematics among their students. Developing a positive disposition toward mathematics involves, in part, developing a meaningful connection with the discipline (Gresalfi & Cobb, 2006). The prospective teachers noticed that teachers in five films (*Invisible Sign, Fever Pitch, Stand and Deliver, 21* and *Good Will Hunting*) provided several meaningful connections to mathematics: by pointing out how it is fun and interesting, by indicating how mathematics is present in the world and by believing students are capable of learning mathematics. Jen found examples of mathematics teaching approaches that she appreciated in the conversational teaching style in Professor Mickey Rosa's college classroom (*21*), Ms. Gray's efforts to help students see mathematics everywhere (*Invisible Sign*) and Ben's interactive, engaging review game (*Fever Pitch*). She wrote,

> I hope to become a math teacher that is constantly engaging my students with different types of activities as well as class discussions; many of these films aligned with this thinking and provided me with ideas of how to do this in the future.

Jen recognized that while the teachers in these films are shown "do[ing] very little mathematics teaching," she identified instructional strategies in the films that she could use to motivate learners. Benjamin noticed that Mr. Escalante modified story problem contexts in *Stand and Deliver* to incorporate humor ("problems dealing with strippers and girlfriends"); as he explained, "we must keep our students' interest," but "there are times when your teaching must be 'not fun.'" Clara described *Stand and Deliver* as an example of believing in students and raising their confidence: "[Mr. Escalante] set high expectations that he believed they all could reach." These prospective teachers noticed and wanted to emulate ways that teachers in these films promoted positive affinities toward mathematics, which could lead to learning of mathematics content.

Strengthening Interpersonal Relationships Through Teaching Mathematics

Departing from the values described in our readings for the course, the theme of interpersonal dynamics between mathematics teachers and students was discussed by two prospective teachers. They observed that mathematics teachers were actively invested in students' lives outside of school in the films *Good Will Hunting* and *Stand and Deliver*. Interestingly, they did not highlight any other films that included similar examples, such as *Invisible Sign*. Benjamin described how Mr. Escalante supported his students academically—providing help before school, staying late to help after school, starting a special summer school program, standing up to testing authorities on behalf of his students—as well as personally, such as when he encouraged students to think about their futures. This resonated with Benjamin: "I didn't become a teacher because of the great pay or get the summers off. I became a teacher to see all of my work and dedication to the field of education pay off in the form of my students' success." In *Good Will Hunting*, the prospective teachers observed how the professor encouraged Will mathematically and conducted research with him, even though he wasn't enrolled in classes. Clara wrote that this example illustrated that "math teachers are passionate about their work, and want to encourage their students to have the same passion because it could lead to great things."

Teaching Mathematics Makes One Odd

Jen was the one preservice teacher who reflected on the degree to which mathematics teachers and those who enjoy doing mathematics were represented as outcasts, focusing on the films *Invisible Sign* and *Mean Girls*. She also noticed that mathematics teachers were represented more positively in the films *Good Will Hunting* and *21*, which contrasted with our own observations of negative portrayals of teachers. She cited the example of the "social suicide" of joining the "Mathlete" team in *Mean Girls*, as the boys who were on the team "do not interact with girls or have much of a life besides doing math." Jen wrote that Cady was recruited for the team "so that the other club members would be able to interact with a girl or at least see one." Jen also observed that in *Invisible Sign*,

> [Mona Gray] was a very strange character . . . [who] uses the method of eating soap to stop herself from enjoying the wonderments of life, such as movies and romance. This shows that doing math can make people themselves very strange and that people who happen to be good at math do not want to participate in having a social life.

In contrast, Jen described the mathematics professors in *21* and *Good Will Hunting* as "cool and grounded," which resonated more with her experiences with mathematics teachers:

> All of my teachers were in essence very normal people who lived lives outside of teaching. I, who happen to be good at math, also live both a social life as well as a life where I perform very well in mathematics . . . Hollywood should try to portray a more positive light on doing mathematics.

Conclusion

We hoped that the experiences of watching these films would encourage preservice teachers to reflect upon why they thought mathematics should be taught in schools. Although in their final papers, they did not challenge their own assumptions about purposes of mathematics teaching, they did share how the films supported and departed from what they valued as teachers. The preservice teachers noticed and appreciated representations of mathematics teaching aligned with promoting social mobility and helping students attain their full potentials, as well as fostering interpersonal relationships with students to support them. They took issue with the idea that odd folks become mathematics teachers, however. We conjecture that these preservice teachers became more aware of their own values through noticing mathematics teachers and teaching in these films. To increase the possibility that preservice teachers will strive to enact their values (or even question them), it is important to increase their awareness about their mathematical assumptions.

Each of these films addressed different potential purposes for teaching mathematics and the values underlying those purposes. Through this Math Movie Club, the preservice teachers were able to contrast values for mathematics teaching from articles that they read prior to watching the films, their own experiences and the various representations of mathematics teaching in the films. This range of perspectives provided opportunities for increasing awareness of their own values; by thinking about their own experiences in relation to the readings and the films, they could make their implicit values more explicit. Prospective teachers considered the personal contexts (e.g., teachers' economic situations, family relationships, other friendships) and social contexts (e.g., the characteristics of the school setting, the students taught, the colleagues worked with, the community in which the school is situated) in which mathematics teachers taught. They also noticed what mathematics teachers in films did as part of their teaching duties (e.g., approaches to delivering content, ways of interacting with students).

While these opportunities to compare and contrast films generated awareness among future mathematics teachers, they would benefit from more explicit opportunities to articulate how they would put their values into practice and to move toward analyzing for any competing conflicts among their own values for teaching mathematics. Given that the preservice teachers were generally not critical of the representations of teaching in the films, in a future iteration of this Math Movie Club, we would like to challenge preservice teachers to move toward critique of the values promoted in the films, values promoted for teaching mathematics in other contexts and their own emerging values.

References

Armstrong, S., Bender, L., Gordon, J., Moore, C., Mosier, S., . . . Weinstein, H. (Producer), & Van Sant, G. (Director). (1997). *Good Will Hunting* [Motion picture]. United States: Miramax Films.

Augustine, N. R., Barrett, C., Cassell, G., Grasmick, N., Holliday, C., . . . Jackson, S. A. (2010). *Rising above the gathering storm, revisited: Rapidly approaching category 5.* Washington, DC: National Academy of Sciences, National Academy of Engineering, Institute of Medicine.

Barrymore, D., Greenspan, A., Netter, G., Posey, A., . . . Thomas, B. (Producers), Farrelly, B., & Farrelly, P. (Directors). (2005). *Fever pitch* [Motion picture]. United States: Fox 2000 Pictures.

Beasley, W., Kavanaugh, R., Spacey, K., Brunetti, D., De Luca, M., Ratner, B. (Producers), & Luketic, R. (Director). (2008). *21* [Motion picture]. United States: Columbia Pictures.

Berfield, J., Edelbaum, J., Ellis, M., Falk, P., Howell, L., . . . Myers, M. (Producers), & Agrelo, M. (Director). (2010). *Invisible sign* [Motion picture]. United States: Silverwood Films.

Bishop, A. J. (2001). What values do you teach when you teach mathematics? In P. Gates (Ed.), *Issues in mathematics teaching* (pp. 93–104). London, UK: Routledge Farmer.

Boaler, J. (1998). Open and closed mathematics: Student experiences and understandings. *Journal for Research in Mathematics Education, 29*(3), 41–62.

Dweck, C. S. (2007). Even geniuses work hard. *Educational Leadership, 68*(1), 16–20.

Eisner, E. W., & Vallance, E. (1974). Five conceptions of curriculum: Their roots and implications for curriculum planning. In E. W. Eisner & E. Vallance (Eds.), *Conflicting conceptions of curriculum* (pp. 1–18). Berkeley, CA: McCutchan.

Ernest, P. (2010). Why teach mathematics? *Professional Educator, 9*(2), 44–47.

Fisher, R., Harris, A., & Jarvis, C. (2008). *Education in popular culture: Telling tales on teachers and learners.* New York, NY: Routledge.

Gieger, J. L. (2007). The myth of the good mathematics teacher. *PRIMUS, 17*(1), 93–102.

Gresalfi, M. S., & Cobb, P. (2006). Cultivating students' discipline-specific dispositions as a critical goal for pedagogy and equity. *Pedagogies, 1*, 49–57.

Guinier, J., Messick, J. S., Michaels, L., Rosner, L., Shimkin, T. (Producer), & Waters, M. (Director). (2004). *Mean girls* [Motion picture]. United States: Paramount Pictures.

Gutstein, E. (2003). Teaching and learning mathematics for social justice in an urban, Latino school. *Journal for Research in Mathematics Education, 34*, 37–73.

Jacobs, V. R., Lamb, L. L. C., & Philipp, R. A. (2010). Professional noticing of children's mathematical thinking. *Journal for Research in Mathematics Education, 41*(2), 169–202.

Keitel, C. (2006). Perceptions of mathematics and mathematics education in the course of history—A review of Western perspectives. In F.K.S. Leung, K. D. Graf, & F. J. Lopez-Real (Eds.), *Mathematics education in different cultural traditions—A comparative study of East Asia and the West* (pp. 81–94). New York, NY: Springer Science and Business Media.

Kinney, L. B. (1942). Why teach mathematics? *The Mathematics Teacher, 35*(4), 169–174.

Labaree, D. F. (1997). Public goods, private goods: The American struggle over educational goals. *American Educational Research Journal, 34*(1), 39–81.

Labunka, I., Law, L., Musca, T. (Producer) & Menéndez, R. (Director). (1988). *Stand and deliver* [Motion picture]. United States: Warner Brothers.

Miller, C. B., & Veenstra, T. B. (2002). Fibonacci: Beautiful patterns, beautiful mathematics. *Mathematics Teaching in the Middle School, 7*(5), 298–305.

Putnam, R. T., & Borko, H. (2000). What do new views of knowledge and thinking have to say about research on teacher learning? *Educational Researcher, 29*(1), 4–15.

Ueno, K. (2006). From Wasan to Yozan—Comparison between mathematical education in the Edo Period and the one after the Meiji Restoration. In F.K.S. Leung, K. D. Graf, & F. J. Lopez-Real (Eds.), *Mathematics education in different cultural traditions—a comparative study of East Asia and the West* (pp. 65–79). New York, NY: Springer Science and Business Media.

Wiseman, R. (2002). *Queen Bees & Wannabes: Helping your daughter survive cliques, gossip, boyfriends, & other realities of adolescents.* New York, NY: Three Rivers Press.

9

I TEACH JIM AND JANE; I DON'T TEACH GYM

Carol A. Smith

The field of physical education was historically based on physical strength and endurance for military preparedness rather than skill development (Spears & Swanson, 1989). Today, the focus of physical education is on taking care of oneself through healthy living; skill development is important but an equal emphasis is placed on a healthy lifestyle. As such, schools and institutes of higher education have moved away from using the term "physical education" in favor of the term "kinesiology" or the study of human movement as a more health-based nomenclature (Brassie & Razor, 1989; Freeman & Woolard, 2012).

Stereotypes in Physical Education

Social media and popular culture, however, influence and shape the perceptions and portrayals of physical educators; these depictions often reinforce negative stereotypes of the profession (Spittle, Petering, Kremer & Spittle, 2012). Since accepted stereotypes create "a set of beliefs about the personal attributes of a group of people" (Stroebe & Insko, 1989, p. 5), these are likely to create negative views of physical educators that make teacher candidates less likely to major in the field. The ubiquity of the media makes movies and television an "inescapable aspect of our modern culture" (Duncan, Noland & Wood, 2002, p. 38) that introduces images that are not easily forgotten. With millions of people seeing negative portrayals of physical education teachers, what is seen in media is too often viewed as truth, regardless of whether it is based in fact (Duncan et al., 2002). It is no wonder that preservice teachers do not want to be categorized with the negatively stereotyped group, even though role models may have initially attracted them to physical education (Spittle et al., 2012).

One prevalent stereotype is that of the physical education teacher as a bully who enjoys seeing students humiliated (McCullick, Belcher, Hardin & Hardin, 2003). Running is used as a punishment, and verbal abuse and put-downs are common (Berg et al., 1995; Carmody et al., 1981; Blum et al., 2000; Levinson, Russo & Russo, 1984). The locker room is a place for humiliation and aggression, as seen in *Carrie* (Monash, Stroller & DePalma, 1976). As a bully, the physical education teacher does little—let alone effective—teaching, often just calling cadence for calisthenics (McCullick et al., 2003). Most instruction is given by yelling, oftentimes with obscenities that ridicule students and insult their physical characteristics. Often, the physical education teacher bullies vicariously by using games like dodgeball in which stronger, more athletic students can dominate or allow those stronger students to bully weaker or less well-liked students. The young male physical education teacher in *Porky's* (Carmody et al., 1981) instigates bullying behaviors and perpetuates situations in which he supports bullying behavior toward the less accepted students by the popular students (Carmody et al., 1981). The teacher's bullying behavior is often reflected in that of athletes; in *Glee* (Woodall, Novick, Silverstein, DelValle & Aguirre-Sacasa, 2009–2015), for example, popular athletes openly throw slushies into other students' faces in the hallways.

The dumb jock is another stereotype often seen in the media's representation of physical education teachers. Most "gym" teachers are relegated to this category; without the benefit of any particular curricular framework, most of them are not depicted as having any ability to teach the content of physical education (Dalton, 2004). The movie *Clueless* (Berg et al., 1995) portrays as clueless not just the lead actress but also the physical education teacher regarding specific curriculum content or understanding of the school environment. In addition, the dumb jock is often portrayed as oversexed, "on the make and muscularly fit" (McCullick et al., 2003, p. 12). This teacher is narcissistically focused on physique and looks and models heterosexual behavior to an extreme. In *Porky's* (Carmody et al., 1981), the young male physical education teacher consistently leers at women and engages in a physical relationship with another teacher in the locker room—which students and teachers hear while they are in the nearby gymnasium. In *Teachers* (Levinson et al., 1984), the male physical education teacher brings young female students into his office; later in the film, we learn three of those students are pregnant.

The physical education teacher is often pigeonholed into the dual role of the coach, a former athlete who is incapable of doing more than train others to play the former sport (Woodall et al., 2009–2015). In the television show *Bad Teacher* (Graynor & Diaz, 2014), the school's physical educator/coach is a pretty boy who does little coaching. McCullick et al. (2003) point out that oftentimes these physical education teachers have "indecipherable" (p. 9) roles since they are rarely portrayed teaching or coaching; most scenes are in the teachers' lounge, cafeteria or athletic field.

Women in physical education have an additional element added to their frequent stereotypes: that of the masculine female. While the need for athleticism and physicality in the profession mean that female physical educators frequently defy "specific constructs of femininity" (Spittle et al., 2012, p. 23), these qualities are greatly exaggerated in fictional female teachers. In *Glee* (Woodall et al., 2009–2015), the successful female football coach is named Shannon Beiste, pronounced "Beast." In *Porky's*, the physical education teacher, named Ms. Balbricker, is ridiculed for her weight and nicknamed "Kong." The lack of stereotypical feminine characteristics often leads to another stereotype, since "in the absence of the traditional notions of heterosexual attractiveness, the character is assumed to be a lesbian" (McCullick et al., 2003, p. 12). In *Clueless* (Berg et al., 1995), commentary on the female physical education teacher concludes, "And in the grand tradition of PE teachers, Miss Stogner seemed to be same-sex oriented." At the very least, female teachers are presented as androgynous, as is Miss Mann in *Scary Movie* (Blum et al., 2000).

Pedagogical Implications

The profession of the physical education teacher is not simply one of fun and games. While movement and exercise are enjoyable, academic content is incorporated in the play. As with other licensed teaching professionals, those certified in physical education are guided by national standards. According to the Society of Health and Physical Educators (SHAPE) America (2015), graduates from a quality physical education teacher education program are able to demonstrate, apply and exhibit

> a variety of motor skills and movement patterns . . . knowledge of concepts, principles, strategies and tactics related to movement and performance . . . knowledge and skills to achieve and maintain a health-enhancing level of physical activity and fitness . . . responsible personal and social behavior that respects self and others . . . [and] the value of physical activity for health, enjoyment, challenge, self-expression and/or social interaction.
>
> *(p. 2)*

Since physical education enjoyment and sport experiences are a primary reason for choosing physical education as a career, awareness and understanding of the stereotypes surrounding physical education are important for preservice teachers. These stereotypes may be stumbling blocks to appropriate perceptions of their future careers, since popular culture clearly supports a negative presentation of physical education teachers that influences how preservice teachers may see themselves and how others view them (Dalton, 2004; Drake & Herbert, 2002; Duncan et al., 2002; Gaudreault, 2014; James-Hassan, 2014; Mitchell & Bott, 2015; McCullick et al., 2003; Spittle et al., 2012). Acknowledging the many negative stereotypes perpetuated by the media, teacher educators must work with preservice teachers to counter negative stereotypes in order to adopt the professional dispositions of physical education teachers (Lawson, 2015).

Professionalism

Physical educators should dress professionally at all times, avoiding coaching attire in the classroom and clothes inappropriate to the classroom regarding length, style or verbiage. Physical educators should work to keep teaching and coaching separate, even though many physical education teachers are coaches—for example, having students refer to the teacher as Mr., Mrs. or Ms. and the coach as Coach in the appropriate setting. The attitude behind teaching and coaching is different, as are styles of facilitating and types of terminology in the professional realm (Drake & Herbert, 2002; Duncan et al., 2002; Gaudreault, 2014; McCullick et al., 2003; Mitchell & Bott, 2015; SHAPE America, 2015; Spittle et al., 2012).

Curriculum

Physical education is the curricular content that provides foundational skills and knowledge for a lifetime (SHAPE America, 2015). Therefore, the curriculum must move beyond the traditional sports-oriented skill development aspect of physical education. While important, athletics is an extracurricular element of physical education, focused on allowing gifted and highly skilled players to continue their participation in the sport (Gaudreault, 2014; James-Hassan, 2014). Foundational knowledge pertaining to health and wellness should be emphasized in addition to learning how to play specific sports or gaining appropriate skills in a variety of lifetime activities. The assessment of learning must also be authentic and credible.

Lifelong Learning

The physical education teacher should attend professional workshops, conferences and seminars to increase content knowledge, learn new pedagogies and develop new curricula to improve programs for students. One benefit of the physical educator's position is the opportunity to teach all students in the school, not just students at a specific level of talent. Learning new pedagogies and staying current with the curriculum standards allow the teacher to teach all with respect and dignity (Gaudreault, 2014; James-Hassan, 2014; Mitchell & Bott, 2015).

Holding high standards of knowledge, skills, behavior and dress is the first step in conquering negative stereotypes of physical education teachers. If truth *is* in the perception, then the visual representation of who we are, the physical manifestation of the knowledge pertaining to the curriculum content and appropriate behavioral actions will be major steps in combating the undesirable typecast. Parents, students, administrators and other teachers must see the teacher in the gymnasium. We may teach Jim and Jane, but we don't teach *gym*.

References

Berg, B. M., Caplan, T., Lawrence, R., Rudin, S., Schroeder, A., (Producers), & Heckerling, A. (Director). (1995). *Clueless* [Motion picture]. United States: Paramount Pictures.

Blum, L., Dalto, E. L., Gold, E. L., Granat, C., Grey, B., . . . Mayes, L. R. (Producers), & Wayans, K. I. (Director). (2000). *Scary movie* [Motion picture]. United States: Dimension Films. Miramax Films.

Brassie, P. S., & Razor, J. E. (1989). HPERD unit names in higher education—a view toward the future. *JOPERD, 60*(7), 33–40.

Carmody, D., Clark, B., Goch, G., Greenberg, H., Kopelson, A., Simon, M. (Producers), & Clark, B. (Director). (1981). *Porky's* [Motion picture]. Canada: Astral Films. 20th Century Fox.

Dalton, M. M. (2004). *The Hollywood curriculum: Teachers in the movies*. New York, NY: Peter Lang International Academic.

Drake, D., & Herbert, E. P. (2002). Perceptions of occupational stress and strategies for avoiding burnout: Case studies of two female teacher-coaches. *The Physical Educator, 59*(4), 170–183.

Duncan, C. A., Nolan, J., & Wood, R. (2002). See you in the movies? We hope not!, *JOPERD, 73*(8), 38–44.

Freeman, W., & Woolard, D. (2012, January). *Defining ourselves: Current major program names in the United States*. Paper presented at the NAKPEHE Conference, San Diego, CA.

Gaudreault, K. L. (2014). "Cool PE" and confronting the negative stereotypes of physical education. *Strategies, 27*(3), 32–35.

Graynor, A., & Diaz, C. (Producers). (2014). *Bad teacher* [Television series]. Los Angeles, CA: Columbia Broadcast System Television Studios.

James-Hassan, M. (2014). Common purposes: Using the common core state standards to strengthen physical education instruction. *Strategies, 27*(6), 8–12.

Lawson, T. (Ed.). (2015). What are key strategies/approaches to prevent using physical activity as punishment in teaching and/or coaching? *JOPERD, 86*(4), 61–63.

Levinson, A., Russo, A., & Russo, I. (Producers), & Hiller, A. (Director). (1984). *Teachers* [Motion picture]. United States: Metro-Goldwyn-Mayer.

McCullick, B., Belcher, D., Hardin, B., & Hardin, M. (2003). Butches, bullies and buffoons: Images of physical education teachers in the movies. *Sport, Education and Society, 8*(1), 3–16.

Mitchell, M., & Bott, T. (2015). Preparing student teachers and beginning teachers for the post-teaching conference. *Journal of Physical Education, Recreation & Dance, 86*(2), 10–13.

Monash, P., Stroller, L. A., De Palma, B. (Producers), & De Palma, B. (Director). (1976). *Carrie* [Motion picture]. United States: United Artists.

SHAPE America. (2015). *The essential components of physical education*. Reston, VA: Author.

Spears, B., & Swanson, R. A. (1989). *History of sport and physical education in the United States* (3rd ed.). Columbus, OH: McGraw-Hill.

Spittle, M., Petering, F., Kremer, P., & Spittle, S. (2012). Stereotypes and self-perceptions of physical education pre-service teachers. *Australian Journal of Teacher Education, 37*(1), 19–42.

Stroebe, W., & Insko, C. A. (1989). Stereotype, prejudice, and discrimination: Changing conceptions in theory and research. In D. Bar-Tal, C. F. Graumann, A. W. Kruglanski & W. Stroebe (Eds.), Stereotyping and prejudice (pp. 3–34). New York, NY: Springer.

Woodall, A. M., Novick, M., Silverstein, K., Del Valle, R., & Aguirre-Sacasa, R. (Producers). (2009–2015). *Glee* [Television series]. Los Angeles, CA: 20th Century Fox Television.

10

WHAT DOES IT MEAN TO BE LITERATE?

Examining School Film Teachers and Their Literacy Values With Preservice Teachers

Shelbie Witte

Thomas Edison once predicted that in place of textbooks, film was destined to revolutionize our educational system (Hays, 1922). Although textbooks continue to be predominant in pedagogy, Edison's prophetic statement has come to pass in many ways. Movies are a powerful and compelling form of popular communication; as members of society, we are constant consumers of popular culture. Popular culture reflects certain truths and interpretations of our society, and reciprocally, it invents and influences societal trends that impact our ways of being, knowing and learning. Whether music, news, fashion, motion pictures or television, all facets of daily life are shaped by the very culture that we malleably mold by our choices. This basic understanding of the reciprocity of popular culture guides the work in teacher preparation in unique ways, for knowledge that emerges from the media-saturated cultural landscape can have a powerful impact on our thinking (Hall, 1980; Kress & Van Leeuwen, 1996; Steinberg & Kincheloe, 1992).

An analysis of what television and film images say about American education, and how they do so, is an area of research for many scholars that highlights links between the rhetorical narrative of American education and its depiction in film and television (Bulman, 2004; Crume, 1989; Dalton, 1995; Trier, 2000, 2001; Williams & Zenger, 2007; Witte & Goodson, 2010). It is also a tool to investigate the evolution of literacy and what society defines as literate through the representations of literacy values and the literacy pedagogy depicted by teachers in school films (Williams & Zenger, 2007; Witte, 2008). The ways in which school film teachers embrace literacy affect how people see literacy and even how they view literacy in relation to themselves and their places in society as literate individuals.

The use of school films with preservice teachers is not new (Trier, 2000). For years, teacher educators have discussed with preservice teachers the characteristics of good teachers and bad teachers, often using school films as depictions of each. What we haven't done, systematically, is make use of popular culture to demonstrate how teachers place value in literacy within the film contexts to create opportunities for professional development. By studying how preservice teachers make sense of the ways in which teachers value literacy in school films, we can explore ways to advance the professional development of preservice teachers and unmask the contradictory images of literacy and learning in school films.

The Approach: Preservice Teachers Examining School Films Through Methods

Preservice teachers in a university English language arts methods course were asked to react, analyze, reflect and apply lessons learned from a sequential and chronological viewing of scenes from school films (Table 10.1) that depict teachers and their literacy values and pedagogies.

Beginning with *Goodbye, Mr. Chips* (Saville & Wood, 1939) and ending with *Freedom Writers* (DeVito et al., 2007), preservice teachers were guided through a shared viewing of key scenes in each film that depict literacy values and pedagogies. Preservice teachers worked through a series of independent and shared writing and discussion activities that highlighted their reactions, analyses, reflections and applications of the knowledge gained (Witte, 2008). By writing and discussing each film scene through the activities detailed ahead, preservice teachers gained insight into the ways in which popular depictions of teachers and literacy events are reflective of the literacy values of society over time. Films in the time periods were selected from a comprehensive list (Witte, 2008), using a process

TABLE 10.1 School Films Used in Methods Course

Time	Film	Director
1930s–1950s	*Goodbye, Mr. Chips* (1939)	Sam Wood
	The Corn Is Green (1945)	Irving Rapper
	Blackboard Jungle (1955)	Richard Brooks
1960s–1970s	*To Sir, With Love* (1967)	James Clavell
	Up the Down Staircase (1967)	Robert Mulligan
	Conrack (1974)	Martin Ritt
1980s	*Teachers* (1984)	Arthur Hiller
	Stand and Deliver (1988)	Ramon Menéndez
	Dead Poets Society (1989)	Peter Weir
1990s	*Dangerous Minds* (1995)	John N. Smith
	Mr. Holland's Opus (1995)	Stephen Hereck
	187 (1997)	Kevin Williams
2000s	*Chalk* (2006)	Mike Akel
	The Ron Clark Story (2006)	Randa Haines
	Freedom Writers (2007)	Richard LaGravenese

of parameters, including the depiction of teachers as main characters, classroom locale and dramatic classification.

Preservice students viewed each scene and responded to it independently, using the following viewing protocol:

REACT: Provide a reader's response to the scene.
ANALYZE: Consider one or more of the following questions:

- How is literacy expressed in the scene?
- What are the components of literacy present in the scene?
- How is the importance of being "literate" expressed in the scene?

REFLECT: What role(s) do(es) the teacher, the school and the student(s) play in the representation of literacy, components of literacy and importance of literacy?
APPLY: Using the lens of a learner and the lens of a future teacher, what lessons can be learned from this representation of teaching, literacy and learning?

After viewing each scene, preservice teachers were provided a written transcription of the scene (Figure 10.1) to aid them in writing their responses to each prompt.

After viewing the film scenes, writing individual responses and sharing in whole-class debriefings throughout the semester, the preservice teachers participated in a

---

Goodbye, Mr. Chips (1939)

[*Bombs explode and sirens wail. A policeman on bicycle rides by while blowing a warning whistle. People on the streets run to cover. A group of the schoolboys is looking out of the window of the school in hopes of seeing some of the battle. Bombs explode and the buildings nearby shake*]

Student #1: Look! There it is! There!

Student #2: Look! Over there!

Student #3: It's the clock, you fool!

Student #4: The guns! They must have spied it.

Teacher: Here! Out of this, you kids! Down to the lower school!

[*He gathers the boys out of the window and guides them downstairs*]

[*Downstairs in the classroom, many of the boys are trying to look out the windows*]

Mr. Chips: Put those blinds down.

[*Sounds of bombs blasting*]

FIGURE 10.1 Excerpt of Scene Transcription

cumulative critical thinking exercise to identify common themes across scenes and decades. Preservice teachers were led through the basic steps of discourse analysis with a model example, highlighting themes and trends that emerged and discussing approaches to interpreting discourse for analysis purposes. A discussion of themes and trends found within the model coding was shared until homogeneity or consensus was achieved to the satisfaction of the group.

Next, the class was divided into groupings of three to code their viewing protocols to identify the common themes across scenes and decades. Once the basic coding was completed, groups shared their themes with textual evidence of the film, scene and discourse provided; as patterns were identified, the film scenes were sorted by theme. After the film scenes were collaboratively grouped according to literacy theme, preservice teachers selected a theme to discuss in further detail in a formal critique essay.

The work discussed in this chapter is drawn from the 2014 cohort of preservice English language arts teachers (names used ahead are pseudonyms). The cohort included 32 students (26 females and 6 males) with 82% of students self-identifying as White, 12% Black and 6% Hispanic, typical demographics for the English Language Arts program at the university. The themes identified in the critique essays and discussed in face-to-face discussions by the 2014 cohort were Literacy and Societal/Ethical Considerations, Literacy and Unorthodox Pedagogy as a Community-Building Practice, Literacy Pedagogy and Media Literacy, Literacy and Textual Connections and Literacy in the Real World. Each theme is discussed ahead.

Literacy and Societal/Ethical Expectations

The scenes selected from *Goodbye, Mr. Chips* (Saville & Wood, 1939), *Teachers* (Levinson, Russo, Russo & Hiller, 1984) and *187* (Davey, Harfield, McEveety & Reynolds, 1997) (Table 10.2) emphasize the importance of literacy by depicting societal and ethical expectations teachers have for their students. When discussing expectations of students with preservice teachers, it is important to emphasize that there are many ways in which we express the literacy expectations we value as educators: through our curriculum, through our teacher behaviors and through our interactions with students (Cook-Gumperz, 1986; Fisher, 2009; Franzak, 2006; Schaafsma, 1990; Tatum, 2006; Zipin & Brennan, 2006).

Kyle highlighted a clear literacy thread between these three scenes in his response, noting,

> I'm really drawn to what each scene represents as important for literate people to know. In *Chips*, of all things to teach teenage boys, I wonder why Latin? Is this the most useful thing these students need to learn? Clearly, in *Teachers*, Mr. Jurel just wants Eddie to be able to read a sentence and in *187*, Mr. Garfield wants Rita to believe in her literacy abilities.

TABLE 10.2 Grouping of Literacy and Societal/Ethical Expectations

	Scene summary
Goodbye, Mr. Chips (1939)	Mr. Chipping (Mr. Chips) leads a class through the reading of *Julius Caesar* in Latin to distract the students while fighter planes bombard the town and bombs strike.
Teachers (1984)	Faced with a meeting with Eddie's self-absorbed mother, Mr. Jurel puts Eddie on the spot to read from a magazine. Despite his struggle, it is apparent that Eddie cannot read and has been passed from grade to grade.
187 (1997)	Mr. Garfield leads a writing conference with Rita, a student struggling to find her way through a gang-centric life. Rita has hopes of being successful but finds ways to anticipate the negative.

In his analysis, Kyle recognized that we have different levels of curricula (Flinders, Noddings & Thornton, 1986; Horn, 2003; Quigley, 1997) and sometimes, while following the curriculum is important, students' inability to use basic literacies effectively is often overlooked. Tayler agreed with this disconnect, emphasizing, "Times have changed and what was considered 'literate' in the past is not what we measure today."

The preservice teachers highlighted the ethical considerations of each of the three scenes, as well. Lashonda asked important questions, such as "Why was Mr. Chips teaching a reading lesson during a siege when it appears the walls could fall down?" and "Couldn't he have at least let them get under their desks?" She then offered a real-life comparison: "I was in a lock down drill once and our teacher made us continue reading from our textbooks. It was 'Rikki-Tikki-Tavvi' and I remember that story and that drill from that year. That's it." Several of the preservice teachers were also flabbergasted that Eddie in *Teachers* is in high school and cannot read. Lashonda stated it simply: "How can someone pass each grade and not be able to read? How does this happen? It's unethical." Especially poignant was Tayler's response to the portrayal of females:

> I know it's way back in time with *Chips*, so there aren't any girls there at the boys' school, but seriously? This is antiquated. And then Eddie's mom is portrayed as someone who doesn't care about Eddie's inability to read and a self-absorbed female worried about money. And then, Rita in *187* is depicted as someone who is used to failing, like the narrative of her life is already planned out for her. I'm so glad the world is different now. Well, at least my part of the world. I guess there are places that aren't. Which makes me sad.

Asking preservice teachers to consider what teachers do as professionals without also considering the expectations of and duties to uphold the societal and ethical considerations of the profession would be incomplete. By providing pre-service teachers opportunities to view the varying degrees to which the profession demands an awareness of, and in some cases an action in response to, these considerations, they are better able to watch for the dynamics and idiosyncrasies at play in their own teaching environments.

Literacy and Unorthodox Pedagogy as a Community-Building Practice

The unorthodox literacy pedagogy approaches found in *The Corn Is Green* (Chertok, Warner & Rapper, 1945), *Conrack* (Frank, Korbitz & Ritt, 1974) and *Dead Poets Society* (Haft, Henderson, Witt, Thomas & Weir, 1989) (Table 10.3) focused the preservice teachers' attention on the practice of building community in order to build literacy. The literature on the importance of building a community of literacy practices is extensive (Bloome, 1986; Grisham & Wolsey, 2006; Moje, Overby, Tysvaer & Morris, 2008; Scardamalia & Bereiter, 2006), but the application of these practices is often difficult to teach preservice teachers without concrete examples, making film clips a useful addition to the classroom.

Meredith found the scene from *The Corn Is Green* instrumental in understanding how important schools are in sharing literacy with communities:

> This scene really illustrates for me the importance of the school to the town. It reminded me of the television show *Little House on the Prairie* where they go to school and have church in the same building. Literacy practices are important in both church and school. This scene, a singing of a hymn in the school, shows that the literacy practice of expression in song is valuable.

TABLE 10.3 Grouping of Literacy and Unorthodox Pedagogy as Community-Building Practice

	Scene summary
The Corn Is Green (1945)	Miss Ronberry leads the class (an eclectic mix of children and adults) in a hymn while Miss Moffat discusses teaching a student Greek and studying/learning Greek only days in advance of teaching a specific student.
Conrack (1974)	Mr. Conroy, after being fired by the local school board for drawing attention to the inequalities prevalent in its district, addresses the town on loudspeaker to plead for both reinstatement and more attention to the inequities prevalent in the schools.
Dead Poets Society (1989)	In dramatic fashion, Mr. Keating brings his class together by showing poetry cannot be analyzed by numbers, as is suggested in the traditional literature textbook, but by savoring the words.

Eric followed the community-building thread from *The Corn Is Green* to *Conrack*, explaining,

> Mr. Conroy tried to teach [the students] the "big picture"' of learning by showing them how to "embrace life openly, to reflect on its mysteries, and to reject its cruelties." His speech symbolizes that there is much more to becoming literate than being taught to read and write.

Both Eric and Meredith recognized the importance of each scene portraying the use of nontraditional methods to reach the communities being taught. The student bodies presented specific challenges, especially in the lack of educational background; as Eric noted, "The traditional model of teaching wouldn't work in either case." Meredith comes back to unorthodox pedagogy in *Dead Poets Society*, reflecting,

> It's unlikely a teacher today could get away with tearing out the pages of the textbook that explains, though archaically, how to analyze poetry . . . and then throwing them in the trash, but this act of civil disobedience builds instant community within the classroom and visualizes for the students the passion Mr. Keating has for helping them learn to "find their own verse," so to speak.

Eric concurs in his analysis, explaining that "in teacher-fandom, this scene is iconic because Mr. Keating does in five very short minutes what we will all hope and dream to do as teachers."

These scenes illustrate for preservice teachers that for many students, literacy is a basic human need and, in some cases, right, to which they have been denied access. From children born in poverty and denied access to equitable literacy education juxtaposed with children born in wealth with every opportunity to develop literacy skills, the students in our classrooms arrive with a multitude of backgrounds. Preservice teachers recognize the need to scaffold and reinforce for all students the literacy opportunities within and beyond the classroom.

Literacy Pedagogy and Media Literacy

Through *Blackboard Jungle* (Berman & Brooks, 1955), *The Ron Clark Story* (Brockway et al., 2006) and *Freedom Writers* (DeVito et al., 2007) (Table 10.4), the preservice teachers recognized that these teachers set out to engage their students in literacy learning by using media literacy and popular culture connections. Most preservice teachers naturally connect the curriculum they are designing for students to contemporary texts and technologies, but they are often more reluctant to do so in practice when faced with prescribed curricula (Buckingham, 1998; Marsh, 2006; Morrell, 2002; Paul, 2000). Making visible the ways in which media

TABLE 10.4 Grouping of Literacy and Media Literacy

	Scene summary
Blackboard Jungle (1955)	Mr. Dadier shows the cartoon "Jack and the Beanstalk" to a difficult-to-reach group of students in order to discuss characterization, plot and theme. (This scene is the first depiction in film of a teacher using multimedia with students.)
The Ron Clark Story (2006)	Mr. Clark introduces the idea of learning all of the U.S. presidents through the memorization of a teacher-created rap.
Freedom Writers (2007)	Ms. Gruwell and her students are impacted by their visit to the Holocaust Museum, as multimedia displays bring the realities of the genocide to life.

literacy can contribute significantly to disengaged students allows preservice teachers the opportunity to build confidence in their pedagogical approaches.

Maria recognized that

> Mr. Dadier initiates lively, meaningful discussions with students about cartoons but these attempts are not without difficulty. Mr. Clark has some reluctant students as well, asking students to learn a rap song in order to know the presidents. Ms. Gruwell struggled with helping the students connect with the events of the Holocaust until she could make it visual for them, at the museum.

Knowing when to use and when not to use ties to popular culture texts is important. Maria noted that the key to success for Mr. Dadier in this scene is his realization that the teens of the 1950s are not the same as the kids with whom he went to school. As Maria explained,

> He knows that the students he teaches enjoy movies. By developing the students' media literacy by showing films, he gets students to let their guards down and to realize that he is not just like all the other teachers. He respects their culture and in turn they begin to respect him.

Eric also recognized that students need to understand how to make judgments about what is depicted in the media based on critical thinking. Doing so requires students to apply what they are learning in school to what they see outside of school (Hull & Schultz, 2002; Lee, 2004):

> What each of the teachers does in the scenes is use [media] to help students see what and why they need to learn things and understand how they relate

to school. That seems like a no-brainer and that teachers would do this often, but maybe it's because they have trouble understanding what media literacy is all about.

As a counterpoint to the enthusiasm of bringing outside literacies into the classroom as a way to engage students, Amy offered a consideration for the cohort to consider:

> While the power of popular culture and media integration is apparent in the scenes, I think we need to also consider the bigger picture of where and why the boundaries between school and home exist. At what point are we bastardizing the literacies that our students value as important?

Amy drew our attention to course readings that discussed the idea of potholes in the process of implementing media literacy as well as the dangers of teachers trespassing in student literacy spaces (Barton, 2001; O'Brien & Scharber, 2008; Witte, 2009), concluding,

> Ultimately, it is a negotiation between the teacher and students as to what is comfortable and what is doable. Teachers must be willing to listen to what students have to say about what they need in order to do what the teacher is asking of them.

Preservice teachers, while often eager to use popular culture and contemporary texts, are sometimes inexperienced in considering the bigger picture of what the inclusion and integration can further in regards to literacy education. Beyond the "attention-getting" engagement aspects of YouTube videos and popular song lyrics, a critical media literacy approach to the inclusion of popular media texts provides teachers with the opportunity to expand their core curriculum in innovative ways.

Literacy and Textual Connections

One important aspect in the preparation of future English teachers is guiding them to find and apply relevant text-to-text connections (Table 10.5) in order to strengthen their lesson plans and curricular decisions. When teachers help adolescents find connections between and within texts, the experiences and background knowledge brought to the texts help students find a purpose in what and why they are reading (Fisher, Frey & Lapp, 2012; Gritter, 2012; Keene & Zimmerman, 1997; L'Allier & Elish-Piper, 2007; Seglem & Witte, 2009).

Rebecca was drawn to the scene highlighted in *Up the Down Staircase* (Pakula & Mulligan, 1967), asking important questions such as "How can we expect students to concentrate on a canonical text like *A Tale of Two Cities* when their basic needs, like sitting in a desk, aren't taken care of?" The preservice teachers questioned

TABLE 10.5 Grouping of Literacy and Textual Connections

	Scene summary
Up the Down Staircase (1967)	Miss Barrett, teaching at an urban high school, introduces *Tale of Two Cities* to her students while being observed by her principal. She scaffolds background knowledge and text-to-self connections in order to illustrate the use of antithesis.
Mr. Holland's Opus (1995)	Mr. Holland, a career music/band/orchestra teacher, helps students trace the connections between classical music and contemporary music.
Chalk (2006)	In a pseudo-fake-umentary, Mr. Lowrey participates in a Spelling Hornet, a teacher/staff event run by students. Structured like a traditional spelling bee, a Spelling Hornet requires the spelling of slang words prevalent in teen vocabularies.

what this scene says about literacy in the 1960s, beyond the racial tensions and Civil Rights movement happening at the time. When literacy is expressed as an ability to read fluently aloud, as well as discussing a text with which students have no connection, they may be deemed illiterate when they are lacking understanding only of background and context.

A lack of background and context in textual origin is also the focus of the scene from *Mr. Holland's Opus* (Cort et al., 1996), with Mr. Holland discussing the origins of rock and roll and tracing them back to classical composers, such as Bach. Rebecca explained, "By showing students how one text scaffolds to the next, students gain an immediate frame of reference for their thinking, a pedagogical approach I will definitely keep in mind as I plan my lessons." The preservice teachers recognized that in order to make these connections, a breadth and depth of knowledge of the texts that will be taught and are available to be taught are critical.

A different perspective of textual connections is offered in the scene from *Chalk* (Akel et al., 2006). As Nikki explained,

> I was one of the people really pushing for this scene to be included in the textual connections theme because I strongly believe that the Spelling Hornet is a great example of how teachers can show students the ways that words matter in the world. Even though slang words aren't a typical text we use in the classroom, they are a part of our students' lives.

By drawing on the schema students have regarding word origins, Mr. Lowery studies and is ultimately successful in learning about a topic that is completely unknown to him. Nikki continued, saying, "Mr. Lowery has modeled for students what a life-long learner looks like and how tackling a new topic, while challenging, has its rewards. He just had to learn how the slang words connected to words he already knew." While the notion of text-to-text/world/self connections is not new to preservice teachers, the film clips help illustrate how these connections are critical in helping students associate their learning from one class and subject to the next, transferring the literacy skills they learn to all aspects of their lives.

Literacy in the Real World

One of the most challenging aspects of preparing preservice teachers is guiding them to appreciate students' needs to understand how what they are learning in the classroom is relevant to their lives outside of school (Alvermann & Hagood, 2000; Freire & Macedo, 2013; Hinchman, Alvermann, Boyd, Brozo & Vacca, 2003; Hull & Schultz, 2002; Purcell-Gates, 2007). *To Sir, With Love* (Clavell & Sloan, 1967), *Stand and Deliver* (Labunka, Law, Musca & Menendez, 1988) and *Dangerous Minds* (Bruckheimer et al., 1995) (Table 10.6) each offer a unique perspective on the importance of connecting literacy to the real world. Shane reflected,

> Mr. Thackeray has an a-ha moment in this scene and so do I. When he says "That's it!" and throws away the textbooks, he has realized that what he is being required to teach is useless to his students. Literacy takes on a whole new meaning than just simply reading and writing well; it means to function well inside of school and outside of school.

Nikki reflected about the *Stand and Deliver* scene, contrasting her own class experience with the one depicted on-screen:

> I know Mr. Escalante's sense of humor doesn't make sense to everyone. Honestly, I would be afraid to say some of the things he said, principal in

TABLE 10.6 Grouping of Literacy in the Real World

	Scene summary
To Sir, With Love (1967)	Mr. Thackeray realizes that the students in his classroom need a curriculum beyond the textbook. He approaches his class with brutal honesty as to what they will need to know in a very short time to be successful adults.
Stand and Deliver (1988)	While trying to explain how an algebraic equation works, Mr. Escalante works with disengaged students struggling to understand how what they are learning in class relates to the lives they will live outside of school.
Dangerous Minds (1995)	Leading her students through an analysis of poetry, Ms. Johnson struggles to reach reluctant students who feel they have no choice in the lives they live, both at school and at home.

the room or not. But I do think he has his students' attention, especially when he helps them see how what they are learning translates to work environments. I never had the opportunity to see how algebra or calculus tied to anything I would do outside of the Saxon textbook. Maybe if I had, I wouldn't be so scared of it now.

The preservice teachers could see many similarities between Mr. Escalante's students and Ms. Johnson's students in *Dangerous Minds*. The need for real-world connections to Dylan Thomas's poem in *Dangerous Minds* leads Ms. Johnson to have a serious discussion with her students about choices. Nikki reacted:

> The students in this scene of *Dangerous Minds* are angry. Their body language and words/lack of words to Mrs. Johnson during the class show that they have absolutely no concept of how this poem and this class mean anything to their real lives. They feel trapped and Mrs. Johnson is trying to help them see that they have every choice.

In his conclusion, Shane also came back to the a-ha moment he mentioned previously with Mr. Thackeray in relation to Mr. Escalante and Ms. Johnson:

> The more I consider it, these scenes are more than just how the students are won over by seeing the real world in what they are learning. These scenes are also about how each of the teachers figured out what the "real world" looks like as a student.

This grouping of film clips, more than any other, helped solidify for preservice teachers the reason why teachers do what they do: prepare students for their future lives. While knowing how to be literate is important for being successful in school, our preservice teachers can clearly see that beyond school, we want the literate lives of our students to continue to grow.

Implications for Teacher Education

By using film as a pedagogical medium, preservice teachers in the cohort identified some important concepts about literacy in their analysis: the need for in-school literacies to acknowledge out-of-school literacies, the importance of media in literacy, the power of student engagement in literacy learning. Although literature in the field discusses these issues, what is currently lacking, and what school films offer, is a pedagogical medium apart and aside from the traditional texts of teacher preparation and professional development. Film offers a common experience that can be shared, evaluated, reflected upon and revisited.

Through examination of depictions of school film teachers and their literacy values, preservice teachers consider the complexities of societal and ethical considerations each can face when providing equitable opportunities for all students to grow in their literate lives. The preservice teachers who consider these clips are also faced with examples of teachers that, despite their best efforts, face real challenges to building engaging and rigorous literacy learning for every student in every class. And certainly, these films allow us to pause and consider alongside our preservice teachers the larger question of the purpose of a literate life altogether. As future English teachers, being able to know the answer to why literacy is important and what a literate life can offer our students could very well be the difference in a student's life trajectory.

School films offer the opportunity to raise collective questions and clarify our thinking through a multimodal experience that is often lost in the traditional curriculum for teacher preparation. School films allow preservice teachers the opportunity to view and better understand the evolution of literacy and our field over time. According to Giroux (2001), film is the site of educated hopes and hyper-mediated experiences that connect the personal and the social by bridging the contradictory.

The complex multiple literacies represented in these films reflect just some of the literacies that can be cultivated in our classrooms. They reflect the emergence of an understanding of these multiple literacies over time, and they remind us of the literacies of all of our students. These films reflect what we have been as educators and how far we have yet to go in bringing forth all of the necessary literacies in all of our students, and for that they serve as instructive reminders of what we are called upon to do as educators.

References

Akel, L., Akel, M., Alvarez, A., Amodei, J., Darbyshire, C. C., . . . Spurlock, M. (Producers), & Akel, M. (Director). (2006). *Chalk* [Motion picture]. United States: Virgil Films and Entertainment.

Alvermann, D. E., & Hagood, M. C. (2000). Critical media literacy: Research, theory, and practice in "New Times." *Journal of Educational Research, 93*(3), 193–205.

Barton, D. (2001). Literacy in everyday contexts. In L. Verhoeven & C. Snow (Eds.), *Literacy and motivation: Reading engagement in individuals and groups* (pp. 23–37), Mahwah, NJ: Lawrence Erlbaum.

Berman, P. S. (Producer), & Brooks, R. (Director). (1955). *Blackboard jungle* [Motion picture]. United States: MGM.

Bloome, D. (1986). Building literacy and the classroom community. *Theory Into Practice, 25*(2), 71–76.

Brockway, J., Burkons, H., Cox, T., Friend, B., Gilad, A., . . . Randall, J. (Producers), & Haines, R. (Director). (2006). *The Ron Clark story* [Motion picture]. United States: Turner Network Television.

Bruckheimer, J., Foster, L., Guinzburg, K., Rabins, S., Simpson, D. (Producers), & Smith, J. N. (Director). (1995). *Dangerous minds* [Motion picture]. United States: Hollywood Pictures.

Buckingham, D. (Ed.). (1998). *Teaching popular culture: Beyond radical pedagogy*. London, UK: UCL Press.

Bulman, R. C. (2004). *Hollywood goes to high school: Cinema, schools, and American culture.* New York, NY: Worth.

Chertok, J., Warner, J. L. (Producers), & Rapper, I., (Director). (1945). *The corn is green* [Motion picture]. United States: Warner Bros.

Clavell, J., Sloan, J. R. (Producers), & Clavell, J. (Director). (1967). *To Sir, with love* [Motion picture]. United States: Columbia Pictures.

Cook-Gumperz, J. (Ed.). (1986). *The social construction of literacy* (Vol. 3). Cambridge, UK: Cambridge University Press.

Cort, R. W., Duncan, P. S., Field, T., James, J., Kroopf, S., . . . Teitler, W. (Producer), & Herek, S. (Director). (1996). *Mr. Holland's opus* [Motion picture]. United States: Buena Vista Pictures.

Crume, M. (1989). Images of teachers in films and literature. *Education Week, 9*(5), 36.

Dalton, M. M. (1995). The Hollywood curriculum: Who is the "good" teacher? *Curriculum Studies, 3*(1), 23–44.

Davey, B., Harfield, D., McEveety, S. (Producers), & Reynolds, K. (Director). (1997). *187* [Motion picture]. United States: Warner Bros.

DeVito, D., Durning, T., Glick-Franzheim, J., Levine, D., Morales, N., . . . Swank, H. (Producers), & LaGravenese, R. (Director). (2007). *Freedom writers* [Motion picture]. United States: Paramount Pictures.

Fisher, D. (2009, April). The use of instructional time in the typical high school classroom. *Educational Forum, 73*(2), 168–176.

Fisher, D., Frey, N., & Lapp, D. (2012). Building and activating students' background knowledge: It's what they already know that counts. *Middle School Journal, 43*(3), 22–31.

Flinders, D. J., Noddings, N., & Thornton, S. J. (1986). The null curriculum: Its theoretical basis and practical implications. *Curriculum Inquiry, 16*(1), 33–42.

Frank, H., Jr., Korbitz, R., Ritt, M. (Producers), & Ritt, M. (Director). (1974). *Conrack* [Motion picture]. United States: 20th Century Fox.

Franzak, J. K. (2006). Zoom: A review of the literature on marginalized adolescent readers, literacy theory, and policy implications. *Review of Educational Research, 76*(2), 209–248.

Freire, P., & Macedo, D. (2013). *Literacy: Reading the word and the world.* New York, NY: Routledge.

Giroux, H. A. (2001). Breaking into the movies: Pedagogy and the politics of film. *Journal of Advanced Composition, 21*(3), 583–598.

Grisham, D. L., & Wolsey, T. D. (2006). Recentering the middle school classroom as a vibrant learning community: Students, literacy, and technology intersect. *Journal of Adolescent & Adult Literacy, 49*(8), 648–660.

Gritter, K. (2012). Permeable textual discussion in tracked language arts classrooms. *Research in the Teaching of English, 46*(3), 232–259.

Haft, S., Henderson, D., Witt, P. J., Thomas, T. (Producers), & Weir, P. (Director). (1989). *Dead poets society* [Motion picture]. United States: Buena Vista Pictures.

Hall, S. (1980). Encoding/Decoding. In S. Hall, D. Hobson, A. Lowe, & P. Willis (Eds.), *Culture, media, language* (pp. 1972–1979). London: Routledge & Kegan Paul.

Hays, W. H. (1922/1974). *Improvement of moving pictures.* National Education Association, Journal of Proceedings and Addresses, Boston. In S. Cohen (ed.), *Education in the United States: A documentary history* (Vol. 4, p. 2205). New York, NY: Random House.

Hinchman, K. A., Alvermann, D. E., Boyd, F. B., Brozo, W. G., & Vacca, R. T. (2003). Supporting older students' in- and out-of-school literacies. *Journal of Adolescent & Adult Literacy, 47*(4), 304–310.

Horn, R. A., Jr. (2003). Developing a critical awareness of the hidden curriculum through media literacy. *The Clearing House, 76*(6), 298–300.

Hull, G. A., & Schultz, K. (Eds.). (2002). *School's out: Bridging out-of-school literacies with classroom practice* (Vol. 60). New York, NY: Teachers College Press.

Keene, E., & Zimmerman, S. (1997). *Mosaic of thought.* Portsmouth, NH: Heinemann.

Kress, G., & Van Leeuwen, T. (1996). *Reading images: The grammar of visual design.* London, UK: Routledge.

Labunka, I., Law, L., Musca, T. (Producer), & Menéndez, R. (Director). (1988). *Stand and deliver* [Motion picture]. United States: Warner Bros.

L'Allier, S. K., & Elish-Piper, L. (2007). "Walking the walk" with teacher education candidates: Strategies for promoting active engagement with assigned readings. *Journal of Adolescent & Adult Literacy, 50*(5), 338–353.

Lee, C. D. (2004). Bridging home and school literacies: Models for culturally responsive teaching, a case for African-American English. *Handbook of Research on Teaching Literacy Through the Communicative and Visual Arts: Sponsored by the International Reading Association, 1,* 334.

Levinson, A., Russo, A., Russo, I. (Producers), & Hiller, A. (Director). (1984). *Teachers* [Motion picture]. United States: MGM/UA Entertainment.

Marsh, J. (2006). Popular culture in the literacy curriculum: A Bourdieuan analysis. *Reading Research Quarterly, 41*(2), 160–174.

Moje, E., Overby, M., Tysvaer, N., & Morris, K. (2008). The complex world of adolescent literacy: Myths, motivations, and mysteries. *Harvard Educational Review, 78*(1), 107–119.

Morrell, E. (2002). Toward a critical pedagogy of popular culture: Literacy development among urban youth. *Journal of Adolescent & Adult Literacy, 46*(1), 72–77.

O'Brien, D., & Scharber, C. (2008). Digital literacies go to school: Potholes and possibilities. *Journal of Adolescent & Adult Literacy, 52*(1), 66–68.

Pakula, A. J. (Producer), & Mulligan, R. (Director). (1967). *Up the down staircase* [Motion picture]. United States: Warner Bros.

Paul, D. G. (2000). Rap and orality: Critical media literacy, pedagogy, and cultural synchronization. *Journal of Adolescent & Adult Literacy, 44*(3), 246–252.

Purcell-Gates, V. E. (2007). *Cultural practices of literacy: Case studies of language, literacy, social practice, and power.* Mahwah, NJ: Lawrence Erlbaum.

Quigley, B. A. (1997). *Rethinking literacy education: The critical need for practice-based change.* The Jossey-Bass Higher and Adult Education Series. San Francisco, CA: Jossey-Bass.

Saville, V. (Producer), & Wood, S. (Director). (1939). *Goodbye, Mr. Chips* [Motion picture]. United States: MGM.

Scardamalia, M., & Bereiter, C. (2006). Knowledge building: Theory, pedagogy, and technology. In K. Sawyer (Ed.), *Cambridge handbook of the learning sciences* (pp. 97–118). New York, NY: Cambridge University Press.

Schaafsma, D. (1990). *Eating on the street: Teaching literacy in a multicultural society.* Pittsburgh, PA: University of Pittsburgh Press.

Seglem, R., & Witte, S. (2009). You gotta see it to believe it: Teaching visual literacy in the English classroom. *Journal of Adolescent & Adult Literacy, 53*(3), 216–226.

Steinberg, J. L., & Kincheloe, S. R. (1992). *Thirteen questions: Reframing education's conversation.* New York, NY: Peter Lang.

Tatum, A. W. (2006). Adolescents' multiple identities and teacher professional development. *Reconceptualizing the Literacies in Adolescents' Lives, 2,* 65–79.

Trier, J. (2000). Using popular "school films" to engage student teachers in critical reflection. Paper presented at the annual meeting of the American Educational Research Association, New Orleans, LA.

Trier, J. D. (2001). The cinematic representation of the personal and professional lives of teachers. *Teacher Education Quarterly, 28*(3), 127–142.

Williams, B. T., & Zenger, A. A. (2007). *Popular culture and representations of literacy*. London, UK: Routledge.

Witte, S. (2008). *What you need, Eddie, is another remedial reading class: A semiotic analysis of representations of literacy in popular school film*. Unpublished dissertation, Kansas State University.

Witte, S. (2009). Twitterdee, twitterdumb: Teaching in the time of technology, tweets, and trespassing. *California English, 15*(1), 23–26.

Witte, S., & Goodson, F. T. (2010). "This guy's dead": Seeking the origins of the dystopian narrative of the American high school in the popular culture. *The High School Journal, 94*(1), 3–14.

Zipin, L., & Brennan, M. (2006). Meeting literacy needs of pre-service cohorts: Ethical dilemmas for socially just teacher educators. *Asia-Pacific Journal of Teacher Education, 34*(3), 333–351.

11

THE HIDDEN CURRICULUM IN ROOM 10

School Mythology and Professional Identity Negotiation in the *Miss Malarkey* Picture Book Series

Sarah Fischer

Two weeks before my first school year as an elementary teacher commenced, I met Miss Malarkey. I was taking a break from sorting the accumulation of school supplies I had inherited from the teacher who had previously occupied my classroom to visit the children's section at the local library to find a read-aloud book for the first day of school. *Miss Malarkey Doesn't Live in Room 10* was displayed on a shelf among other humorous titles chronicling classroom life, such as the popular *Miss Nelson Is Missing!* by Harry Allard and *First Day Jitters* by Julie Danneberg. The book takes up a familiar, yet seldom articulated, belief among young children that teachers' lives do not extend beyond the school building. Its sophisticated humor, requiring an experienced reader to pay careful attention to both text and illustration to "get it," was an aspect I thought would appeal to my class of third graders. I was right: *Miss Malarkey Doesn't Live in Room 10* was well-liked by my students that year and those that followed.

Written by retired teacher Judy Finchler and illustrator Kevin O'Malley, the picture books in the popular *Miss Malarkey* series employ a first-person limited perspective narrator in six of the seven books, an unnamed student who matter-of-factly narrates the everyday experiences in Miss Malarkey's first-grade classroom for the reader. The series includes:

- *Miss Malarkey Doesn't Live in Room 10* (1995)
- *Miss Malarkey Won't Be in Today* (1998)
- *Testing Miss Malarkey* (2000)
- *You're a Good Sport, Miss Malarkey* (2002)
- *Miss Malarkey's Field Trip* (2004)
- *Miss Malarkey Leaves No Reader Behind* (2006)
- *Congratulations, Miss Malarkey!* (2009)

While my third graders connected with the observational humor presented by the narrator (the student perspective) and the juxtaposition of O'Malley's illustrations with the text (often representing the teacher's point of view), the resulting layer of irony and sarcasm is entertaining to adults, too, particularly educators.

The *Miss Malarkey* books were an ideal resource for meeting course goals when I began teaching undergraduate children's literature and reading methods courses for preservice elementary teachers. Not only are they popular with children and teachers, but also they exemplify the sophisticated interdependence of text and illustration in children's picture books and provide opportunities to critically and, in this case, reflexively examine the ideological assumptions implied within texts. I have used the books as read-alouds at the beginning of a semester to aesthetically engage students in various course topics, such as reader identity or literacy-rich environments. Later in the course, we revisit the series as a whole class and in small groups to "read against the text" (West, 1994), deconstructing ideological assumptions and literary devices.

After we study the concept of implied reader and the interdependence of text and illustration in children's picture books, I have found that the preservice teachers are empowered to consider their agency as professionals; our discussions of *Miss Malarkey* scaffold their developing critical insight into the political discourses that will shape the contexts in which they teach. As culturally constructed artifacts, children's books are also read and understood within a sociocultural context. While there are ideological aspects of the *Miss Malarkey* books I find personally problematic—like stereotypes of substitute teachers and assumptions about boys and video games—the series is rich in content for analysis by teacher educators. Situating these picture books as cultural artifacts with multiple implied readers and multiple narratives, this chapter explores the use of the series to scaffold elementary preservice teachers' critical and reflexive discussions around school mythology and professional identity negotiation.

Reading Children's Picture Books

As adults being reacquainted with children's literature, it is important for preservice teachers to learn to assume the role of text's *implied reader*, the ideal reader constructed by "the apparent 'attitude' of the narrative toward the reader" (Tyson, 2006, p. 187). The implied reader embodies what a text assumes a reader should know and be able to do in order to engage in the reading experience. Nodelman and Reimer (2003) write,

> Texts assume that readers possess a body of knowledge of literature and life, what reader-response theorists call "repertoire." The implied reader of a text has in his or her repertoire the factual, cultural, and literary knowledge the

text refers to, and that knowledge enables the implied reader to understand the text.

(p. 17)

Regarding ideologies assumed of the implied reader, Sarland (2005) concludes that actual readers have three options when they read. Readers can

assume the ideology of the text and subsume it into their own reading; they can miss or ignore the ideology of the text and import their own ... or they can question the text in order to reveal the underlying ideology.

(p. 42)

Child readers exercise this agency when they read, but, because texts for children are seen as important vessels for imparting the ideologies of the adults who created them, the notion of implied reader has significant consequences for the study of children's literature. Preservice teachers need the ability to recognize the dominant cultural values a text either reinforces or disrupts if they want to select classroom literature that respects children as knowing meaning-makers and capable critical thinkers (Chambers, 1996).

The unique characteristics of successful children's picture books, particularly the complex interdependence of text and illustrations, can result in the construction of multiple implied readers. As with Finchler's books published between 1995 and 2009, a text may even assume both an implied child reader and an implied adult reader. Nodelman (2008) describes the complexity of considering the implied reader in the study of picture books, specifically:

In picture books the division in the implied audience is confirmed and reinforced by the fact that books contain both words and pictures. The viewer they imply knows not only what kind of information to expect from each of these two different media, each requiring a different set of assumptions, but also how to put the information together into a whole.

(p. 258)

Picture books have the potential to offer multiple narratives with which the reader can engage and interpret: one constructed by the text, one represented visually by the illustrations and one comprising the compositional whole of the text and illustration together.

Studying contemporary examples reveals that illustrations may *depict* details already included in the text (Lewis, 2001), *elaborate* on the text by providing the reader with new information (Schwarcz, 1982) or *contradict* the information provided by the text (Nikolajeva, 2003). Illustrations move a story along and give it depth. To be "absorbed" into a narrative, the reader must develop the ability to linger over an illustration, "plumbing its depths, understanding its multiple dimensions and messages, interrogating the feelings of its characters" (Moebius, 2011, p. 171). This ability is developed when readers acknowledge the sociocultural context in which picture book images were created, enabling them to consider alternative meanings (Kress & van Leeuwen, 1996; Op de Beeck, 2011). Studying the images of "teacher" in children's picture books with preservice teachers means providing opportunities to discuss the dominant political and sociocultural ideologies that are either reinforced or challenged through the work of the author and illustrator and the ways our own experiences influence our seeing.

The Hidden Curriculum in Room 10

The interplay of the text (child-student perspective) and illustrations (adult-educator perspective) in the *Miss Malarkey* series engages the reader with multiple juxtaposed narratives as a comedic device. The child narrator welcomes readers into Miss Malarkey's classroom to take on an emic perspective of the classroom's hidden curriculum. An often invisible but central force in the life of a classroom, the hidden curriculum is characterized by all of the things students learn in school without being intentionally taught, including the sociocultural values implied by the structure and implementation of formal instruction (Posner, 2004). Similarly, as preservice teachers and teacher educators engage in the series, we are also being instructed by a hidden curriculum of sorts: the cultural representation of teacher identity and positioning. By taking up the roles of the various implied readers in the *Miss Malarkey* series with some degree of self-awareness and intentionality, preservice teachers are challenged to reflect on their developing professional identity.

School Mythology

When I first encountered *Miss Malarkey Doesn't Live in Room 10* as a new teacher with limited classroom experience, I engaged with the narrative aesthetically rather than critically and was intrigued by Finchler and O'Malley's use of a first-person limited narrator to represent a culturally specific school mythology (see books by Finchler and O'Malley from 1995 to 2009 in the references). Similarly, preservice teachers see their own experiences as students in the narrator's familiar accounts of classroom life; our initial discussions of the series are often focused on these kinds of personal identification responses. By analyzing the juxtaposition of the child narrator's interpretation of classroom events through the text with the elaborative details of the teacher perspective available to the reader through the illustrations, the preservice teachers are challenged to reflect on their transition from this perceived "narrow" student perspective of formal school structures to the broader horizons afforded to the teacher. Through this kind of content analysis, preservice teachers are able to critically engage with their own assumptions and explicitly consider a number of teacher myths that emerge throughout the series.

Myth #1: Teachers Live at School

In *Miss Malarkey Doesn't Live in Room 10*, the narrator documents his daily observations of Miss Malarkey that have led him to conclude she must live at the school. When he arrives at school early in the morning, assignments are already written on the blackboard and work from the day before is already graded. Because he has never seen inside the Teacher's Room, it must be where the teachers sleep. This myth is challenged when Miss Malarkey moves into his apartment building but the book ends with "Next year I'll have Mrs. Boba. Mrs. Boba doesn't live in my building. I guess she lives in Room 12!" (Finchler, 1995, p. 32). This is the only book in the series in which school mythology is taken up directly as the premise of the narrative. Because it is also the first book in the series, the recognition that a school mythology exists among the students at Youngstown Elementary becomes part of the implied reader's repertoire as we engage with the subsequent books. It invites the reader to continue to question the idea of representation and reflect on the humor in our own perspectival limitations.

Preservice teachers are amused by the possibility of being seen as a mythic figure to their students, a perspective they had also held as children. Many find the notion contrary to their developing teaching philosophy and express their belief in a more personal, transparent relationship between teacher and student in which the image of teacher as sole authority becomes diluted. They find it striking that, throughout the series, the reader is privileged to very little informal dialogue between Miss Malarkey and her students, giving them the sense that she might be too distracted by the formal curriculum to recognize the conclusions her students are drawing.

Myth #2: Teachers' Closets Magically Produce Materials

In *Miss Malarkey Leaves No Reader Behind* (reminiscent of No Child Left Behind), Miss Malarkey helps her students progress in the new reading campaign their school has adopted. Principal Wiggins has challenged the student body to read 1,000 books by June. The narrator avoids reading at all costs but Miss Malarkey is relentless in finding a book he will love. The text conveys the passage of time as the narrator, quite unappreciatively, recounts the books Miss Malarkey gives him to try, month after month, with no success.

Flipping through the book, preservice teachers are immediately drawn to the classroom's changing physical landscape throughout the year. While Miss Malarkey is smiling on every page, O'Malley's illustrations give the adult reader the impression that she must be completely exhausted by the end of the year, often being depicted in motion or carrying huge piles of books in her arms, each intended for a particular child. Every month, she puts together an interest-based reading list to send home, like "October Is Scare Up a Good Book Month!," and adorns the walls with handmade signs for extra encouragement, such as "Let a book be your Valentine!" and "*MAY* you always love reading!"

While preservice teachers are charmed by the way the first-person limited narrator worked to construct the teacher as mythic figure in *Miss Malarkey Doesn't Live in Room 10,* they are surprised to find themselves bothered that he neglects to recognize all of the time, money and energy Miss Malarkey has invested to encourage his reading in *Miss Malarkey Leaves No Reader Behind.* As children, they do not recall ever really thinking about where their classroom materials originated, only that, like Mary Poppins's carpet bag, the teacher's closet always seemed to magically have whatever the class needed.

Myth #3: Teachers Do Not Have Bosses

Analyzing the use of the first-person limited narrator throughout the series also reinforces a familiar childhood perception that teachers' autonomy is boundless, and therefore everything they say and do comes from their inherent authority. Through the eyes of the narrator, Finchler (1995, 1998, 2000) and Finchler and O'Malley (2002, 2004, 2006, 2009) position Miss Malarkey as the only adult in the school who seems poised and professional—perhaps even the one keeping things together.

In *You're a Good Sport, Miss Malarkey,* we learn Miss Malarkey comes to be appointed the school's soccer coach when her predecessors prove ineffective: Principal Wiggins keeps losing his toupee and Mr. Fitanuff talks over the students' heads. Though she knows little about soccer before taking the job, she is able to bring the team together, enhance the students' enjoyment and reprimand the crowd of overly competitive parents. The narrator explains, "All the parents are given lollipops before the games to help keep them from yelling" (Finchler & O'Malley, 2002, p. 28). O'Malley's accompanying illustration of the well-behaved parents is reminiscent of a group of toddlers sucking on their pacifiers.

We also see iterations of this myth in *Testing Miss Malarkey,* a book about the weeks leading up to the students' annual standardized assessment. Any parent whose child has ever expressed their belief in the unquestionable authority of a teacher's words by arguing something like, "But, my teacher said . . ." would find the narrator's similar sentiments humorously familiar in this book. He describes Miss Malarkey's behavior following her announcement of the approaching test: She *says* the test is nothing to worry about, but she has begun biting her nails and keeping the class in from recess to work on test skills. While the narrator notices her strange behavior, he takes Miss Malarkey at her word. At home, he relaxes by playing video games, justifying the activity by saying, "But Miss Malarkey said THE TEST wasn't that important. She said it wouldn't affect our report cards" (Finchler, 2000, p. 7). Though he expresses an unshakable confidence in his teacher's clout throughout the series, O'Malley's illustrations portray a second narrative that at times contradicts the perception that Miss Malarkey answers to no one but herself.

Professional Identity Negotiation

Since the overall narrative of the series flows between the permeable boundaries of school-home-community, readers observe Miss Malarkey both in and out of school. By analyzing this metanarrative, questions begin to surface regarding teachers' pressure to balance the ethical obligations and responsibilities of personal and professional lives. Our analyses of O'Malley's illustrations and the culturally dominant images of "teacher" he seems to challenge through the visual equivalent of hyperbole led us to reflexively consider the implications of Miss Malarkey's experiences for our own identity negotiation.

Miss Malarkey as Renegade

As suggested by Myth #3, we get the sense from the narrator that Miss Malarkey answers to no one. However, in our book discussions, a number of images of "teacher" depicted throughout the series give the preservice teachers pause. These illustrations became the central focus of a discussion of Miss Malarkey's courage to walk the line between what she believes a teacher should be for her students and what taxpayers might consider grounds for disciplinary review.

Surprisingly, one illustration that caught the attention of the preservice teachers was one of the concluding images of *Miss Malarkey Leaves No Reader Behind*, in which Miss Malarkey hugs the narrator to congratulate him on finally finishing a book. They admired the way she ensured her students knew they were valued and cared about but were concerned Miss Malarkey could not physically touch her students without risking lawsuits. But as Miss Malarkey hugs the narrator, the reader can see she is holding a note from the child's parents. The intimacy of its words seems to support the appropriateness of the hug for the preservice teachers: "He loves the book! You are the greatest! Thank you so much, Carol & Bob" (Finchler & O'Malley, 2006, p. 30).

Another of these illustrations appears in *You're a Good Sport, Miss Malarkey*. Miss Malarkey has been putting in overtime to coach her students' soccer team, but the parents' unruly behavior at the games is a problem. We examined her increasingly frustrated characterization in O'Malley's illustrations and wondered at what point she would abandon her professionalism to set things straight. (In *Miss Malarkey's Field Trip*, her patience is tested with an inattentive parent chaperone but she remains composed.) At the climax, she finally explodes and we learn that "Miss Malarkey threw her soccer book into the air and yelled—ARE YOU PEOPLE CRAZY?" (Finchler & O'Malley, 2002, p. 25). She gives the adults lollipops to keep them quiet (and perhaps to soften the consequences of her outburst), and the reader is never told whether any complaints were made to the school board. While the preservice teachers acknowledged these interpretations were influenced by their personal experiences, rather than any threat to Miss Malarkey's job security implied in the narrative landscape of the series, they felt both anxious that she might be senselessly reprimanded and empowered by her audacity.

Miss Malarkey as Political Activist

Miss Malarkey's devotion to her students is often complicated by outside political forces. Even when this tension flies below the radar of the narrator, readers who closely examine the illustrations will find the irony. When the IPTU (say that quickly a few times!) tests arrive at school in an armored vehicle driven by a uniformed officer, strange things begin to happen at school. Miss Malarkey says the test is not important, but the art and physical education teachers have abandoned their curriculum to teach shading "those little circles" (Finchler, 2000, p. 14) and relaxation yoga. Principal Wiggins posts signs (assumed to be made by Miss Malarkey) that say, "Stay calm" and "Breathe deeply" but is losing his toupee over #2 pencils. Through it all, it is up to Miss Malarkey to protect her students from the pressure she feels herself and maintain a child-centered learning environment. At the end of the book, the narrator finally acknowledges what the reader has observed in the illustrations all along: "Miss Malarkey looked wiped out, and she didn't even take THE TEST" (Finchler, 2000, p. 28). There is an obvious disruption between the teaching philosophy Miss Malarkey characterizes in the other books and what she feels compelled to do in the weeks leading up to the assessment, but as an activist for the holistic well-being of her students, she positions herself as a buffer between Principal Wiggins's intense data-driven obsession and her students; she works tirelessly to establish a positive IPTU material culture around the school and, with constant verbal and nonverbal cues, is vigilant to keep her students' confidence high and anxiety low.

This kind of classroom activism is also exemplified in *Miss Malarkey Leaves No Reader Behind* as Miss Malarkey pushes back against corporate influences on her classroom instruction by nurturing authentic relationships with her students. The school's participation in a new campaign, *Everybody Reads in America*, has Principal Wiggins quantifying what every student reads. From some remote location, the off-putting "Montgomery County School Board and the President's Council on Reading Advancement and Promotion Assessment" gives Miss Malarkey recommended book lists to send home with her students, all of which could likely be purchased at the school's "Elastic Book Fair." Meanwhile, Miss Malarkey works to offset the competitive nature of the program by inspiring her students with books they are intrinsically motivated to read, often including parents in the process.

This layer of the series constructs an implied reader whose repertoire includes the discourse of educational policy. The publication timeline of the *Miss Malarkey* books parallels critical junctures in the push for accountability in public education in the United States, most notably the No Child Left Behind Act of 2001. The timely 2000 publication of *Testing Miss Malarkey* is the series's most explicit commentary on high-stakes testing. Having experienced standardized assessments as students, and having read about contemporary educational policy in their coursework, the preservice teachers are often anxious to engage in an analysis of this book. By framing our consideration of Miss Malarkey's professional identity negotiation with discussions of the current political climate in education, we are able to meaningfully engage in and reflect on these ideological interpretations.

Miss Malarkey as Teacher of the Year

Miss Malarkey sacrifices many things to be a superstar teacher. She spends what seems like all of her personal time finding books for her students and coaching the soccer team. She endures public scrutiny by having to post her students' reading progress on the bulletin board outside of her classroom. After calling in a sick day, she worries so much about her students that she goes into school in her robe and pajamas to check on them before the end of the day. Therefore, it always comes as a surprise to the preservice teachers when (in Disney-fashion) the series ends with Miss Malarkey getting married in *Congratulations, Miss Malarkey!*

With one of her students living in her apartment building, noticing everything from the way she takes out the garbage to her red painted toenails, they wonder how she could even feel comfortable bringing home a date. Throughout the first six books, the reader is given the impression that even outside of school Miss Malarkey's first love is her students. All things considered, it becomes difficult to imagine Miss Malarkey (the now presumed "Mrs. Fulla-Malarkey") talking to her new husband, Bob Fulla, about anything other than her students, all of whom are invited to the wedding.

By the end of the series, Miss Malarkey has never been formally recognized for the personal sacrifices she has made to hold the school together and ensure her students feel loved and valued. The preservice teachers feel that all of her efforts are worth it, however, because as readers, we know she makes a lasting impact in the life of at least one of her students. In the final book in the series, the narrator finally acknowledges, "Miss Malarkey is the best teacher I've ever had" (Finchler & O'Malley, 2009, p. 32).

Conclusion

Thinking about children's picture books as culturally constructed artifacts that reinforce and/or challenge dominant cultural assumptions through both written and visual modes of communication has important implications for future elementary teachers. Nodelman (2005) writes,

> Making ourselves and our children more conscious of the semiotics of the picture books through which we show them their world and themselves will allow us to give them the power to negotiate their own subjectivities—surely a more desirable goal than repressing them into conformity to our own views.
>
> *(p. 138)*

Preservice teachers must negotiate their own subjectivities as they transition from a limited student perspective of "teacher" to a phenomenal repositioning of professional identity throughout their teacher preparation programs. Culturally constructed images of "teacher" can be found in many popular children's picture books, like the *Miss Malarkey* series, and many employ comedic devices to represent the traditionally unchallenged teacher-student power dichotomy. These picture books not only represent cultural assumptions about teacher identity and the field of education that preservice teachers and teacher educators can deconstruct together, but also, as texts intended for children, present interesting opportunities to consider the role of children's culture and child agency in teacher positioning. Examining picture books through the lens of implied reader can be a meaningful way to scaffold preservice teachers' critical understanding of their future roles as educators, while also inspiring them to engage in similarly rich literature-based discussions with their own students.

References

Chambers, A. (1996). *Tell me: Children, reading, and talk.* Portland, ME: Stenhouse.

Finchler, J. (1995). *Miss Malarkey doesn't live in room 10.* New York, NY: Walker.

Finchler, J. (1998). *Miss Malarkey won't be in today.* New York, NY: Scholastic.

Finchler, J. (2000). *Testing Miss Malarkey.* New York, NY: Walker.

Finchler, J., & O'Malley, K. (2002). *You're a good sport, Miss Malarkey.* New York, NY: Walker.

Finchler, J., & O'Malley, K. (2004). *Miss Malarkey's field trip.* New York, NY: Walker.

Finchler, J., & O'Malley, K. (2006). *Miss Malarkey leaves no reader behind.* New York, NY: Walker.

Finchler, J., & O'Malley, K. (2009). *Congratulations, Miss Malarkey!* New York, NY: Walker.

Kress, G., & van Leeuwen, T. (1996). The semiotic landscape: Language and visual communication. In *Reading images: The grammar of visual design* (pp. 15–42). New York, NY: Routledge.

Lewis, D. (2001). Modern picturebooks: The state of the art. In *Reading contemporary picturebooks: Picturing text* (pp. 1–30). New York, NY: Routledge Falmer.

Moebius, W. (2011). Picture book. In P. Nel & L. Paul (Eds.), *Keywords for children's literature* (pp. 169–173). New York: New York University Press.

Nikolajeva, M. (2003). Picturebook characterisation: Word/image interaction. In M. Styles & E. Bearne (Eds.), *Art, narrative and childhood* (pp. 37–50). Stoke on Trent, UK: Trenthem Books.

Nodelman, P. (2005). Decoding the images: How picture books work. In P. Hunt (Ed.), *Understanding children's literature: Key essays from the second edition of the International Companion Encyclopedia of Children's Literature* (2nd ed., pp. 128–129). New York, NY: Routledge Taylor & Francis.

Nodelman, P. (2008). *The hidden adult.* Baltimore, MD: Johns Hopkins University Press.

Nodelman, P., & Reimer, M. (2003). *The pleasures of children's literature* (3rd ed.). Boston, MA: Allyn & Bacon.

Op de Beeck, N. (2011). Image. In P. Nel & L. Paul (Eds.), *Keywords for children's literature* (pp. 117–120). New York: New York University Press.

Posner, G. (2004). *Analyzing the curriculum* (3rd ed.). New York, NY: McGraw-Hill.

Sarland, C. (2005). Critical tradition and ideological positioning. In P. Hunt (Ed.), *Understanding children's literature* (2nd ed.). New York, NY: Routledge Taylor & Francis.

Schwarcz, J. (1982). Relationships between text and illustration. In *Ways of the illustrator: Visual communication in children's literature* (pp. 9–20). Chicago, IL: American Library Association.

Tyson, L. (2006). *Critical theory today: A user-friendly guide* (2nd ed.). New York, NY: Routledge, Taylor & Francis.

West, A. (1994). Reading against the text: Developing critical literacy. *Changing English: Studies in Culture and Education, 1*(1), 82–101.

PART III

Imaging the Teacher as Savior

The mediocre teacher tells. The good teacher explains. The superior teacher demonstrates. The great teacher inspires.

—William A. Ward

Forget it, these are minorities. They can't learn and they can't be educated. With all due respect, sir, I'm a White lady; I can do anything.

—"Nice White Lady"

I had some teachers that I still think of fondly and were amazing to me. But I had other teachers who said, "You know what? This dream of yours is a hobby. When are you going to give it up?" I had teachers who I could tell didn't want to be there. And I just couldn't get inspired by someone who didn't want to be there.

—Hilary Swank

12

MOVING BEYOND THE TEACHER SAVIOR

Education Films, Teacher Identity and Public Discourse

Carey Applegate

Three Snapshots of Teaching

Scrolling through my Facebook feed this morning, I came across a tribute that a former student had left for one of my educator friends. The student had written, "Thank you for lighting the way! You are a great teacher." In the attached image was a large cartoon teacher-candle, literally pouring itself into the small, empty schoolchildren-candle-shells; written in the foreground was this: "A good teacher is like a candle—it consumes itself to light the way for others."

On campus last fall, my education students and I were analyzing the movie *Freedom Writers* (DeVito et al., 2007) in our course on urban education in popular culture. Together, we problematized the good vs. bad binary depictions of the main character, Erin Gruwell, and the other teachers in her school. My students talked about everything that the main character had gained in her role as a teacher during the film, and then everything she had lost or sacrificed. We challenged the film's time line, its singular perspective and its character compositions, as compared to the book's much more nuanced narrative. However, at the end of our discussions, most of my predominantly White, middle-class, female students could not (or would not) shake their foundational belief that urban students needed to be saved and that the ideal person to do this was a teacher much like them. Gruwell was a good teacher, they wanted to be good teachers and that was what good teachers did.

Two weeks ago, after observing a dynamic, engaging writer's workshop led by one of my strongest teacher candidates (TCs), I sat down with her and her cooperating teacher to chat about her lesson and how things were going in her placement. As I turned to beam at my TC, she burst into tears. "I'm so sorry," she said, trying to compose herself. "I didn't know." She paused and gathered her thoughts.

"I didn't know how much power and pressure there was in teaching. I thought those teaching stories were real. What if I mess up? What if I ruin their lives?"

Metaphors and the Development of Teacher Identity

What interests me most about the three snapshots I have offered is how teachers are being read within the context of popular culture transposed onto real-world teaching scenarios. In each situation, the people involved used a metaphoric lens provided by a popular culture narrative—an image, a film, books—to shape their perception of not only the teaching profession but also their own identities. We do this all the time without realizing it: Teaching is a war or a battle; we are in the trenches. It's a calling or a mission; we are missionaries. Students are wild animals—or, in a more disturbing turn, uncivilized tribes of people—who are need of discipline, instruction and civilization. Once tamed, students can become part of a classroom family, with their teacher taking the role of the head of the family.

Teachers and nonteachers alike use metaphors like these routinely when discussing education, even if we don't consciously hear ourselves doing it. Sometimes a candle is just a candle. Unless the candle is a teacher. And then things get a little more complicated. As a linguistic concept, metaphors provide insight into our own lives and values. As linguists George Lakoff and Mark Johnson (1980) explain, "A large part of self-understanding is the search for appropriate personal metaphors that make sense of our lives" (p. 233). In other words, we select metaphors that resonate with us; as we use them to reinforce our own identities and belief systems, some of those metaphors begin to shape social structures and policies. This process occurs through the interaction between three different types of metaphors: linguistic metaphoric expressions, conceptual metaphors and generative metaphors.

Lakoff and Johnson (1980) describe metaphoric linguistic expressions as comparisons between two divergent things; from our earlier examples, for instance, "A good teacher is like a candle—it consumes itself to light the way for others." This is the basic, sentence-level structure for what we generally think of as a metaphor: *one object* "*is*" *another object*.

Linguistic metaphoric expressions evolve into what we think of as conceptual metaphors, which both shape and reflect the speaker's thoughts about the source object—the teacher, in our foregoing example. With the candle example, the self-sacrificial consumption directly stated in the second half of the expression—"it consumes itself to light the way for others"—promotes the conceptual metaphor that *teaching* is self-*sacrifice*. With conceptual metaphors, we have analogical reasoning that is reflective of the relationship between two objects or people. Often, we see patterns of time, movement, embodiment or some other component of the human experience with this kind of metaphor. Embedded in this conceptual metaphor, for instance, is a particular understanding of what teaching should look like; it involves transference of energy or life force or power at the expense of the teachers to promote the well-being of their students.

Finally, in some situations, conceptual metaphors become so ingrained in how we think about different concepts (or people or organizations) that they start to shape personal and/or community structure and policies. As these conceptual metaphors evolve, they become generative metaphors, which refer "both to a certain kind of product—a perspective or frame, a way of looking at things, and to a certain kind of process—a process by which new perspectives on the world come into existence" (Schön, 1979, p. 254). Once the conceptual metaphor of teaching as sacrifice becomes a relatively well-accepted foundational ideology within an educational organization, we often see this start to shape some of its structural frameworks and policies. The easiest places to see these generative metaphors at play would usually include an organization's model of teacher assessment and their often-enforced school policies. Where are their priorities? Who and what are valued? Who and what are not? What do their policies say about their understanding of teachers and learners? About the purpose of education? This interplay between language, ideas and practice occurs within conversations about education, teachers and the teaching profession at both the national and individual levels.

Education Films, Metaphor and Public Discourse

On the surface, the films *Freedom Writers* (DeVito et al., 2007) and *Dangerous Minds* (Bruckheimer et al., 1995) are truly inspirational stories. A teacher learns how to teach; her students go on to college and success; their legacy inspires other teachers and students across the nation. Like many other teacher movies, these films are based on true stories; *Dangerous Minds* is taken from LouAnne Johnson's memoir about her first years in teaching, and *Freedom Writers* is based on a book describing Erin Gruwell's work with students in her first years as a teacher. However, unlike those books, the movies have been molded to fit— and shape—the public narrative around what it means to be an urban educator. In her memoir *My Posse Don't Do Homework*, Johnson (1993) shares many struggles with her reader; she doesn't always succeed with her students—in fact, some of her students are downright hostile. *Freedom Writers* is based on the book *Freedom Writers Diary* (Gruwell & The Freedom Writers, 1999) in which the students tell the majority of the story. Their voices are clear and distinct from each other, and they provide a dialogic account of their home- and school lives.

With the transition from print to screen, the way that these stories are told shifts. Linguistic and cognitive metaphors—"school is a war zone" and "teaching is a mission or a calling," for example—influence the characterization of teachers, students and schools in the films. This, in turn, promotes specific kinds of pedagogies and educational structures through generative metaphors; in this case, the films portray very traditional pedagogies, poor administrative structures and a problematic understanding of teacher effectiveness as being radically progressive and innovative.

The War Zone

Both movies begin with a montage of scenes that depict the communities in which they are set as war zones. The first lines in *Freedom Writers* are news clips from the Los Angeles riots of 1992, and they explicitly use linguistic metaphors to draw parallels between the city itself and civil war: "There have been shots fired . . . total civil unrest . . . the city resembles a war zone . . ." Scenes of looting mobs, buildings on fire, police sirens and an intense heartbeat pulse are background to the audience's reminder that there were "over 120 murders in Long Beach in the months following the Rodney King riots" and that "gang violence and racial tension [had reached] an all time high."

Similarly, *Dangerous Minds* opens with black-and-white shots of chaos on the streets: images of memorializing graffiti honoring those who have been killed, homeless collecting cans in shopping carts and casual drug deals—all as students of color file onto a school bus. Coolio's (Coolio, Wonder, Rasheed & Sanders, 1995) lyrics to "Gangsta's Paradise"—"As I walk through the valley of the shadow of death/I take a look at my life/And realize there's nothing left./'Cause I've been blasting and laughing so long/That even my momma thinks that my mind has gone"—offer the first linguistic metaphors to set the movie's tone: This space is like an insane asylum, this community is a wasteland and the rhetoric of casual violence is pushed to the forefront of the narrative. With both of these movies, the audience is primed to read the film through a war-tinted lens within the first five minutes.

In the context of these war zones, students are framed as members of tribes who instinctively understand an almost animalistic competition for survival within each group. In *Freedom Writers*, Eva breaks this social Darwinism down for the audience: "It looks like this: one tribe drifting quietly into another's territory, as if to claim what isn't theirs. An outsider looking in would never see it but we can feel it." Behind her words, a bass beat provides a heartbeat. This power struggle is fundamental to their identities as well as the audience's understanding of how dangerous the "tribes" are, reinforced through glimpses of mob fights, several shootings and interpersonal conflict between characters. In *Dangerous Minds*, the audience is clued into this social dynamic in similar scenes: students yelling and pounding on desks on Johnson's first day, chasing her out of the classroom and making not-so-sly innuendos at her; we are also witnesses to student fights, overtly sexualized teenagers and heightened violence outside of the school walls. The power struggle is ongoing; even without the explicit voice-over, it is clear that one of the films' messages about these students is that they need to be shaped into productive members of society by teachers who care enough to commit to the long, arduous task of helping their students evolve from thugs into scholars. In this cognitive metaphor, their role is fairly passive: They are expected to become civilized. Colonized, even. Compliant, definitely.

Playing into the war-zone metaphor is the depiction of teacher LouAnne Johnson as a protective warrior. Johnson has clearly chosen to immerse herself in the school with the express purpose of saving her students. She explicitly tells one of her more challenging students that she is trying to save him as she shelters him from somebody who has been threatening him: "You asked me once how I was gonna save your life. This is it. This moment." Her role as a teacher-warrior is accentuated by her history with the Marines. She also incorporates that training into her English classroom in unconventional ways, using a karate lesson to engage her students in the classroom activities that she is leading. Grammar lessons that she designs integrate connections to the violent elements of her students' lives: A lesson on verbs changes the sentence "We are going to die" into "We choose to die," while another grammar lesson commands, "Never shoot a homeboy." Her pedagogy in the classroom begins with connecting with her students in ways that accentuate her understanding of them as, if not enemy combatants, at least unaligned individuals to be cautiously engaged.

Embedded in the war-zone metaphor is an expectation that school—and the people who walk its halls every day—is not only unsafe but inherently dangerous. Anything can happen and violence should be expected. When this is the expectation, we tend to see other fragments of war at school: parole officers and security guards, metal detectors, a focus on structure and order in the classroom, a structural emphasis on authority and power, quiet learning activities and very traditional pedagogies. When these frameworks and expectations become part of professional development trainings and education books for current and future teachers, it is time to consider the impact that those models can have on our students and teachers, both in the classroom and in their out-of-classroom lives.

The Mission Field

Both *Dangerous Minds* (Bruckheimer et al., 1995) and *Freedom Writers* (DeVito et al., 2007) also promote another powerful, and popular, conceptual metaphor about education: teaching as a calling or mission. For teachers who are called to be "education missionaries," there are numerous parallels with expectations of religious missionaries: that teachers will make sacrifices for their students, that school is a "mission field" and that teachers' primary role is to use the transformative power of education to save their students. The missionary metaphor is a slight variation on the teacher-savior metaphor, in that the savior metaphor *can* have religious implications (but doesn't have to), while the missionary metaphor almost always involves religious or spiritual elements.

While LouAnne Johnson's dominant role is that of warrior-hero, she also exhibits many of the characteristics of the missionary teacher. She chose to give up a career in the military for one in the classroom because she felt called to be a teacher. Her interactions with her only friend and mentor, Hal, are almost entirely related to teaching. She is never seen with friends or family, she never dates—she doesn't even have a cat. She is alone, solely defined in her role as teacher.

Similarly, Erin Gruwell's character in *Freedom Writers* (DeVito et al., 2007) is invested in sacrificing parts of her life to be more involved with her students and in her teaching. While she begins her teaching career as a married woman with strong ties to her father, Gruwell's long nights away from home—either at one of her multiple part-time jobs or volunteering her time with her students—cause a rift to form in her relationship with her husband. (This is different, however, from the story told in *Freedom Writers Diary* [Gruwell & The Freedom Writers, 1999], in which she works part-time jobs during her student teaching and does not address her divorce at all.)

Over the course of the movie, it becomes clear that her husband is not as invested in her students or her mission, and he resents the intrusion of her teaching in his life. She does not choose her husband over her students when asked to do so—"I finally realized what I'm supposed to be doing and I love it. When I'm helping these kids make sense of their lives, everything about my life makes sense to me. How often does a person get that?"—and their marriage ends in divorce. She has no friends at work or outside of work. While she does maintain a relationship with her father, the audience is led to believe that this is primarily because he has become heavily invested in her students' lives, picking them up for field trips and giving his daughter advice about how to approach volatile situations. In almost all other regards, she is alone in her struggle to provide a positive learning environment for her students.

Both of the teachers in these films demonstrate their understanding of the school as a "mission field" on numerous occasions. In their first meeting, Gruwell cheerfully explains to her department chair that she wants to fight for her students, to keep them from getting lost in the court system, and she is willing to make sacrifices to ensure that she accomplishes her mission. She spends time and money that she does not have, and then works additional jobs in order to buy books and classroom supplies that the school will not provide. In *Dangerous Minds* (Bruckheimer et al., 1995), we see Johnson approaching her teaching in similar ways. She continuously sacrifices time and money to be with her students; as a reward, for example, she takes several students to an expensive restaurant and treats them to dinner and etiquette lessons. Throughout the film, the audience is shown glimpses into her home life: grading papers, sheltering a student from a rival gang and visiting students' homes to encourage them to return to school. This student-based life is her life outside of school.

In addition, this metaphor is very clearly aligned with that of purity or innocence. Both Johnson and Gruwell enter their classrooms as young, untested teachers, and they hold onto their faith in their students. Despite being warned and questioned about wearing her pearl necklace to class, for example, Gruwell insists that none of the students would try to steal it. Johnson, in response to a colleague asking her why she stayed for another year, smiles and says, "They gave me candy and called me their light." These moments in the film emphasize the reverence and hope that they have for their missional charges. Neither has children, except for the students who become part of their classroom family. In both cases, they are celibate and, by the end of *Freedom Writers* (DeVito et al., 2007), single.

In addition, these two teachers are driven to save their students from not only the poverty and gang violence in their communities but also harmfully neglectful bad teachers and administrators. Gruwell intervenes multiple times on behalf of her students in ways that align her with civil rights activists; her allusions to the Freedom Riders and the social justice movements of the 1960s make this reference for her, as do the pedagogical allusions to Anne Frank and Miep Gies. Johnson and Gruwell are both strong advocates for their students' educational and personal development, and they are willing to advocate for their students in confrontations with their colleagues. Johnson, in response to the death of a beloved student, confronts her administrator about his ambivalence when the student reached out for help. When an administrator refuses to interfere with departmental politics and create a looped classroom so that her students can stay together for another year, Gruwell takes the fight to the school board and wins. Part of the teachers' responsibility in their roles as student advocates is to challenge the power structure within their districts to ensure that the students are, in fact, saved.

Finally, at the end of the mission, the missionaries leave. Missionaries are not necessarily expected to be long-term members of the community that is their mission field; this reality, however, is often tucked into a movie's footnote and rarely addressed in the plot itself. In real life, both Johnson and Gruwell left teaching within a few years of their movies' time line ending. At the end of *Freedom Writers* (DeVito et al., 2007), the footnote explains that Gruwell left high school teaching in order to join her students at a local college; since then, Gruwell has created professional development resources that tie into the movie, and she and her former students have created a foundation to spread the message of the Freedom Writers. Although *Dangerous Minds* (Bruckheimer et al., 1995) omitted this piece of information from the narrative, LouAnne Johnson taught for five years before leaving for graduate school; she, too, released several books for teachers about effective teaching. What's interesting is that these facts about how the real teachers' lives evolved beyond the movie are not inherently important to the message of the films. Only the moment, in the context of the (fictionalized) narrative, matters.

Much later, in an email to a graduate student, Johnson (2007) reflected, "I had very little input into the movie and much of it is fiction, at times so far removed from fact to be ridiculous." One of the concerns with an emphasis on teaching as a mission is that the expectations for perfection and self-sacrifice are too high to meet consistently in real life. Not only does this place undue internal pressure on novice teachers to play a role that doesn't exist, it also implies that the level of sacrifice demanded of good teachers is appropriate. Since these movies continue to be used as models for 21st-century education reform and because their tie-in professional development resources are still referenced in educational circles, we must reconsider our roles in the uncritical fandom that we have communally developed around these films and how, exactly, teachers and teacher education programs can be involved in reshaping the conversation.

Teacher Metaphors in Public and Personal Discourse

During the 2015 primaries, Wisconsin governor and candidate for the Republican presidential nomination Scott Walker compared his leadership experiences engaging with Wisconsin teachers' and firefighters' unions with combating terrorists in the Middle East. "If I can take on 100,000 protestors, I can do the same across the world," he told an audience at the Conservative Political Action Conference (Campbell, 2015). Similarly, news-anchor-turned-education-reformer Campbell Brown began the Partnership for Educational Justice, which challenged teacher tenure by helping seven parents file lawsuits against the State of New York; as part of an interview with Stephen Colbert, Brown argued that the teachers' unions had antiquated priorities and were trying to silence the education reformers supporting these parents (Brown, 2014). In these examples, two well-funded and politically connected individuals flip the script and position themselves as small-but-mighty heroes facing off against impossibly violent and imposing forces.

Public discourse about teachers often reveals a binary in the popular imagination: Teachers are good or bad; they are driven by love for their students or by a desire for money; they can inspire their students to succeed or they can torment their students into hopelessness and frustration. Teachers who are political are generally characterized as bad teachers using their political affiliations, often with union thugs, to save their ill-earned jobs. Teachers who are passionate about their subject matter and about helping kids learn are characterized as good teachers who shape tomorrow's generation by leading them to success in the classroom. We see these kinds of characterizations in other venues, too, like the education-inspiration boards on Pinterest, where bright and beautiful visual placeholders allude to teachers as heroes, warriors, surrogate parents, artists and gardeners. Comedians Key and Peele added to the public conversation with a "Teaching Center" sketch that envisioned an alternate reality in which teachers, instead of pro-sports players, garnered public respect and financial gain through their profession (Comedy Central, 2015).

These oversimplifications in the media and in public discourse are not uncommon. The teacher-savior/hero metaphor, in particular, has become a strong storyline for popular films, advertisements and public service announcements; it has also been at the center of much criticism for its overly simplified depiction of teachers (Alsup, 2006; Bauer, 1998; Bulman, 2005; Fisher, Harris & Jarvis, 2008; Giroux, 1997, 2002, 2008; Klaustrophobic, 2007; Liston & Renga, 2015). As Janet Alsup (2006) explains,

> the dark side, and also the fundamental irony, of such constructions is that only rarely are teachers the recipients of it in American culture. Because

standards of performance are so high, and the price of service is so great, few teachers are awarded this hero status; the rest are labeled mediocre at best, or simply inadequate.

(pp. 20–21)

In addition to shaping cultural expectations about practicing teachers and education, these metaphors also help to develop the emerging teaching identities of novice educators (Johnson, 2006). According to Bullough, Knowles and Crow (1992),

Metaphors form the basis of the stories that are acted out and define the situational self when first becoming a teacher . . . Emerging as a teacher is, therefore, a quest for compelling and fitting metaphors that represent who beginning teachers imagine themselves to be as teachers.

(p. 8)

So, not only do metaphors about education directly impact teachers' self-perception and worldview(s), they also influence novice teachers' emerging teaching personas and subjectivities. Much of the work exploring teacher identity and growth during methods classes and student teaching leads scholars to the conclusion that self-identity and metaphor are both key factors in a novice teacher's development.

More recently, Vadebonvoeur and Torres (2003) conducted a study of surface and generative metaphors used by preservice teachers and in-service teachers. The results of this study—and the metaphors used by both types of teachers—reflect identity as it is shaped by experience and perspective. For example, the preservice teachers' metaphors cast the teacher in the following ways: teacher as gardener, giver of knowledge, agent of change and mediator of culture; each of these metaphors reflect a larger, generative metaphor of teaching as either "transmission" or "transformation" (p. 94). From the preservice teachers' perspectives, teaching was largely driven by the *teacher's* work; the students, while important, were secondary. The in-service teachers in this study, however, described teaching through action- or process-oriented metaphors: teaching as building a home, teaching-researching as rafting, teaching and learning as quilting. Their generative metaphors reflected learning as a collaborative process with students as "co-builders," "co-workers" and "co-researchers" (p. 96).

In terms of education, then, the metaphors that we create or adopt about teaching, about ourselves as teachers and about our students, become part of our schemas that then become part of our worldview and our own self-perception. When these metaphors are at work in public spaces—especially through popular texts that often embed cultural and critical stances into the texts themselves—they influence how the public perceives education and those who are involved in it.

Implications for Teacher Education Programs

Much of public discourse about education pits good teachers against bad teachers; while the good teachers are warriors and missionaries for education, the bad teachers exist in a nebulous space of "not that." When Campbell Brown and other education reformers are pressed for specifics about what makes a bad teacher, their definitions fluctuate: students' low test scores, poor teacher-student relationships, a lack of creativity and passion in the classroom, inadequate dedication to students . . . the list could go on for pages, and it is rarely supported by education theorists or researchers, much less classroom teachers. Aside from a glaring credibility issue, the problem with how they frame education reform is that the way that they are conceptualizing education itself is fundamentally flawed.

And They're Not Alone

Educators are culpable, too. We regularly incorporate war-zone and mission-field metaphors into teacher education, and we perpetuate the binaries that we criticize. Traditional student-teaching models privilege a missional approach with a slight war-zone twist. Most education programs require teacher candidates to work hundreds of hours of unpaid on-the-job training, while not working any outside jobs and still paying full tuition. Many student teachers are under intense observation by their cooperating teachers and university supervisors, people who could make or break their careers. In addition, teacher candidates walk through the good teacher/bad teacher minefield of teaching dispositions and skills, sometimes without the tools to effectively navigate their journey.

Throughout this chapter, I have used a fairly linear approach in my discussion of how metaphors work: Linguistic expressions work together to shape cognitive metaphors about how something functions or exists, and those cognitive metaphors provide a foundational understanding for creating frameworks and systems via generative metaphors. The reality is that this process is complex and messy and recursive in nature, and we can't reboot the system to simply change how we think about education.

As teacher educators, we can, however, push back against the actual linguistic, cognitive and generative frameworks that we ourselves use in our work with students, with teachers, with the public and with policy makers. In response to some of the issues discussed in this chapter, I would suggest teacher education programs consider some—or all—of the following actions:

1. Get education majors actively and meaningfully involved in schools as soon as humanly possible. Have them tutor individual students, lead small-group discussion sessions, respond to student work. Repeat and add complexity throughout the rest of their program.
2. Require a low-credit Introduction to Education class of first-year education majors. Run it as a seminar. Engage them in analysis of education issues,

including education metaphors. Make time for reflection about their personal education narratives and beliefs about education. Remix and create new education metaphors.

3. Develop intentional and collaborative learning communities that involve community teachers, professors, teacher candidates and education students. Share perspectives. What does it mean to be a good teacher? A bad teacher? Where are the degrees of difference in this spectrum? Is it even a spectrum?

4. Encourage students to search for counternarratives that complicate the single story of the teacher savior.

5. Dig deeply into programmatic structures and policies. How are they reinforcing problematic conceptions of education? How are they resisting oversimplification? How are they helping students, faculty and community educators to become innovative in their teaching?

6. Consider how to reduce the financial burden on future teachers, especially during student teaching. Investigate paid teaching internships.

7. Reconsider the structure of student teaching: collaborative teaching models, length of time, assessment structures, professional development models and additional areas suggested by students, cooperative teachers and faculty.

8. Start conversations with people whose opinions about education make us uncomfortable and use those conversations to reflect on our approaches to and outcomes of teacher preparation.

Some of these actions are grounded in my own teaching and research (Applegate, 2003, 2013; Applegate, Magnafichi & Musolf, 2010) while others involve structural changes and programmatic reforms that are, quite frankly, more than a little tricky. We must start somewhere, however, to create the metaphors that present teaching as we know and want it to be—far from the war zones and missionary fields of our fictional counterparts.

References

Alsup, J. (2006). *Teacher identity discourses: Negotiating personal and professional spaces*. Mahwah, NJ: Lawrence Erlbaum.

Applegate, C. (2003). *Carpe Diem* in the Mississippi Delta. *English Journal, 93*(1), 24–28.

Applegate, C. (2013). Just like "Freedom Writers": One teacher's personal narrative about working with hip hop in the classroom. *International Journal of Critical Pedagogy, 4*(3), 55–68.

Applegate, C., Magnafichi, A., & Musolf, K. (2010, November). *Developing a pedagogy of empowerment*. National Council of Teachers of English (NCTE) Convention. Orlando, FL.

Bauer, D. M. (1998). Indecent proposals: Teachers in the movies. *College English, 60*(3), 301–317.

Brown, C. (2014, July 31). Interview by S. Colbert. *The Colbert report* [Television series]. Retrieved from http://www.cc.com/video-clips/2mpwlv/the-colbert-report-campbell-brown

Bruckheimer, J., Foster, L., Guinzburg, K., Rabins, S., Simpson, D. (Producers), & Smith, J. N. (Director). (1995). *Dangerous minds* [Motion picture]. United States: Hollywood Pictures.

Bullough, R. V., Jr., Knowles, J. G., & Crow, N. A. (1992). *Emerging as a teacher.* London, UK: Routledge.

Bulman, R. C. (2005). *Hollywood goes to high school: Cinema, schools, and American culture.* New York, NY: Worth.

Campbell, C. (2015, February 26). Scott Walker: If I can handle 100,000 protestors, I can defeat ISIS. *Business Insider.* Retrieved from http://www.businessinsider.com/scott-walker-if-i-can-handle-protesters-i-can-defeat-isis-2015-2

Comedy Central [Screen name]. (2015, July 28). *Key & Peele—Teaching Center* [Video file]. Retrieved from https://www.youtube.com/watch?v=dkHqPFbxmOU

Coolio, Wonder, S., Rasheed, D., & Sanders, L. (1995). Gangsta's paradise. On *Gangsta's paradise* [CD]. New York, NY: Tommy Boy.

DeVito, D., Durning, T., Glick-Franzheim, J., Levine, D., Morales, N., . . . Swank, H. (Producers), & LaGravenese, R. (Director). (2007). *Freedom writers* [Motion picture]. United States: Paramount Pictures.

Fisher, R., Harris, A., & Jarvis, C. (2008). *Education in popular culture: Telling tales on teachers and learners.* New York, NY: Routledge.

Giroux, H. A. (1997). Race, pedagogy, and Whiteness in *Dangerous Minds. Cineaste, 22*(4), 46–49.

Giroux, H. A. (2002). *Breaking in to the movies: Film and the culture of politics.* Malden, MA: Blackwell Press.

Giroux, H. A. (2008). Hollywood film as public pedagogy: Education in the crossfire. *Afterimage, 35*(5), 7.

Gruwell, E., & The Freedom Writers. (1999). *Freedom Writers diary: How a teacher and 150 teens used writing to change themselves and the world around them.* New York, NY: Broadway Books.

Johnson, K. (2006). The Millennial teacher: Metaphors for a new generation. *Pedagogy: Critical Approaches to Teaching Literature, Language, Composition, and Culture, 6*(1), 7–24.

Johnson, L. (1993). *My posse don't do homework.* New York, NY: St. Martin's Press.

Johnson, L. (2007, June). My thoughts on the movie *Dangerous Minds*, which was (very very loosely) adapted from my book, *My posse don't do homework* [Email]. Retrieved from http://www.louannejohnson.com/files/My_Thoughts_re_the_movie_Dangerous_Minds.pdf

Klaustrophobic. (2007, July 7). *Nice White lady* [Video file]. Retrieved from http://youtu.be/ZVF-nirSq5s

Lakoff, G., & Johnson, M. (1980). *Metaphors we live by.* Chicago, IL: University of Chicago Press.

Liston, D. P., & Renga, I. (2015). *Teaching, learning, and schooling in film: Reel education.* New York, NY: Routledge.

Schön, D. A. (1979). Generative metaphor: A perspective on problem-writing in social policy. In A. Ortony (Ed.), *Metaphor and thought* (pp. 137–163). Cambridge, UK: Cambridge University Press.

Vadebonvoeur, J. A., & Torres, M. N. (2003). Constructing and reconstructing teaching roles: A focus on generative metaphors and dichotomies. *Discourse: Studies in the Cultural Politics of Education, 24*(1), 87–103.

13

REVISIONIST FILMS

Detaching From Teacher as Hero/Savior

Chea Parton

> I hope I will be at least half a good [sic] of a teacher as Erin Gruwell. She inspires me, and I hope I can inspire my students one day to do something amazing for themselves.
>
> —Speer, 2014

Movies as sites of public pedagogy (Giroux, 2001) are places of learning where moviegoers in all of their complicated intersections of identity—age, race, class, gender, sexuality, profession, interests, passions—ingest information about themselves and their cultures as it is reproduced for them on the screen. For preservice teachers, films about teachers construct and reconstruct powerful cultural notions and ideals about what it means to occupy the position of "teacher" in society (Bulman, 2005; Dalton, 2010; Weber & Mitchell, 1995). In examining teacher films, preservice teachers have the opportunity to examine their future selves using films that are "very real and meaningful artifacts of our culture" (Bulman, 2005, pp. 1–2), as well as "deeply a part of our society . . . [with] . . . much to teach us about the social and cultural worlds we live in" (p. 3). These opportunities to examine understandings of how they should be and who they will be as teachers are especially important as preservice teachers build and develop a teacher identity (Alsup, 2006). Therefore, reading teacher films is a viable way to help preservice teachers interrogate the teacher as a social construct and the ways that Hollywood resists or reifies societal beliefs about that construct (Bulman, 2005; Dalton, 2010; Mitchell & Weber, 1999; Raimo, Devlin-Scherer & Zinicola, 2002; Weber & Mitchell, 1995). As Weber and Mitchell (1995) assert, films contribute to a "cumulative cultural text of teacher" (p. 19), whereby each new film adds to how preservice teachers and society understand who teachers are and what teachers do.

Teacher Films for Preservice Teachers: Traditional and Revisionist

The bulk of films designated as "teacher films" can be broken into two major categories: traditional and revisionist. In traditional teacher films, teachers are lionized as crusaders for knowledge, fighting administrators, fellow faculty, family and societal expectations in order to inspire their students to live good—that is, educated—lives. These teachers are viewed as heroes or saviors (Bulman, 2005; Dalton, 2010) who sacrifice themselves for the greater good of their students. In revisionist teacher films, teachers are problematized, having personal/moral problems that run counter to the more traditional narratives. In a revisionist film, teachers may be unkempt, deal with drug addictions, have sexual relationships with students, cheat on standardized tests or care little about their students. Revisionist teacher films intentionally question the traditional narrative, revising and problematizing the depiction of a good teacher. While traditional films tend to highlight the sacrifice and heroic qualities of teachers, revisionist films serve as counternarratives, highlighting instead the humanity of teachers, which includes imperfections, poor choices and struggles.

Films like *Blackboard Jungle* (Berman & Brooks, 1955), *Stand and Deliver* (Labunka, Law, Munca & Menéndez, 1988), *Dangerous Minds* (Bruckheimer et al., 1995) and *Freedom Writers* (Devito et al., 2007) fit into the traditional teacher film category. Bulman (2005) and Dalton (2010) categorize these films as "Teacher as Hero" or "Teacher as Savior" films; they follow a predictable arc in which the teachers sacrifice greatly to reach the adolescents in their classrooms, making pupils better students as well as better people in the process. In Bulman's (2005) framework, hero teachers are characterized as lone figures who ignore the cynicism of veteran teachers, speak directly to the hearts of students and inspire them to aspire to White middle-class values. Likewise, Dalton's (2010) framework characterizes savior teachers as outsiders who experience tension in their relationships with administrators as they devise personal curriculum for students and become personally involved with them.

The savior teachers from these films present preservice teachers with a construction of *reel* teachers (Mitchell & Weber, 1999) that is very difficult for *real* teachers to attain. Though such narratives—some of which are based on true stories—are inspiring, this particular construction of teacher is oversimplified and exaggerated, developed by how much of their time, their lives and their selves the teachers are willing to sacrifice for their students. While these films ostensibly attempt to cast a positive light on what teachers do and are, they instead render teachers in caricature, highlighting and overemphasizing certain attributes while underemphasizing or altogether ignoring others.

For preservice teachers who are actively learning and incorporating information and experience into their ideas and understandings of the teacher, watching traditional teacher films without the opportunity to question and interrogate the representation and depiction of the teacher in the film is troublesome. Who wouldn't want to be the teacher immortalized in film who saves her students while leading them to success? Unfortunately, preservice teachers (like the burgeoning young teacher featured in the epigraph) aspire to achieve the feats that Hollywood presents to them while failing to consider what is on the other side of the screen. For example, in *Freedom Writers* (DeVito et al., 2007) Erin Gruwell achieves her meteoric success in the classroom during a four-year period, and then promptly leaves to design curriculum on and give speeches about that success. Although the film presents her sacrifice of time, energy and marriage for her students, it fails to note that she is no longer teaching students like those featured in the film. Preservice teachers should grapple with the incongruities between what happens on the screen and what happens in real life, questioning how both come to bear on the formation of their identities and how they think about themselves as and in the role of teacher. The same is true for revisionist counter-narratives played out on the big screen.

Revisionist films such as *Detachment* (Brody et al., 2011), *Half Nelson* (Boden et al., 2006), *The English Teacher* (Achour et al., 2013) and *Bad Teacher* (Dietrich et al., 2011) undertake to revise those traditional teacher depictions in some way. The heroes in these films are inherently flawed: They are disheveled; they don't want personal relationships with students; they do drugs; and they teach for undesirable reasons, such as earning money for breast augmentation surgery. While Erin Gruwell struggles to keep her kids off drugs and out of gang violence in *Freedom Writers* (DeVito et al., 2007), Dan Dunne teaches his students about dialectical relationships while struggling with a drug addiction in *Half Nelson*. While LouAnne Johnson reaches her students by throwing out pedagogical theory and donning a leather jacket in *Dangerous Minds* (Bruckheimer et al., 1995), Henry Barthes avoids connecting to his students by bouncing around from school to school as a perennial substitute teacher in *Detachment*.

Revisionist films and teachers are memorable—often shockingly so—to viewers in the opposite way of traditional teacher films. They confront the idea that teachers should be paragons of morality and decency, featuring teachers with problems and desires both inside and outside the classroom that force preservice teachers to think about how person and pedagogy converge when defining a good and bad teacher. While preservice teachers will likely not aspire to adopt Mr. Dunne's drug habit, does that mean that they shouldn't aspire to adopt his pedagogy? While they will likely care about their students and want to help them inside and outside the classroom, is it acceptable to do so in the way that Ms. Halsey does in *Bad Teacher* (Dietrich et al., 2011)? What is the difference? Why is one acceptable and the other not? Asking preservice teachers these questions and allowing the space to confront the issues presented in revisionist teacher films can help them unpack and tease out the different representations of teachers in film, comparing and contrasting them to gain a better understanding of the way society views, understands and constructs the role of teacher as well as how that construction connects to, converges with or diverges from their own views and understandings of the teacher.

These films focus on opposite ends of the spectrum: While traditional hero/savior teacher films typically focus on the inspiring, caring nature of teachers, revisionist films emphasize the imperfections and selfishness that can exist in teachers. Each genre renders teachers in caricature. Traditional teachers sweetly sacrifice everything for their students while they fight valiantly to help them achieve White middle-class values. Revisionist teachers do their best to get past their drug habits and ulterior motives for teaching to teach their students something (if anything) of value. Situated as they are, traditional teacher films create caricatures to which real teachers aspire, while revisionist films seek to problematize the oversimplified goodness of traditional teachers by giving would-be "good" teachers "bad" qualities.

As preservice teachers tackle the (in)accuracies of traditional teacher films, they must also have occasion to interact with revisionist teacher films. Reading, analyzing and discussing films that consciously critique depictions of teachers provide preservice teachers more than a single view, a single understanding or a single depiction of what it means to be a teacher. Without exposure to this complexity, preservice teachers ingest only the oversimplified and prevailing narrative of the traditional savior teacher, learning that sacrifice is normative, that good teachers give up their personal lives for their students and that they should be saintly paragons of virtue and morality for their students. Preservice teachers need to consider what it means to be a teacher as well as what it means to be a good teacher from both sides of the traditional/revisionist spectrum. Are the flawed teachers of revisionist films still good teachers even if they're imperfect people? Is it possible that just as there are a "variety of good lives to live" (Grant, 2012, p. 1095), there are a variety of ways to be a good teacher? If revisionist films are to be believed, the answer to both is yes.

Reading Revisionist Films: *Detachment*

In *Detachment*, Adrien Brody plays the role of Henry Barthes, a permanent and highly sought after substitute teacher. In the film, Barthes's experiences as a teacher in one school illustrate his detachment from those around him. Barthes in many ways is presented in contrast to traditional hero teachers like Erin Gruwell and Jaime Escalante. He avoids connecting to anyone, including his students, and lives a life of solitude. Barthes rides the bus, visits his ailing grandfather in the nursing home and frequently recalls memories of his mother's suicide. He is soft-spoken and poker-faced, claiming he has no feelings that can be hurt. He does not exhibit much energy, charisma or passion for teaching. He shows up to school to do his job and go home; he encourages students who don't want to be there not to come to class. Constantly quoting from Camus's *The Plague*, Barthes has a bleak outlook on the world; though he eventually tries to show compassion and caring for his students and the teenage prostitute he takes in, he is ultimately unsuccessful in saving any of them.

Despite the contrast between this teacher and his traditional movie counterparts, critics struggle to read Barthes's character or summarize it outside of the context and conventions of traditional teacher films. Tribeca Films (2011) summarized the film thusly:

> In Director Tony Kaye's *Detachment*, Academy Award® winner Adrien Brody stars as Henry Barthes, *an educator with a true talent to connect with his students*. Yet Henry has *chosen to bury his gift*. By spending his days as a substitute teacher, he conveniently avoids any emotional connections by never staying anywhere long enough to form an attachment to either students or colleagues. When a new assignment places him at a public school where a frustrated, burned-out administration has created an apathetic student body, *Henry quickly becomes a role model as a teacher who actually cares about the wellbeing of these students*. In finding an emotional connection to the students but also fellow teachers and a runaway teen, he finds that he's not alone in a life and death struggle to find beauty in a seemingly vicious and loveless world.
> *(Tribeca Films, 2011, emphasis mine)*

Though the film situates him as a revisionist teacher, critics and moviegoers have difficulty reading Barthes's character outside of the confines of traditional hero teacher tropes. Though he is clearly flawed and unwilling to connect, this viewer/critic sees him (re)form into a traditional teacher who cares about his students, who rejects the administration by refusing to teach mandated curriculum and who becomes a role model intent on saving the adolescents around him by teaching them about the flaws in the construction of society. So, is Henry Barthes truly a revisionist teacher? Is he a traditional teacher in antihero form? Or, like his students, is he just misunderstood?

Keeping the Traditional Tropes

To completely invert or revise all traditional teacher tropes would be to create an unrecognizable narrative; thus revisionist films must complete their revisions within a narrative framed by traditional teacher film conventions. *Detachment* (Brody et al., 2011) handles this by merging some traditional tropes with revisionist tropes. For example, like his traditional hero/savior counterparts, Barthes is a lone figure and outsider; he speaks directly to his students' hearts and devises a personal curriculum for them (Bulman, 2005; Dalton, 2010). However, Barthes's character also revises traditional tropes. He accepts, rather than rejects, the cynicism of veteran teachers; he does not form personal connections with students; he has no run-ins with administrators; he encourages students to question rather than accept the values of White middle-class culture (Bulman, 2005; Dalton, 2010).

While teachers in other films are outsiders due to race, class or gender, Barthes is an outsider due to his transience and his substitute status. Not only is he new to the school and neighborhood, and thus an outsider to the students, he is not a "real" teacher and so exists as an outsider to the teachers, as well. He is a good sub, however, one the principal says comes "highly recommended," yet despite his position as a good sub, Barthes is not a member of the teaching community in the school or the teaching community writ large. As he explains directly to audience members in a vlog-like monologue, "I'm a substitute teacher—there's no real responsibility to teach. Your responsibility is to maintain order, make sure nobody kills anybody in your classroom, and then they get to their next period" (Brody et al., 2011). Because Barthes himself views his relationship to the teaching community as one of outsider, he solidifies that as his position among the teachers and students in the building.

Despite his outsider and detached status, Barthes still does his best to impart knowledge to the students under his supervision. His methods, though a bit unorthodox, reach students, evidenced in their demeanor toward him in class and their protestations when he tells them he's leaving. This characteristic qualifies him as a hero/savior teacher because he speaks directly to students about issues that matter. He talks about real things, like caring about each other enough not to call each other names such as "dyke," like questioning the world around them so as not to ingest the belief that women are "bitches" and "whores," like not giving into the media-propagated assertions that they need to change themselves, have plastic surgery or be thin to be worthy of life (Brody et al., 2011). Speaking about such serious and important topics in honest language, Barthes engages his students, and they all look at him admiringly attentively from their seats. Wondering how teachers are "supposed to reel kids in with classic literature if they don't believe [they] have something meaningful to share," for his first assignment, Barthes asks his students to write what people would say about them at their funeral. He reads the first one he receives while students laugh—"He just fucks their shit up and the ladies cry for me at the funeral because I ain't around to dicks that split up raw and shit and my boys alls get faded smokin' that skunk shit and fuck" (Brody et al., 2011)—giving the student who wrote it a facetious thumbs-up after he's finished. Though the words are harsh, the tone is light, and viewers can tell that students appreciate his cavalier attitude. However, the tone changes to reflect the weighted meaning of the next one he reads:

> She used to be a sweet girl. She never seemed dissatisfied with her life, and why should she have been? Her mother and I gave her everything she needed. So why did she become so angry—so miserable and mean all of a sudden? We don't know. Frankly it doesn't reflect on us. We were good parents, but still she repaid us for all we've done by killing herself. Stupid, selfish child; now she'll never get into Princeton.
>
> *(Brody et al., 2011)*

As the camera pans across the body of students in the classroom, they are all focused on the words of the eulogy, the looks on their faces as somber and serious as the music playing in the background.

Mr. Barthes wants to teach his students something that matters, which may explain why he ignores the principal's directive upon arriving at the school. On Barthes's first day, the principal tells him, "Teach the curriculum, *most importantly*" because he is charged with the task of getting students "up to grade level" (Brody et al., 2011). This standards-focused perspective does not align with Barthes's student-focused belief that "we have such a responsibility to guide our young so that they don't end up falling apart, falling by the wayside, becoming insignificant." Rather than follow her directive, Barthes teaches his students about the dangers of anti-intellectualism and ubiquitous assimilation. In a spontaneous lesson, Barthes uses the Orwellian concept of doublethink from *1984* to teach students about doublethink and its connection to their daily lives:

> Doublethink. To deliberately believe in lies, while knowing they're false. Examples of this in everyday life: "Oh, I need to be pretty to be happy. I need surgery to be pretty. I need to be thin, famous, fashionable." Our young men today are being told that women are whores, bitches, things to be screwed, beaten, shit on, and shamed. This is a marketing holocaust. Twenty-four hours a day for the rest of our lives, the powers that be are hard at work dumbing us to death.
>
> *(Brody et al., 2011)*

With lessons like this, Barthes speaks to students about societal issues connected to a text they've read in a discourse with which they're familiar. The swear words he uses are traditionally considered inappropriate for classroom use, but he uses them so his students might relate to the lesson in a more concrete way since that language (as evidenced multiple times throughout the film) is a large component of their everyday discourse. He continues to engage them by including himself in the fight against doublethink:

> So to defend *ourselves*, and fight against assimilating this dullness into *our* thought processes, we must learn to read. To stimulate *our* own imagination, to cultivate *our* own consciousness, *our* own belief systems. *We* all need skills to defend, to preserve, *our* own minds.
>
> *(Brody et al., 2011, emphasis mine)*

Including himself in this proclamation, Barthes equates himself to his students because they all have a common enemy. In situating himself in this manner, he wears this trope of the traditional hero teacher.

Revising the Traditional Tropes

While Barthes does demonstrate certain characteristics typical of traditional hero/savior teachers, he does not keep all of them. Rather than resist the cynicism of veteran teachers, Barthes accepts that "the system is fucked" while rejecting a teaching-is-life attitude (Brody et al., 2011). He encourages students to question and reject aspects of White middle-class culture, rather than aspire to them, despite his lack of personal involvement with students. While he does not teach to the test as ordered, he has no run-ins with administrators.

Instead of rejecting the negative attitude of veteran teachers like traditional hero teachers, Barthes joins them in lamenting the state of the educational system. Reflecting on the lack of parents at parent/teacher conferences, Barthes says,

> I actually felt quite at home—that there were no parents. I thought, how appropriate; it was like a moment of insight into the fucking problem in the first place. Some of us believe that we can make a difference and then sometimes we wake up, and we realize we failed.
>
> *(Brody et al., 2011)*

Rather than entertain optimistic or hopeful notions that he can somehow make it better for his students next year if he just works a little harder, Barthes acknowledges the system's failure and does nothing to fix it. Instead, he rejects it, maintaining and prioritizing his personal identity over his professional one. For example, when he meets one of his colleagues for the first time, she introduces herself as Ms. Madison, a signifier of her professional identity, but he introduces himself as Henry Barthes, privileging his personal name over his professional name. While this may seem a small and innocuous happenstance, Ms. Madison further demonstrates the personal/professional divide when she confesses that she doesn't even "know what to do with herself" when she's not in the classroom (Brody et al., 2011). She is Ms. Madison, teacher first; he is Henry Barthes, person first. The structure of the film itself echoes this fact: Most of the footage is not of Barthes in the classroom or interacting with students, as would be typical in a traditional teacher film. Instead, most of the scenes in the film are devoted to his interactions with his grandfather, showing tough love to the teenage prostitute he takes in, meandering around the city and delivering monologues about life to the camera.

Just as Barthes questions the role of some of the typical middle-class conventions of school, he encourages his students to question and even reject aspects of White middle-class culture. One scene features an intense lecture on refusing to accept the beauty standard and gender inequality. He rails on television and the media for constantly presenting society with preconstructed values, saying, "How are you to imagine anything if the images are always provided for you?" (Brody et al., 2011). He implores students to think for themselves instead of blindly following and falling into the cultural values that are already in place, asking them to detach from what they are fed in order to consider what could be.

Traditional hero/savior teachers frequently refuse to teach the lackluster and formulaic curriculum mandated by their administrators and find themselves in trouble because of it. In that these lessons urging students to question the structure of society are not part of the formal curriculum, Barthes operates within traditional teacher tropes; however, because he is not questioned or reprimanded by the administration, he also exists outside of them. Barthes also refuses to teach the curriculum that will reportedly get his students up to grade level, yet suffers no repercussions. Rather than an intrusive administrator, Barthes's principal is being forced out of her position as a sacrifice to test scores and property values; she fades into the background—very literally blending in with the red lockers in one scene—and doesn't give Barthes any trouble over his delinquency.

Ironically, as he asks his students to detach from society, he is becoming more attached to them. Initially, Barthes does not want to be personally involved with his students, which clearly breaks with the hero/savior tradition. He says, "I spend a lot of time trying not to deal ... not to commit" (Brody et al., 2011). In this particular circumstance, however, he finds himself wanting to attach but isn't allowed to do so. When he tries to connect with Meredith, a suicidal student desperate to be valued by someone, Ms. Madison walks in as Meredith is crying and trying to hug Barthes who is awkwardly (and unsuccessfully) trying to comfort her. Interrupted by Ms. Madison, Meredith runs out of the classroom while Ms. Madison accuses Barthes of inappropriate behavior, asking, "Why were you touching her?" While his hero/savior counterparts dance with, eat with and hug their students after class, Barthes isn't afforded the opportunity to comfort a student who desperately needs the attention of her teacher. Later in the film, on his last day at the school and as Meredith serves cupcakes to faculty and students in the courtyard, Barthes tries once again to comfort her and reassure her that "[he] know[s] that it's really tough for [her] right now" but that "it won't always be that way" (Brody et al., 2011). She interrupts him to comment on the irony that it is his last day (because she has also decided that it is her last day) and to say good-bye, having already made up her mind to eat a poisoned cupcake of her own making. She dies while only Barthes tries to literally save her, performing CPR until the paramedics arrive. Unlike the traditional teacher hero, the teacher's attempted attachment to one particular student is not enough to save her from her emotionally abusive father, horrible home life or society's expectations of her (mind and body).

Revising the Teacher With Preservice Teachers

Despite retaining some of the tropes of traditional teacher films, *Detachment* (Brody et al., 2011) serves as a counternarrative to the construct of the teacher as savior. Analyzing revisionist films like *Detachment* provides preservice teachers the opportunity to think about teaching from the other side of Hollywood. Asking them to problematize the ways in which they'll be expected to embody the tropes of the traditional teacher (and avoid the personal/professional issues of revisionist teachers) provides preservice teachers time to question what they believe teachers are and what teachers do. Because teaching is often integrated into teachers' personal identities (Alsup, 2006), preservice teachers need to explore who society believes them to be as teachers as well as how that is (dis)connected to who they believe themselves to be. Viewing revisionist and traditional films, critically analyzing those films and discussing their understandings with classmates provide preservice teachers with a different experience than merely watching the films on their own. The exchange of thoughts and information in the setting of a methods course creates a more critical and scholarly atmosphere for deconstructing the perceptions and images of the teacher presented in such films. The coursework and reading they do, the films they see and school visits and practicums they complete throughout their teacher preparation programs all work together to shape and inform the beliefs and understandings they have about their identity and work as teachers. Reading revisionist films like *Detachment* and considering how they contribute to the cumulative cultural text of teacher (Weber & Mitchell, 1995) through dialogue with classmates, professors and critical literature provide preservice teachers with the opportunity to interrogate aspects of the traditional text of teacher (i.e., sacrifice is normative) and confront both traditional and nontraditional depictions of who teachers are and what teachers do, shaping their teacher identities in a more informed way.

References

Achour, A., Bederman, M., Chausse, M. E., Chausse, P., Curits, R., . . . Tagger, M. (Producers), & Zisk, C. (Director). (2013). *The English teacher* [Motion picture]. United States: Mirabelle Pictures.

Alsup, J. (2006). *Teacher identity discourses*. Mahwah, NJ: Lawrence Erlbaum.

Berman, P. S. (Producer), & Brooks, R. (Director). (1955). *Blackboard jungle* [Motion picture]. United States: MGM.

Boden, A., Corwin, C., Dey, D., Gray, H., Korenberg, R., . . . Walker, J. K. (Producers), & Fleck, R. (Director). (2006). *Half Nelson* [Motion picture]. United States: Hunting Lane Films.

Brody, A., Frigeri, M., Gubelmann, B., Hausen, D., Kohn, B., . . . Sterling, P. (Producers), & Kaye, T. (Director). (2011). *Detachment* [Motion picture]. United States: Paper Street Films.

Bruckheimer, J., Foster, L., Guinzburg, K., Rabins, S., Simpson, D. (Producers), & Smith, J. N. (Director). (1995). *Dangerous minds* [Motion picture]. United States: Hollywood Pictures.

Bulman, R. (2005). Hollywood goes to high school: Cinema, schools, and American culture. New York, NY: Worth.

Dalton, M. M. (2010). *The Hollywood curriculum: Teachers in the movies* (2nd ed.). New York, NY: Peter Lang.

DeVito, D., Durning, T., Glick-Franzheim, J., Levine, D., Morales, N., . . . Swank, H. (Producers), & LaGravenese, R. (Director). (2007). *Freedom writers* [Motion picture]. United States: Paramount Pictures.

Dietrich, C., Eisenbert, L., Householter, D. B., Kacandes, G., Kasdan, J., . . . Stupnitsky, G. (Producers), & Kasdan, J. (Director). (2011). *Bad teacher* [Motion picture]. United States: Columbia Pictures.

Giroux, H. (2001). Breaking into the movies: Pedagogy and the politics of film. *Journal of Composition Theory, 21*(3), 583–598.

Grant, C. (2012). Cultivating flourishing lives: A robust social justice vision of education. *American Educational Research Journal, 49*(5), 910–934.

Labunka, I., Law, L., Musca, T. (Producer), & Menéndez, R. (Director). (1988). *Stand and deliver* [Motion picture]. United States: Warner Bros.

Mitchell, C., & Weber, S. (1999). Reel to real: Popular culture and teacher identity. In *Reinventing ourselves as teachers* (pp. 164–188). Philadelphia, PA: Routledge.

Raimo, A., Devlin-Scherer, R., & Zinicola, D. (2002). Learning about teachers through film. *The Educational Forum, 66*, 314–322.

Speer, L. (2014). *[Msg 11].* Message posted to https://www.youtube.com/watch?v=Thd8xw_poNo

Tribeca Films. (2011). Tribeca film acquires US rights to Tony Kaye's *Detachment.* Retrieved from https://tribecafilm.com/press-center/tribeca-film/press-releases/129463653

Weber, S., & Mitchell, C. (1995). "That's funny, you don't look like a teacher": Interrogating images, identity and popular culture. New York, NY: Routledge.

14

DECONSTRUCTING A NEW TEACHER SAVIOR

Paladins and Politics in *Won't Back Down*

Ashley Boyd

On the first day of each semester, I begin my secondary English methods course with a discussion of portrayals of teachers in popular media. My students have a ready repertoire of school-related films and answer rapidly when asked to name and describe the pedagogues in them, remembering well Erin Gruwell in *Freedom Writers* (DeVito et al., 2007) and Jaime Escalante in *Stand and Deliver* (Labunka, Law, Musca & Menéndez, 1988). When I ask, however, why it is important to consider these images in terms of their own teaching, they become more reticent. Hollywood depictions, they share, are the kinds of teachers they aspire to be. Beyond that, they see little need to discuss such images. To think of those figures otherwise, in any sort of analytical way, is a disruption of their burgeoning teacher identities. They hope to inspire their students in ways similar to those teachers, to motivate unreachable youth through their charisma and care. Many of them plan to achieve this feat yearly in a lifelong career.

It is my contention, however, that we must encourage our preservice teachers to think otherwise. I have elsewhere documented how the images created in school films influence teacher candidates in detrimental ways and have posited the crucial need to critically consider the treatment of education in popular media outlets in teacher education courses, especially those with aims for social justice (Boyd, 2014; Boyd & Senta, in press). Characterizing teachers as figures who rescue students from their dismal lives, these films reinscribe norms of Whiteness (Giroux, 2002b), pathologize students of color (Hughey, 2010) and create unrealistic expectations for teachers (Farhi, 1999).

In this chapter, I continue this line of argument by examining the film *Won't Back Down* (Flaherty et al., 2012) and the construction of a new type of teacher savior. I argue that this more recent version of the teacher savior is a figure who impacts education broadly, as opposed to more individualistic heroes in films of the past. I then examine the political agenda proffered in the film as it relates to education and teaching, particularly the topic of charter schools and the privatization of education. Finally, I end by suggesting ways that teacher educators can bring images of the teacher savior to the forefront of preservice candidates' cognizance and engage those students in critique of such social scripts.

The Teacher Savior: An Established Model

Scholars have well-documented traditional notions of the "teacher savior" image in school-related films (see, e.g., Ayers, 2001; Dalton, 1999; Farber & Holms, 1994). Generally, such movies involve a White, heterosexual, middle-class female who, as Hughey (2010) describes, is "charged with teaching a majority nonwhite, low-income, 'at risk' classroom" (p. 475). In these storylines, the teacher is typically seen with only one group of students, has no personal life and uses unconventional methods to reach overnight success with students (Giroux, 2002a; Trier, 2001). Often, the gallant figure teaches English, and in movies such as *Dangerous Minds* (Bruckheimer et al., 1995) and *Freedom Writers* (DeVito et al., 2007), we see how the teacher makes poetry and writing come alive for her inner-city students. Allegedly using students' experiences, these teachers find ways to encourage their charges to "care" about school when before they did not; they secure guardian approval from parents who do not "see" the value of education; they engage in dynamic pedagogies that oppose the "boring" methods of their uncaring colleagues. Ridden with deficit discourse (Brown, 2013), then, the trope is a person who works tirelessly to win over her students and inspire them toward a successful life, all in virtually one school year (Farhi, 1999). The message becomes clear: "White teachers alone are capable of bringing order, decency, and hope to those on the margins of society" (Giroux, 2002b, p. 156). As Cann (2015) points out, these stories are largely at odds with research showing "the backgrounds and identities of the White teacher saviors do not align with the backgrounds and identities of teachers shown to successfully increase student achievement" (p. 303) in the types of classrooms shown in the films nor do their pedagogies align with what research has shown works for students of color, such as culturally relevant pedagogy (Ladson-Billings, 2006) and critical caring (Antrop-González & De Jesús, 2006).

Perhaps most outstanding and largely unquestioned in the teacher savior image is its reflection of the institution of Whiteness, a conclusion documented by a number of scholars. Cann (2015), drawing on critical race theory (Cole, 2012), explores how these popular films reinforce and uphold systems of privilege. She states,

> Whiteness is rationalized as necessary and celebrated for its intrusions into Black and Brown spaces for the purpose of saving low income urban youth of color. The *White savior industrial complex* proposes band-aid solutions in

the form of White saviors, ignoring the deeper entrenched forms of institutional racism.

(p. 291)

Images of the superteacher allow viewers a way to cognitively resolve educational
inequity without having to challenge the dominant narratives in society (Delgado, 2011). Furthermore, Brown (2013) extends the savior paradigm to include
a reflection of the neoliberal agenda, as the teachers' push for students to attend
college helps them to "access material gain and social mobility" (p. 130). Brown
(2013) further argues it "includes a moneyed logic intertwined with the liberal
agenda of tokenistic diversity and equality that is suspiciously absent of a critique"
(p. 130). Drawing on similar ideas of Whiteness and the secular savior as connected to neoliberalism, Giroux (2002b) notes one lesson from *Dangerous Minds*
(Bruckheimer et al., 1995) is "citizenship can be constructed for students of color
as a function of choice linked exclusively to the marketplace" (p. 148). The parallel aspects of the White teacher savior thus extend well beyond mere plot points
and perpetuate systems of oppression that are key to the operation of our society.

Overview of Film

Won't Back Down (Flaherty et al., 2012), purportedly based on real events, catalogs
the story of concerned parents who fight to take over their children's "failing"
elementary school in order to implement a new environment with caring teachers and relevant curriculum. Dissatisfied with the treatment of their children's
psychological and educational needs at their current school and frustrated by
futile attempts to gain access to the local charter school, the protagonists petition
school board authorities for approval to construct a new school. The film stars
two female protagonists, one White and one Black: Jamie Fitzpatrick (Maggie
Gyllenhaal), the determined and outspoken mother whose daughter Malia struggles relentlessly with her reading abilities and bullying by peers, and Nona Alberts
(Viola Davis), who doubles as a mother and teacher at the school in question and
battles not only her son Cody's ability to achieve academically but also a crumbling marriage with her husband.

Most of the plot is devoted to combating union officials for rights to take over
the school as well as to winning the hearts of the school's current teachers, who
are portrayed as paralyzed by a system that guarantees their benefits while con-
stricting their autonomy. Other major parts of the film include an actor representing Teach for America, whose pedagogy of singing and dancing contrasts with the
drab methods of other teachers, the unfair principal, whose ethics become questionable, and the evil union leader, whose strategies include borderline blackmail
to thwart the mothers' efforts. In the end, and after tireless efforts, coercion and
setbacks, the mothers succeed in their quest and a charter school is born.

A Conflicted Teacher Savior

The character of Nona Alberts at first seems to defy many of the established characteristics of the superteacher trope (Farhi, 1999; Michie, 2012). First, rather than being a White savior, she is a woman of color, and by her appearance in the film, she lives an upper-middle-class lifestyle. The character of Jamie Fitzpatrick is visibly impressed with Alberts's objectified capital (Bourdieu, 1986), particularly her spacious home and the material goods within. Second, Alberts does not, as many teacher saviors do, believe that her coworkers simply do not care about the students in their classrooms. She goes to great lengths to recruit colleagues whom she perceives as "good" teachers for the school she envisions. In fact, when lobbying for their support in a faculty meeting, Alberts appeals to their intrinsic desire to teach, which she believes prompted them to become educators, saying, "This could be our chance to be the teachers we always hoped to be." Third, rather than viewing parents as antagonists or inconsequential to her goals, she works to solicit students' guardians' approval and participation in her mission, going door-to-door with Fitzpatrick to gain their confidence. She tells one parent, "Change the school, you change the neighborhood," after the parent expresses her concern with ongoing issues in their area. In these ways, Alberts diverges from what is traditionally represented in film as the teacher hero.

And yet, in other ways, Alberts fits the mold of the teacher savior. She mirrors the conversion narrative (Bauer, 1998) through which she comes to want the best for her students. In the beginning of the film, she teaches in a monotonic voice from a seated position at her desk while removing her nail polish. We quickly learn that Alberts, however, was once passionate about teaching: We watch as she sorts through a box of mementos, which includes news clippings that document her receipt of a "Teacher of the Year" title and colorful materials used in her previous classrooms. Once Alberts connects to the school change agenda, her teaching becomes markedly livelier. We see her walking around the classroom, engaging students in a call-and-response pedagogy (Lee & Majors, 2003), instilling pride for their school's namesake and giving hugs as they leave the classroom.

Continuing her adherence to the teacher savior archetype, she works against the odds, persevering in a system that is constructed as uncaring and cold. When told to wait for the school to change, she and Fitzpatrick repeat throughout the film that their children do not have time to wait. Alberts reflects the narrative that the kids in this school suffer from dismal lives and need to be rescued, and she directly mentions the school-to-prison pipeline at a rally to gain community support. Furthermore, Alberts works against an administration plagued by bureaucracy, including an administrator who forces her to change attendance records and later suspends her for doing so when it benefits him. Finally, as many heroic teachers constructed in film (Ryan & Townsend, 2012), she sacrifices her personal time and her relationships in numerous ways to advocate for her educational cause. In a rocky relationship from the outset, Alberts and her husband separate during the film and she focuses all of her energy on developing ideas for the new school. The only instances in which we see her interacting socially are in situations related to the school: at a celebration with colleagues who decide to join the cause, for example, or meeting with Fitzpatrick to work in her home on writing the new school proposal.

The New Teacher Savior: Structure and Politics

Despite these conflicting elements, I argue that the teacher savior script nonetheless persists as a backdrop in *Won't Back Down* (Flaherty et al., 2012) in even more potent ways. In fact, this hero is even more "larger than life" than in typical renditions, and her greatness shines in two specific ways. To begin, Alberts operates on a broader level than has previously been depicted. Whereas most teacher saviors are paladins of justice for individual students, chiefly operating at their classroom level (Michie, 2012), Alberts is rarely seen as a pedagogue. In fact, there are only two scenes of her teaching in the film, both described earlier: one in which she is indifferent and another in which her teaching has been revolutionized. Instead, she is a teacher activist, working to overthrow an entire failing system. We see her at a neighborhood rally, at the district school board office and talking with colleagues in the faculty lounge or at meetings. Her axiom throughout the film is that what is most vital are expectations of students. If teachers demand more, she argues, students will rise to the occasion. Teachers are ostensibly limited, however, in being able to maintain and work in the name of these expectations by a system that restricts their time investments and autonomy. As a result, she implies, teachers lose their appetite for actually helping students.

The culprit of this broken system and teachers' ensuing apathy, Alberts avows, is the teachers' union. In order to achieve the desired school, she tells her peers, one in which the practice of sound pedagogies and student-driven curriculum is the norm, they will have to forego union membership. Alberts has "ideas" for a new school and, although those are ambiguously referred to throughout, the school board member to whom Alberts appeals approves of them upon reading the new school proposal. A sufficient majority of the board follows suit in the public vote. Nona Alberts, then, saves *all* of the students in the school. She saves her colleagues who desperately want to teach an unscripted curriculum. And she saves education from its worst enemy: teacher unions.

Alberts's embodiment of anti-unionism is the second exceptional addition in this newly constructed teacher savior image. Again, her battle is on structural, rather than individualistic, grounds and the political agenda of privatization is evident. Throughout the film, Alberts clashes with colleagues who feel she has betrayed their trust, peers who, although unhappy, feel the teachers' union guarantees their interests and their job safety. The union leader is a consistent force in the film, a representative of the obstacles impeding a sound education for the students in Alberts's school. Cavanagh (2012), referencing the treatment of unions in the film, tells us, "They are all that stands in the way of the sale of our public education system to the highest bidder and that is precisely why they are being attacked" (para. 3). Unions, the film posits, give educators license to disengage from teaching. They restrict curriculum and make both students and those surrounding them unable to perform.

The message toward unions in the film echoes current rhetoric in the media. When teacher unions in the state of Washington organized walkouts in the spring of 2015 to protest underfunding and class sizes, *The Seattle Times* labeled the move "antagonistic to students" (Riley et al., 2015). Republican senator Michael Baumgartner (2015) said of the situation, "It remains unfortunate that they use school kids as pawns in their political games." Berliner and Glass (2014) note,

> Anti-union sentiments have taken root in the public narrative about teachers, often showing up in newspaper articles, political debates, and popular documentaries . . . The message is always clear: Unions protect bad teachers and hurt students. In Arizona, for example, this rhetoric is common in legislature and newspapers, even though the conservative Fordham Institute ranks the Arizona union as the weakest/least influential union in America (Winkler, Scull, & Zeehandelaar, 2012). The unfortunate part of this antiunion campaign is that the public has heard the message so often and from so many sources, it has begun to believe it, when in fact the message isn't just deceptive, it is entirely not true.
>
> *(p. 78)*

Untrue as it may be, when framed in such a way, the natural conclusion is to create one's own school so as to escape bureaucracy and union constraints, which is just what occurs in *Won't Back Down* (Flaherty et al., 2012). Never mind the slew of critiques of charter schools, including their support of segregation, for-profit status, refusal to serve students with special needs, glaring student attrition rates and reproduction of meritocratic ideals, to name a few (Lack, 2009; Ravitch, 2010; Wilson, 2010). Teachers in charter schools are typically not members of traditional unions (Brill, 2011), and thus they are supposedly freed from the negativity shown in *Won't Back Down*. The appeal to viewers' emotions with an eschewed notion of equality is palpable, and by the end, we are cheering for the dismantling of public education and the institution of a charter school before we even realize what's happened. We are led to believe in a "postracial" society in which both mothers experience a cause that transcends barriers of race and social class. The false sense of diversity and equality in the neoliberal agenda for which Brown (2013) critiqued the teacher savior image thus remains, yet in a newer, more nuanced way.

Deconstructing the Teacher Savior in Teacher Education

Just, then, as we have worked to deconstruct individualistic approaches to "rescuing" students in other popular films, so must we engage our preservice teachers in consideration and critique of conceptions presented in recent films such as *Won't Back Down* (Flaherty et al., 2012). The images promoted of this new teacher savior are just as harmful to teacher candidates and the collective psyche as traditional notions, especially when they offer a false binary where the only options are unions or charter schools.

It is perhaps no coincidence that *Won't Back Down* (Flaherty et al., 2012) was partially funded by Walden Media, the company that also financed the controversial documentary *Waiting for Superman* (Birtel et al., 2010) that carried much the same sentiment. In my previous work (Boyd & Senta, in press), I have engaged preservice teachers with the latter film to deconstruct rhetoric that places blame for failing school systems on teachers and unions in a manner similar to what I propose here with *Won't Back Down*. In order to accomplish this, I create alternative short film texts in which I juxtapose particular scenes from popular media with others from documentaries (Boyd, 2014; Boyd & Senta, in press). Drawing on the work of James Trier (2003, 2004), I employ film texts about schools with teacher candidates as pedagogical strategy and use these films to encourage critical dialogue among students as well as to prompt them to reflect and build their own future identities as teachers.

One pedagogical practice I enact to lead students through an examination of the nuanced example of the teacher savior begins with first asking students to consider what teachers should know and be able to do. This provides a basic list to which to return throughout continued discussion and academic exercises. I then prompt students to compose reflections on their own personal experiences with teachers, introducing them to Lortie's (1975) theory of the apprenticeship of observation and expanding this to include what they witness as consumers of mass media.

Next, students view a series of juxtapositions from films, which I created for the work of deconstructing the teacher savior. I use films such as *Freedom Writers* (DeVito et al., 2007), *Dangerous Minds* (Bruckheimer et al., 1995) and *Mr. Holland's Opus* (Cort et al., 1995) spliced with documentaries from real teaching contexts, including *The First Year* (Friedman et al., 2001) and *Hard Times at Douglass High* (Raymond & Raymond, 2008). I match specific discursive features throughout scenes in the new film text, such as language that focuses on resources in schools, pedagogical practices and attitudes toward students. These are interwoven to upset romantic ideals of teachers often portrayed in mainstream texts. I have found it useful to include text on-screen prior to each segment in such a way that labels these contrasts directly for students. For instance, I include a title slide "Lack of Resources" before two contrasting scenes, one from *Freedom Writers* where the protagonist says she will buy all of her students' books herself and one from *The First Year* where an elementary teacher breaks into tears at the sight of a playground at a wealthy school, lamenting that his students do not even have swing sets on which to play at his school. Additional juxtapositions continue to show glamorized versions of teachers' responses to educational situations alongside realistic illustrations of the same topics, such as stories of success and working with difficult students. As a final piece for emphasis, I show my students the *MADtv* spoof "Nice White Lady" (EyeLook2U, 2011), a parody of the popular film *Freedom Writers* that ends with an Erin Gruwell look-alike telling her negative, discouraging, alcohol-drinking principal, "With all due respect, sir, I'm a White lady. I can do anything." Although humorous, it helps students to name the teacher savior image easily.

I then ask students to generate a list of qualities of the teachers presented in these Hollywood films. We compare this list with our original ideas of what teachers should know and be able to do, and we then discuss how the documentaries challenge *both* the qualities exhibited in film and our own lists, prompting students to consider where our own ideals of teachers originate and if we expect teachers to be superhuman as well. Once students have become familiar with the traditional teacher savior, I ask them to view *Won't Back Down* (Flaherty et al., 2012) in its entirety, noting, as I have done earlier, how Nona Alberts is similar to and different from what we have established as the typical superteacher. Once students have identified how Nona Alberts is like the traditional teacher savior, I have them focus on their list of differences. What message, I ask, could her differences be constructing? If she defies the archetype, what does her persona lead us to believe about teaching and education? I then task students, having seen my juxtapositions previously, to find their own elements of media that speak back to the message in the film. Having scaffolded this for them with established school films and using the title slides mentioned previously in my own film, students more readily understand the mission before them. As an extension, they can choose one ideological message on which to focus, such as unions being responsible for school failure, and find alternative images to support their counterclaim. In this way, students are creating and practicing the reconstructive element that scholars have cited as dire in critical media pedagogy, moving beyond critique and into production (Morrell, Duenas, Garcia, & Lopez, 2013).

Students' final course assessment is a rendering of their teacher self as a result of their experiences in the course and the mediation of their dispositions upon entering the course with what they have since encountered. I ask them to create an artistic project to illustrate that self, accompanied by a written statement. For example, one student submitted a three-dimensional representation of a tree with "apples" that both had fallen (symbols of notions from which she had unsubscribed) and were growing on the tree (symbols for what she had learned), all related to her perspectives on teaching. Many students note the importance of self-reflection to their teacher identity, especially as it relates to what they bring to the classroom in terms of values and background. Often they mention, in critical ways, the teacher saviors they saw in film, and they interrogate what is presented as common sense in educational arenas. They also talk about their desires to be culturally responsive, authentic and personally balanced.

Through the use of film, I thus engage students in critique of the popular as well as planning for their future selves. While it is never my hope to quell my students' passion or aspirations to make a difference, I do want them to hold realistic expectations for themselves and their students. In addition, I want them to be able to articulate a response to the political agenda set forth in popular media regarding education—such as that presented in *Won't Back Down*—since, as pieces of public pedagogy, these films affect our shared attitudes and actions toward educational equity.

There is no doubt that the teacher savior is an established trope in both media and the collective psyche. The presentation of that savior, however, is altering in response to current rhetoric that advocates the privatization of schools and the dissolution of teacher unions. As these manifestations evolve, so will our preservice teachers imbibe and integrate them into their budding teacher identities. Thus, it is crucial that those of us who work in teacher education devote attention in our courses to exploring and disrupting those stances so that our preservice teachers discern the institution of education as a contested field, one that is not immune to politics, so that as a result of this recognition, they envision futures in which they can engage in praxis for equity.

References

Antrop-González, R., & De Jesús, A. D. (2006). Toward a theory of critical care in urban small school reform: Examining structures and pedagogies of caring in two Latino community-based schools. *International Journal of Qualitative Studies in Education, 19*(4), 409–433.

Ayers, W. (2001). A teacher ain't nothin' but a hero: Teachers and teaching in film. In P. B. Joseph & G. E. Burnaford (Eds.), *Images of schoolteachers in America* (2nd ed., pp. 201–210). Mahwah, NJ: Lawrence Erlbaum.

Bauer, D. (1998). Teachers in the movies. *College English, 60*(3), 301–317.

Baumgartner, M. (2015, April 23). In *Facebook* [political page]. Retrieved July 14, 2015, from https://www.facebook.com/VoteBaumgartner/posts/1077808518902771

Berliner, D., & Glass, G. (2014). *50 myths and lies that threaten America's public schools: The real crisis in education.* New York, NY: Teachers College Press.

Birtel, M., Chilcott, L., Hindmarch, E., Katz, M., Skoll, J., . . . Wyermann, D. (Producers), & Guggenheim, D. (Director). (2010). *Waiting for Superman* [Motion picture]. United States: Walden Media.

Bourdieu, P. 1986. "The forms of capital." In J. G. Richardson (Ed.), *Handbook of theory and research for the sociology of education* (pp. 241–258). Westport, CT: Greenwood Press.

Boyd, A. (2014). Dètournement as anti-oppressive pedagogy and invitation to crisis: Queering gender in a pre-service teacher education classroom. In J. Trier (Ed.), *Detournement as pedagogical praxis* (pp. 107–128). Rotterdam, Netherlands: Sense.

Boyd, A., & Senta, A. (in press). Towards structural attribution: Using détournement with pre-service teachers to challenge the teacher savior myth. In L. M. Nicosia & R. A. Goldstein (Eds.), *Through a distorted lens: Media as curricula and pedagogy in the 21st century.* Rotterdam, Netherlands: Sense.

Brill, S. (2011). *Class warfare: Inside the fight to fix America's schools.* New York, NY: Simon and Schuster.

Brown, A. (2013). Waiting for superwoman: White female teachers and the construction of the "neoliberal savior" in a New York City public school. *Journal for Critical Education Policy Studies, 11*(2), 123–164.

Bruckheimer, J., Foster, L., Guinzburg, K., Rabins, S., Simpson, D. (Producers), & Smith, J. N. (Director). (1995). *Dangerous minds* [Motion picture]. United States: Hollywood Pictures.

Cann, C. N. (2015). What school movies and TFA teach us about who should teach urban youth: Dominant narratives as public pedagogy. *Urban Education 50*(3), 288–315.

Cavanagh, J. (2012). The truth behind *Won't Back Down. Huffington Post: Education.* Retrieved from http://www.huffingtonpost.com/julie-cavanagh/wont-back-down_b_1906434. html

Cole, T. J. (2012, March). The White savior industrial complex. *The Atlantic.* Retrieved from http://www.theatlantic.com/international/archive/2012/03/the-white-savior-industrial-complex/254843/

Cort, R. W., Duncan, P. S., Field, T., James, J., Kroopf, S., . . . Teitler, W., (Producers), & Herek, S. (Director). (1995). *Mr. Holland's opus* [Motion picture]. United States: Buena Vista Pictures.

Dalton, M. (1999). *The Hollywood curriculum: Teachers and teaching in the movies.* New York, NY: Peter Lang.

Delgado, C. (2011). Freedom writers: White teacher to the rescue. In E. Marshall & Ö. Sensoy (Eds.), *Rethinking popular culture and media* (pp. 226–229). Milwaukee, WI: Rethinking Schools.

DeVito, D., Durning, T., Glick-Franzheim, J., Levine, D., Morales, N., . . . Swank, H. (Producers), & LaGravenese, R. (Director). (2007). *Freedom writers* [Motion picture]. United States: Paramount Pictures.

EyeLook2U. (2011, January 19). *MADtv nice White lady* [Video file]. Retrieved from https://www.youtube.com/watch?v=JaewfHk9KiA

Farber, P., & Holms, G. (1994). A brotherhood of heroes: The charismatic educator in recent American movies. In P. Farber, E. Provenzo & G. Holm (Eds.), *Schooling in the light of popular culture* (pp. 21–39). Albany: State University of New York Press.

Farhi, A. (1999). Hollywood goes to school: Recognizing the superteacher myth in film. *The Clearing House, 72*(3), 157–159.

Flaherty, M., Johnson, M., Palmer, A. M., Schmidt, R., Willians, T. (Producers), & Barnz, D. (Director). (2012). *Won't back down* [Motion picture]. United States: 20th Century Fox Film.

Friedman, J., Guggenheim, D., Kheshgi, S., Murphy, J., Schachter, J. (Producers), & Guggenheim, D. (Director). (2001). *The first year* [Motion picture]. United States: Public Broadcasting Service.

Giroux, H. (2002a). Culture, class, and pedagogy in *Dead Poets Society.* In *Breaking into the movies: Film and the culture of politics* (pp. 75–99). Hoboken, NJ: Wiley-Blackwell.

Giroux, H. (2002b). The politics of pedagogy, gender, and Whiteness in *Dangerous Minds.* In *Breaking into the movies: Film and the culture of politics* (pp. 136–169). Hoboken, NJ: Wiley-Blackwell.

Hughey, M. W. (2010). The White savior film and reviewers' reception. *Symbolic Interaction, 33*(3), 475–496.

Labunka, I., Law, L., Musca, T. (Producers), & Menéndez, R. (Director). (1988). *Stand and deliver* [Motion picture]. United States: Warner Bros.

Lack, B. (2009). No excuses: A critique of the knowledge is power program (KIPP) within charter schools in the USA. *Journal for Critical Education Policy Studies, 7*(2), 127–152.

Ladson-Billings, G. (2006). "Yes, but how do we do it": Practicing culturally relevant pedagogy. In J. Landsman & C. Lewis (Eds.), *White teachers/diverse classrooms: A guide to building inclusive schools, promoting high expectations, and eliminating racism* (pp. 29–41). Herndon, VA: Stylus.

Lee, C. D., & Majors, Y. J. (2003). Heading up the street: Localised opportunities for shared constructions of knowledge. *Pedagogy, Culture, and Society, 11*(1), 49–68.

Lortie, D. (1975). *Schoolteacher: A sociological study.* Chicago, IL: University of Chicago Press.

Michie, G. (2012). *We don't need another hero: Struggle, hope and possibility in the age of high-stakes schooling.* New York, NY: Teachers College Press.

Morrell, E. Dueñas, R. Garcia, V., & López, J. (2013). *Critical media pedagogy: Teaching for achievement in city schools.* New York, NY: Teachers College.

Ravitch, D. (2010). *The death and life of the great American school system: How testing and choice are undermining education.* New York, NY: Basic Books.

Raymond, A., & Raymond, S. (Producers/Directors). (2008). *Hard times at Douglass High.* United States: HBO documentaries.

Riley, K., Blethen, F. A., Blethen, R., Dudley, B., Higgins, M., . . . Tan, T., & Torres, B. (2015, May 18). Students lose instruction in Washington Education Association walkouts. *The Seattle Times.* Retrieved from http://www.seattletimes.com/opinion/editorials/students-lose-instruction-in-washington-education-association-walkouts/

Ryan, P. A., & Townsend, J. S. (2012). Promoting critical reflection in teacher education through popular media. *Action in Teacher Education, 34*, 239–248.

Trier, J. (2001). The cinematic representation of the personal and professional lives of teachers. *Teacher Education Quarterly, 28*(3), 127–142.

Trier, J. (2003). Designing school film "videocollages" as pedagogical texts in pre-service education. *Taboo, The Journal of Culture and Education, 7*(1), 31–46.

Trier, J. (2004). Dètournement as pedagogical praxis. *Journal of Thought, 39*(4), 35–52.

Wilson, T. (2010). Civic fragmentation or voluntary association? Habermas, Fraser, and charter school segregation. *Educational Theory, 60*(6), 643–664.

15

CHALK

Overwriting the Savior Narrative

Walter E. Squire

Despite the preparation provided by teacher education programs, the first year of employment for a new teacher can be especially intense and exhausting, if not disheartening. Moir (1999) presents this first year as a five-stage development: from anticipation, through survival and disillusionment, to rejuvenation and reflection. While the sheer volume of work may explain the movement from anticipation to survival phase, other contributors are certainly at play, from the sudden loss of the support system preservice teacher education provides to the need to devise coping strategies as novice teachers (Keogh, Garvis, Pendergast & Diamond, 2012). In educating students with backgrounds different from their own, new teachers must adjust to new environments and "bridge differences they face with their students" (Shoffner & Brown, 2010, p. 90). There are also ingrained expectations of dramatic and instantaneous success when preservice teachers move from being students to full-time teachers, perhaps in part due to cinematic representations of educators.

Due to the seeming verisimilitude of screen images and sounds to those off-screen, film is a particularly effective means of conveying ideology, regardless of whether the conveyance is intentional. Ryan and Kellner (1990) suggest that this verisimilitude results in "an illusion that what happens on the screen is a neutral recording of objective events, rather than a construct operating from a certain point of view" (p. 1). In the introduction to *Reel to Real: Race, Sex, and Class at the Movies* (1996), hooks notes that "cinema assumes a pedagogical role in the lives of many people" (p. 2). Whereas hooks focuses upon race, sex and class in her collection of essays, one might also look at what films teach audiences about teaching and teachers. Preservice teachers can benefit from an interrogation of cinematic narratives featuring educator protagonists, for such interrogation not only can prepare preservice teachers for potential student, parent and community expectations but also may indicate the degree to which preservice teachers share those expectations. Since many educator screen narratives focus upon first-time teachers, examinations of them are particularly useful for exposing expectations.

The Savior Narrative in Teacher Films

While educators often feature tangentially in films with adolescent protagonists, films with educators as protagonists tend to be "savior" narratives within which, through great personal sacrifice, educators transform resistant students. While various scholars and critics have dubbed such educator protagonists "charismatic" (Farber & Holm, 1994), "superteachers" (Farhi, 1999) and "teacher heroes" (Barlowe & Cook, 2015), I share the terminology "savior" with Trier (2001, p. 133) since these educators are singled out for their specialness that amounts to possession of a "gift."

Protagonists in savior educator narratives generally are new to the teaching profession or at least new to the school depicted on-screen. Richard Dadier in *Blackboard Jungle* (Berman & Brooks, 1955) and LouAnne Johnson in *Dangerous Minds* (Bruckheimer et al., 1995) come to the teaching profession from the military—the Navy and the Marines, respectively. Mark Thackery in *To Sir, With Love* (Clavell & Sloan, 1967) was previously a communications engineer. At the beginning of *Freedom Writers* (DeVito et al., 2007), first-time teacher Erin Gruwell mentions that she had previously considered going to law school.

Key facets of the savior narrative include immense sacrifice, the replacement of teacher preparation and planning with epiphany or "light-bulb moments," immediate success after initial resistance by students and a lack of productive interaction between the savior teacher and other educators. In fact, savior narratives are driven by conflict, that conflict accentuated by the savior teacher often being new to teaching. Additionally, the savior teacher may acknowledge how students' environments impact their education but that acknowledgment generally informs pedagogy minimally. During the course of *Blackboard Jungle* (Berman & Brooks, 1955), for example, Richard Dadier is beaten and knifed by a few of his students. Student resistance to his teaching begins on his first day, when one class member throws a baseball at the chalkboard as Dadier writes on it. Yet, when he shows an animated version of *Jack and the Beanstalk* to his students to spark a discussion on ethics, a lesson that the viewer never sees Dadier planning, students immediately respond without hesitation. While Dadier empathizes with a couple of other first-year teachers at his high school, *Blackboard Jungle* depicts experienced educators as cynical or in denial. Dadier empathizes with the economic conditions his students face, but, unless his assumption that they can be reached only through children's popular culture is based upon their economic situations, class does not seem to play a role in his pedagogy nor do the diverse ethnicities of his students, other than to lecture them on the unacceptability of slurs.

In some cases, the sacrifice on the part of savior educators is physical. The savior teacher as sacrificial body is exemplified by Scott Voss, a biology teacher at

Wilkinson High School in *Here Comes the Boom* (Ewing et al., 2012) who competes in mixed martial arts fights in order to fund the music program at his school. The most dramatic of all sacrifices is that experienced by Freida J. Riley in *October Sky* (Cramer, Franco, Gordon, Sternberg & Johnston, 1999), who dies of Hodgkin disease shortly after her students win top prize at the national science fair. Frequently, the sacrifice is emotional and relational. Teachers in savior narratives are often single, sometimes having lost a spouse, as has the widowed Dr. Joshua Larabee in *Akeelah and the Bee* (Brown et al., 2006) and LouAnne Johnson, who divorces and has an abortion prior to the action of *Dangerous Minds* (Bruckheimer et al., 1995). When the savior educator enters the classroom while still in a relationship, that relationship frequently suffers, as between Erin Guwell and her husband, Scott Casey, who divorce by the end of *Freedom Writers* (DeVito et al., 2007).

Teachers in these narratives may also sacrifice their finances or even their careers for students. Throughout *Dangerous Minds* (Bruckheimer et al., 1995), LouAnne Johnson pays for various incentives and rewards for her students, from candy bars to a trip to an amusement park and dinner at a fancy restaurant. Erin Gruwell takes on two part-time jobs in addition to her full-time teaching position to pay for more books for her students in *Freedom Writers* (DeVito et al., 2007). Most significantly, John Keating is fired in *Dead Poets Society* (Haft, Witt, Thomas & Weir, 1989), his sacrifice all the more messianic for he is falsely implicated by a Judas-like student, whose red hair further matches him to some traditional presentations of Judas Iscariot (Baum, 1922).

These narratives suggest that teaching is an occupation which demands everything of the teacher. In order to be effective, a teacher must give all of her time and attention to students, at all times of the day, as well as possibly her wealth, body and even life. Savior narratives thus portray the teaching profession as a mixture of two other professions: the priesthood and the military. Just as celibacy is required of Roman Catholic clergy, the strong tendency of savior educators to be single or to have their relationships collapse suggests that teaching and any sort of home life are incompatible, for the effective teacher must devote her full attention, even after hours, to her students. The willingness of educator saviors to sacrifice their bodies or even their lives connects them to members of the military. As one preservice teacher mentions in Trier's (2001) study, these films "probably cause the average American to think that a teacher should be some super teacher ready to give up his [or her] life for the profession. Nobody expects this from other professionals . . ." (p. 133, brackets and ellipses in original)

While savior narratives devote ample attention to the sacrifices made by educators, they seldom devote any attention to those educators developing lesson plans. Understandably, screenwriters and directors might deem attention to such labor too slow-paced, as would be the attention to the evaluation of student work, and contrary to their purposes of maintaining heightened dramatic action over the course of one and a half to two hours. The effect of such absence, though, is to suggest that good teachers are effective because, through epiphanies or light-bulb moments, they know instantly how to reach their students. Thus, no preparatory work is shown in *Dangerous Minds* (Bruckheimer et al., 1995) before LouAnne Johnson decides to match her students' experience to Bob Dylan lyrics. Seemingly, savior narratives present effective teachers as essentially different from other educators and even hostile to their colleagues' pedagogies, as demonstrated by John Keating having his students rip the introductions from the literature texts on the first day of class in *Dead Poets Society* (Haft et al., 1989).

Corollary to the lack of planning in savior narratives is teachers' often immediate success after initially encountering resistance by students, which depicts those teachers as "capable of permanently changing lives in a short period of time" (Farhi, 1999, p. 157). That immediate success within these screen narratives is all the more surprising given the extremity of that initial resistance. When students enter Erin Gruwell's classroom for the first time, several turn their desks so that their backs face her and then they engage in conversations among themselves while one student thinks, "I give this bitch a week." Within the first few minutes of *Stand and Deliver* (Labunka, Law, Musca & Menéndez, 1988), a student throws a crumpled-up piece of paper at Jaime Escalante and yells, "Read this paper, esé!" Another student asks, "Can we talk about sex?" Escalante answers, "If we discuss sex, I have to give sex for homework," to which yet another student responds, "You know, I can get you fired for saying that." Yet, once the savior teacher employs innovative, or at least unusual, pedagogies, resistance tends to cease very quickly. Not only do students become interested in their education but also, through the unusual methods, students seldom stumble in their facility with academic and critical skills. The short duration of cinematic narratives is one reason for instantaneous success replacing incremental and fluctuating development of skills. Another is the tendency for popular film to have closed endings. There is no doubt in the minds of protagonists, their students or the viewing audience of "finished business" and "[t]hat the game has been won" (Farber & Holm, 1994, p. 168), but such conclusive endings do not allow for students' continued future development and may create expectations for similar immediacy in offscreen classrooms.

If the closed endings of these films indicate that student academic success is dependent upon dynamic individuals who single-handedly change education, there is also a suggestion in savior narratives that teachers do not develop over time but actually become less effective over time. The savior educator's colleagues often are cynical and inhibit or even sabotage her efforts. Upon meeting Mark Thackeray in *To Sir, With Love* (Clavell & Sloan, 1967), a fellow teacher remarks, "So you're the new lamb for the slaughter," and after Thackeray has had a rough first few days of teaching he adds, "Don't worry, the worst is yet to come ...These little bastards have a multitude of tricks." *Lean on Me* (Avildsen, Schiffer, Seelig & Twain, 1989) begins with Joe Clark learning the union he started has agreed to Clark being transferred from Eastside High in exchange for its members receiving salary increments. Such antagonism highlights the independence of the savior educator while at the same time rendering consultation impossible. The savior teacher has no network of support and there is no "suggestion of shared work among adults of good will to achieve any transformative ends together" (Farber & Holm, 1994, p. 171).

Although savior narratives celebrate charismatic individualism, some protagonists do attempt to link students' circumstances and experiences to curricular goals. However, these attempts fall short of culturally responsive teaching. In LouAnne Johnson's classroom in *Dangerous Minds* (Bruckheimer et al., 1995), students analyze Bob Dylan's "Mr. Tambourine Man," in part due to the subject matter of the song, which she thinks speaks to her students' experiences. But culturally responsive teaching not only "builds bridges of meaningfulness between home and school experiences" but also "teaches students to know and praise their own and each other's cultural heritages" and "incorporates multicultural information, resources, and materials" (Gay, 2000, p. 29). Through the foregrounding of Bob Dylan and Dylan Thomas alone as poets worthy of study, *Dangerous Minds* neglects the cultural heritage of Johnson's African American and Latina/o students, a neglect made all the more apparent by the film's predominantly rap and soul soundtrack.

The teacher presented in these savior movies is fully formed as an educator before ever entering the classroom, assumedly without any training, and reaps the reward of instantaneous success for employing novel and apparently impromptu pedagogies. Such representations are disingenuous and divorced from the actual reality of teaching, which is a continuous process of training, planning, implementing, reflecting, consulting and revising. Using teacher movies with preservice teachers, as others have shown, has worth because they make manifest expectations students, parents and preservice teachers themselves may have internalized as well as provide a site for communal interrogations of such expectations.

Chalk: Not the Typical Teacher Movie

Screening and discussion of savior film narratives in the preservice classroom can result in "students examining their assumptions, beliefs, and knowledge about a range of educational issues" (Trier, 2001, p. 129), but the closed nature of these narratives may lead students merely to reject as unrealistic the celebration of complete sacrifice and immediate successes instead of providing students the opportunity to posit more effective approaches than those they see teachers implement on-screen. More instructive would be a film narrative that presents earnest and devoted teachers who struggle but frequently fall short of their goals. *Chalk* is such a film. Released in 2006, *Chalk* (Akel et al., 2006) is a mockumentary—a fictional narrative filmed in documentary style—set at a high school in Texas. *Chalk* focuses upon one academic year in the careers of three teachers— Mr. Lowrey, Coach Webb, Mr. Stroope—and one administrator, Mrs. Reddell. By devoting attention to multiple teachers as well as an administrator, *Chalk* avoids the simplicity of savior narratives, which tend to collapse all nonprotagonist educators and administrators into allies and foes (Farber & Holm, 1994, p. 169). Rather, the film replicates the educational experience of students—who experience numerous teachers with diverse pedagogies—as well as downplays to some degree rivalries between teachers and administrators through including both perspectives in Reddell, a first-year assistant principal who previously was the school's choir director.

The faux documentary style of *Chalk* (Akel et al., 2006), which relies heavily upon the handheld camera, connects the fictional school in *Chalk* to documentaries and news footage of actual schools rather than to the fantasized settings and cinematic techniques of savior narratives, thus allowing more readily for student and teacher viewers to reflect upon the relationship between what they see on-screen and their own experiences. The first several minutes of the film jump from classroom to classroom, to administrator's office, to teacher's lunchroom without narration, mimicking the direct cinema of Frederick Wiseman, noted for his documentaries of institutions, including *High School* (Wiseman, 1968). That *Chalk* is a fictionalized documentary rather than a standard feature film also determines its range. Instead of presenting highly dramatic and unusual events for audiences to experience vicariously, *Chalk* depicts the everyday world of education experienced by administrators, students and teachers throughout the United States. Whereas savior narrative films display extraordinarily turbulent classrooms, if not entire schools in violent chaos, students in *Chalk* are generally at worst silent and bored. The one teacher who has discipline problems within his classroom, Lowrey, is a first-year history teacher who comes to the profession from computer engineering. The students in his class do not seem to pick on him for being a novice teacher; rather, his reactions to standard pranks, like a student hiding his chalk, are excessive, for he is quick to anger. Lowrey exhibits a common characteristic of novice teachers, who often focus upon "concerns about classroom management and control . . . and student challenges to their developing sense of self-determination" (Keogh et al., 2012, p. 57). Moments when Lowrey struggles with classroom management are ideal places to stop the film and ask preservice teachers: Why does Lowrey act as he does? How might Lowrey have acted differently? Since he has already acted, what might Lowrey do now?

As Reddell is a first-time administrator, her struggles may also be worthy of examination by preservice teachers. The teachers in *Chalk* (Akel et al., 2006) do sacrifice, but Assistant Principal Reddell in particular sacrifices time. At the beginning of the school year, she learns that her new position will demand even more of her time than does teaching. Another assistant principal informs her, "I usually get here about six-thirty in the morning and I leave around eight in the evening. I'm here on Saturday from about oh seven o'clock until about three." Later, in a video diary, Reddell reports that because of her late school hours, when she gets home, "I'm exhausted and, um, my husband is asleep. Uh, and I'm going to go to sleep soon, too. . . . I haven't had sex in three weeks." Reddell's marriage is suffering due to her new workload, but others within the film report relationship difficulties that are tangentially related to teaching, not stemming from a notion that an individual cannot be fully engaged as an educator and maintain a relationship also. Reddell's sacrifice is a side effect rather than a necessity of her employment. Her situation can prepare preservice teachers for potential extracurricular consequences during the period of adjustment to the first year's workload while also providing students an opportunity to consider how she might take steps to protect her relationship and home life during that stressful first year.

While planning is not presented in depth within *Chalk*, the consequences of its absence are presented. The affable teacher Stroope is first seen making a joke after greeting each student at the door: "So, Mr. Stroope is my name, history's my game—no, that was really corny, wasn't it? Could you imagine if I really used that?" Stroope excels at interaction but not at education, precisely because he is an extremely lax and unprepared teacher. In a meeting with an administrator, he admits his continuing difficulty with formulating and submitting lesson plans. The administrator explains, "The point is to know before you teach." While the incompetency of Stroope stretches *Chalk*'s credibility, he begins to redeem himself in a video diary reflection toward the end of the film. After he does not win the Teacher of the Year award, he acknowledges that his desire for recognition has superseded his commitment to his students: "What kind of leader am I? I wouldn't follow someone like me. I'm just hoping, you know, with this class I can teach the rest of this year and I'm not a lame duck." Preservice teachers might reflect upon Stroope sacrificing education itself for his own ambitions by considering their own desires and how those desires might forward or inhibit their efficacy as teachers.

If *Chalk* (Akel et al., 2006) treats planning somewhat meagerly, it does excel at indicating that success in the classroom, however that may be defined, is incremental and intermittent. Throughout the course of a full year, Lowrey moves from being authoritarian, beginning the first day of class by asserting demands of students ("In my class, you will always always always [sic] need paper") while at the same time being uncomfortable around them, to genuinely interacting with them. While Lowrey achieves some modicum of success, somewhat more experienced educators reveal what they feel they need to improve. In her video diary, Coach Webb acknowledges, "I need to be encouraging rather than coming down on people or them feeling like I'm coming down on them." For Reddell, a year removed from teaching, the lesson is knowing her limits: "We can only do so much. We've got to do what we can to be accountable and to teach these kids what we can, but it does not start in the school." Through presenting even the most accomplished educators within a school as being uncertain yet constantly striving, *Chalk* resists the implication of savior narratives that certain individuals possess a gift for teaching that assures success, even in the absence of planning.

Chalk (Akel et al., 2006) also presents the benefits of community. Whereas the savior educator is a lone wolf who seems to know instantaneously how to reach every student, with feedback from other educators and administrators perceived as thwarting the protagonist's achievements, the first-year teacher Lowrey recognizes his own inadequacies. After getting angry at a student for hiding chalk, Lowrey researches classroom management within the school library at his next break. Later in the year, Lowrey has his worst altercation with a student, over a cell phone, resulting in the two trading profanities and the student being ordered out of the classroom. Lowrey's demeanor after the event, including holding his face in his hands, indicates he is upset in part with his own behavior. Lowrey is still acclimating and his colleagues humorously suggest to him that he may be taking the actions of his students too personally. During a happy hour get-together, he reports to them that when he reprimanded a student in the hallway, the student called him "an f-ing c-sucker." Lowrey's reticence to repeat the student's actual words is mocked gently by his colleagues. One teacher asks, "Did he say it like that? Did he say f-ing c-sucker?" and Reddell adds, "Like a see[r]-sucker suit?" Their levity points out that while tempers will flare and some students will respond with verbal hostility at some point, Lowrey need not let himself be unsettled. This community guidance and encouragement of Lowrey continues to the end of the film, when, at a lunch meeting, Webb asks Lowrey, "What will you do differently that you didn't do this year?" Lowrey admits that he's not sure he will return the next year. The group tries to encourage him, with Reddell saying, "You really have come a far way, Mr. Lowrey."

Viewing *Chalk* With Preservice Teachers

One way in which Lowrey has come a far way is in his developing as a culturally responsive teacher. Early in the year in an attempt to quell a classroom dispute and to demonstrate the inclusiveness of American democracy, he asks a series of questions, including "Are Black people people?" Though well-intentioned, the question is insulting when asked by the White teacher Lowrey of his multiracial classroom, for he does not also question White privilege by asking, "Are White people people?" However, though Lowrey begins as an unconfident teacher who demands respect and frequently loses his temper, he subsequently does, as a developing culturally responsive teacher, "purposefully (and humbly) try to learn from his students, his fellow teachers, and his community" (Shoffner & Brown, 2010, p. 98), including parents. He especially learns from his own students, including learning elements of their interracial youth culture. His students persuade him to enter the Spelling Hornet, a yearly event during which students quiz faculty on the spelling "of slang words . . . that the kids use every day but we don't know what they mean." Lowrey wins the Spelling Hornet due to the joint effort of his students and himself, Lowrey claiming to his colleagues that "I, um, had three students who regularly came [to tutor me], two religiously, and several others who would like hand in words—'and don't forget this one.'" After his success, his students then encourage him to freestyle rap with them during a class period. These two vignettes demonstrate that Lowrey has learned that to gain respect from and teach students, he must demonstrate to them that he respects and is willing to learn their languages and their knowledges. Lowrey has learned that education is an interaction and a transaction, whereby knowledge is created and interchanged between willing and interested parties. Too frequently protagonists in savior narratives compel students to learn through the sheer force of their personalities rather than humble themselves for the benefit not only of their students' education but also of their own.

Unfortunately, Lowrey seems to buy into the messianic narrative of education. In his final video diary entry before leaving the profession he opines, "Being a teacher is, is, it's a gift. Maybe it's something you can learn, but no one's taught me, you know." By focusing upon the extraordinary rather than the ordinary, upon the rare occasions when a teacher is able to radically alter students' academic interest and abilities within the first year of teaching, savior narratives build unrealistic expectations not only within students and parents but also within novice teachers who, like Lowrey, may not recognize the important incremental progress they are making as educators, even if colleagues and administrators praise their efforts and successes.

Viewing and responding to *Chalk* (Akel et al., 2006) within the preservice classroom can aid new teachers' development through the processes of constructive critique and reflection. Whereas other screen narratives often dichotomize educators as immediately effective saviors and ineffective cynics, *Chalk* presents teachers as earnest yet flawed. This imperfection opens a space for interrogation by preservice teachers, such as when Lowrey struggles with classroom management. Students in the preservice classroom might attempt to answer why Lowrey acts as he does, how he might have acted differently and what he might do following actions of his that are ineffective or even damaging. Likewise, Reddell's increased workload provides students an opportunity to consider how she might take steps to protect her relationship and home life during her stressful first year as an administrator. Furthermore, the maintenance of video diaries by the four protagonists of *Chalk* highlights the importance of reflection, which can be especially beneficial to preservice (Gomez, Allen & Clinton, 2004) and beginning teachers (Shoffner & Brown, 2010), including in the format of online group discussions (Keogh et al., 2012).

References

Akel, L., Akel, M., Alvarez, A., Amodei, J., Darbyshire, C. C., . . . Spurlock, M. (Producers), & Akel, M. (Director). (2006). *Chalk* [Motion picture]. United States: Someday Soon Productions.

Avildsen, J. G., Schiffer, M., Seelig, D., Twain, N. (Producers), & Avildsen, J. (Director). (1989). *Lean on me* [Motion picture]. United States: Warner Bros.

Barlowe, A., & Cook, A. (2015). From blackboard to smartboard: Hollywood's perennially misleading teacher heroes. In D. Liston, & I. P. Renga (Eds.), *Teaching, learning, and schooling in film: Reel education* (pp. 25–55). New York, NY: Routledge.

Baum, P. (1922). Judas's red hair. *Journal of German and English Philology, 21*(3), 520–529.

Berman, P. (Producer), & Brooks, R. (Director). (1955). *Blackboard jungle* [Motion picture]. United States: Metro-Goldwyn-Mayer.

Brown, J., Burns, M., Butan, M. Cuban, M., Fishburne, L., . . . Wagner, T. (Producers), & Atchison, D. (Director). (2006). *Akeelah and the bee* [Motion picture.] United States: Lionsgate Films.

Bruckheimer, J., Foster, L., Guinzburg, K., Rabins, S., Simpson, D. (Producers), & Smith, J. N. (Director). (1995). *Dangerous minds* [Motion picture]. United States: Hollywood Pictures.

Clavell, J., Sloan, J. R. (Producers), & Clavell, J. (Director). (1967). *To Sir, with love* [Motion picture]. United Kingdom: Columbia British Productions.

Cramer, P., Franco, L. J., Gordon, C., Sternberg, M. (Producers), & Johnston, J. (Director). (1999). *October sky* [Motion picture]. United States: Universal Studios.

DeVito, D., Durning, T., Glick-Franzheim, J., Levine, D., Morales, N., . . . Swank, H. (Producers), & LaGravenese, R. (Director). (2007). *Freedom writers* [Motion picture]. United States: Paramount Pictures.

Ewing, M. P., Falsetto, G., Garner, T., Giarraputo, J., James, K., . . . Sussman, J., (Producers), & Coraci, F. (Director). (2012). *Here comes the boom* [Motion picture]. United States: Happy Madison Productions.

Farber, P., & Holm, G. (1994). A brotherhood of heroes: The charismatic educator in recent American movies. In P. Farber, E. Provenzo, & G. Holm (Eds.), *Schooling in the light of popular culture* (pp. 153–172). Albany: State University of New York Press.

Farhi, A. (1999). Hollywood goes to school: Recognizing the superteacher myth in film. *The Clearing House, 72*(3), 157–159.

Gay, G. (2000). *Culturally responsive teaching: Theory, research, and practice.* New York, NY: Teachers College Press.

Gomez, M. L., Allen, A-R., & Clinton, K. (2004). Cultural models of care in teaching: A case study of one pre-service secondary teacher. *Teaching and Teacher Education, 20,* 473–488.

Haft, S., Witt, P., Thomas, T. (Producers), & Weir, P. (Director). (1989). *Dead poets society* [Motion picture]. United States: Touchstone Pictures.

hooks, b. (1996). *Reel to real: Race, sex, and class at the movies.* New York, NY: Routledge.

Keogh, J., Garvis, S., Pendergast, D., & Diamond, P. (2012). Self-determination: Using agency, efficacy and resilience (AER) to counter novice teachers' experiences of intensification. *Australian Journal of teacher Education, 37*(8), 46–65.

Labunka, I., Law, L., Musca, T. (Producers), & Menéndez, R. (Director). (1988). *Stand and deliver* [Motion picture]. United States: Warner Bros.

Moir, E. (1999). The stages of a teacher's first year. In M. Scherer (Ed.), *A better beginning: Supporting and mentoring new teachers* (pp. 19–23). Alexandria, VA: Association for Supervision & Curriculum Development (ASCD).

Ryan, M., & Kellner, D. (1990). *Camera politica: The politics and ideology of contemporary Hollywood film.* Bloomington: Indiana University Press.

Shoffner, M., & Brown, M. (2010). From understanding to application: The difficulty of culturally responsive teaching as a beginning English teacher. In L. Scherff & K. Spector (Eds.), *Culturally relevant pedagogy: Clashes and confrontations* (pp. 89–112). Lanham, MD: Rowman & Littlefield.

Trier, J. (2001). The cinematic representation of the personal and professional lives of teachers. *Teacher Education Quarterly, 28*(3), 127–142.

Wiseman, F. (Producer & Director). (1968). *High school* [Motion picture]. United States: Zipporah Films.

PART IV

The Teacher Construct as Commentary

You're destroying America. Yeah. Look at you, with your chalk-stained irregular blouses from Loehmans and your Hyundai with its powered steering and its windshield. I guess bugs hitting you in the face doesn't cut it for old Mr. Chips. (Mr. Holland? Whoever the Dead Poets guy was? Alright, forget it.) Three months' vacation every summer. Special textbooks with all the answers in them. And who outside of Google employees have both a cafeteria and a gymnasium? At their workplace. Don't think we don't know about those shiny red apples you get day after day after day after day. You think those apples grow on trees, mister? Well, I don't because I don't have all the answers in a book. The point is this: The greed that led you into the teaching profession has led to the corruption of it.

—Jon Stewart

Teachers are the only professionals who have to respond to bells every forty-five minutes and come out fighting.

—Frank McCourt

Can teachers successfully educate children to think for themselves if teachers are not treated as professionals who think for themselves?

—Diane Ravitch

16

FILMS, GOVERNMENTALITY AND AGENCY IN THE STRUGGLE OVER READING EDUCATION

Patrick Shannon

In this chapter, I describe my efforts to help teacher education candidates locate themselves within the 60-year debate concerning equity and excellence through reading education in the United States. I begin with popular films to represent the public arena in which the debate takes place and to develop easier access to the competing curricular and policy positions involved. Despite the evidence of a growing income achievement gap in the United States (Reardon, 2011) and continuing high test scores for middle- and upper-class American students internationally (Carnoy & Rothstein, 2013), federal and state officials and their business partners stress higher standards, tougher tests and tighter lessons *for all students*, as if these were the only possible steps for school reform (Shannon, 2013). I want teacher candidates to consider alternatives before they begin teaching because some alternatives promise quite different futures for students, teachers and society.

This is a first step in a larger agenda to disrupt the tidy efforts to produce "good readers" and "good teachers" through the construction and normalization of "official" or "best practices" routines of reading education. Too often, our pre-service teachers seek to fit seamlessly into these efforts, demonstrating what Foucault (1991) called governmentality. As part of the governing apparatus, schools are tasked with the legitimate practices of helping all children and youth to learn to read and write for pleasure, occupation and citizenship within certain political, social, cultural and ethical boundaries. The apparatus of schooling includes laws, polices, bureaucracies, certifications, credentials, standards, floor plans for classrooms, tests and commercial curricula, to be sure, but also the requisite mentalities and dispositions for all involved to make learning to read and write in appropriately bounded ways run smoothly and normally at school. By viewing, analyzing and discussing scenes about reading education, we explore the possible mentalities and dispositions that create the boundaries in which reading occurs.

Fidelity to the apparatus is maintained through the perpetuation of fear of a reading crisis in America. All participants in reading education must assume their positions responsibly in order to prevent economic and societal breakdown because "Johnny can't read," "we have a rising tide of mediocrity" or "Asian nations want their kids to excel." Under these putative conditions, to deviate from the pull of the apparatus is to contribute to the crisis and to weaken society. Collectively, then, participants hone the system; individually, each engages in continuous self- and professional development in order to forestall the consequences of the crisis. How reading, learning, teaching and "the crisis" are represented and framed in films invites us to engage in different ways of thinking about ourselves, our relationships with others and the apparatus of reading education.

I use scenes from the films *My Fair Lady* (Warner & Cukor, 1964), *Dead Poets Society* (Haft, Henderson, Witt, Thomas & Weir, 1989), *A League of Their Own* (Abbott et al., 1992) and *The Color Purple* (Guber et al., 1985) in order to explore the values among competing discourses concerning the past, present and future of reading education in the United States. Gee (2001) defined discourse as "a socially accepted association among ways of using language, of thinking, and of acting that can be used to identify oneself as a member of a socially meaningful group" (p. 21). Each discourse "involves a set of values and viewpoints in terms of which one must speak and act" (p. 22). These sets of values and viewpoints— discourses—are not only internally defined but also relational—aligned and oppositional—to other discourses. Before we delve into the materiality of the apparatus, we unpack the films' "identity kit[s], which comes complete with the appropriate costume and instructions on how to act and talk so as to take on a particular role that others will recognize" (p. 21). By critically engaging these films and naming the discourses they convey, the teacher candidates can harness their agencies within governmentality to analyze how the discursive representations work in order to position themselves, to locate themselves among these discourses and to make choices about where they wish to stand as teachers of reading.

Film as Public Pedagogy

Public pedagogy is a label for the curricula and teaching that take place informally in the public sphere outside formal educational settings (Sandlin, Schultz & Burdick, 2009). In my experience, teacher candidates accept the concept and agree to its potential impact on people's understanding of themselves, the world and how it works. Yet, most balk at my efforts to connect public pedagogy to anything that they consider to be entertainment: amusement parks, reality television, Facebook, even film. Although they concede that documentaries are intended to inform, if not teach, through a point of view, they separate documentaries from Hollywood films along these lines. Most hold fast to the notion that the movie industry is almost exclusively meant to entertain them.

I have no interest in policing teacher candidates' pleasures, but I think it is an ethical and pedagogical mistake to ignore the ways that films teach the public and teachers about reading education. Films re-present the world to viewers, who must see through the surface images in order to recognize that every aspect of any film is based on explicit choices (Hall, 1997). Nothing is left to chance; every sound, image, gesture, light exposure and camera angle is planned, rehearsed, shot and edited in order to achieve expected effects for each scene. The meanings of the scene are certainly open to interpretations, but the intention for the scene is fixed in the minds of the filmmakers (Barthes, 1975). This requires careful coordination of efforts among scores of film workers, who frame the viewers' gaze for them and hold it steady according to the plan (Hall, 1997). The coordination requires technical expertise through professional discourses as well as allegiance, at least temporarily, to social discourses—ideologies—that name, explain and legitimize the subjects, social practices and purposes depicted (Bakhtin, 1992). The film pedagogy need not be heavy-handed, and the film crews might not be consciously discussing the social discourses speaking through them on each particular subject; however, pedagogical strategies and ideologies are nonetheless there in the text they produce (Kellner & Share, 2007).

Public pedagogies of film weave stories that offer viewers positions within their ideological narratives. They teach the public about the purposes, parameters and practices of our lives, setting standards of normality and inviting us to accept the positions they lay out for us (Davies & Harre, 1990). By design, films engage viewers' intellects and emotions simultaneously, displaying ideas, values and desires that we can audition in our continuous construction of our identities as learners, teachers, parents, taxpayers and citizens. Moreover, those displays mediate our relationships with others in our private and public lives—at least for a time. For the teacher candidates, the films offer possibilities of who and how they might be in schools and communities. By interrogating these stories, taking up the subject positions they produce and the norms the films present as unquestionable, teacher candidates can become agentic in the negotiations of reading education before and after they achieve certification to teach.

Viewing Clips; Naming Discourses

Before the teacher candidates and I settle in to watch the film clips together, we draw a chart with film titles across the top and a list of questions down the side: What is reading? What is it for or what does it do? What is learning? What is teaching? Who needs to be taught? Who should teach them? We stop to complete a row after each five- to six-minute segment of *My Fair Lady* (Warner & Cukor, 1964), *Dead Poets Society* (Haft et al., 1989), *A League of Their Own* (Abbott et al., 1992) and *The Color Purple* (Guber et al., 1985) (always used in this order). Patricia Crawford (now the associate chair of the Instruction and Learning Department at the University of Pittsburgh) and I picked these popular films because we believe that they represent distinct discourses about reading education (although none of the films are about reading per se). We selected the scenes from the films in order to highlight their lessons about reading education. Of course, the films cannot be reduced to scenes we selected. However, because many classes of teacher candidates have noticed the separate sets of values about reading education in each, and even commented on cross-references of the respective values among the films, we are confident that the films' lessons on reading education are meant to be distinct, and we have not imposed these interpretations on the films.

My Fair Lady

We use the 1964 version of *My Fair Lady* (Warner & Cukor, 1964), an update of a 1938 musical and an adaptation of Shaw's *Pygmalion* (1913). It is a commentary on the rigidity of social class systems (British in this case) and the roles of social capital within upward mobility. Stuffy professor Henry Higgins bets his new colleague Colonel Pickering that he can turn a nearby flower girl into a society pillar, primarily by changing the tone and quality of her speech. Flower girl Eliza Doolittle appears at Higgins's residence the next day, ready to pay for speech lessons that will enable her to secure a job in a local flower shop. The romantic plot unfolds from Higgins's contemptuous indifference toward Eliza until he grows accustomed to her face, and she to his. We concentrate on four early scenes totaling roughly five minutes: Higgins's bet at Covent Garden after an opera, instruction at Higgins's house, an exchange among four characters about the nature of the instruction and a quiet exchange among Higgins, Doolittle and Pickering, which ends with the singing of "The Rain in Spain."

The teacher candidates adopt a variety of strategies to track the questions across these clips. Some take furious notes; others list phrases or single words as symbols; many stare at the screen silently. When the clips end, I ask them to take a few minutes to jot answers to the questions, providing evidence from the scenes for their answers; if they can't think of an answer, "then cheat" by looking on a neighbor's sheet or talking with a peer. I'm for this type of cheating because it shows that this is a low-stakes endeavor and we are in this together. Typically, the first comment is that *My Fair Lady* (Warner & Cukor, 1964) is about language, not reading, and they are not certain how they should address the questions. Not meaning to be flippant, I respond, "Pretend that language and reading are related."

From Higgins's explanations and actions, the teacher candidates conclude that reading is the mastery of subskills in order to unlock the meaning of the greatest ideas of the Western world (England primarily). To justify their conclusions, they offer Higgins monitoring Eliza's vowel pronunciation, his insistence that the instructional intensity will not stop until she does it perfectly and that, eventually, this work will lead her to the works of Shakespeare and Milton. The bet itself provides the evidence of who are the teacher and taught. A teacher must be an expert with a clear understanding of what it means to be educated; the lower classes are the most in need of these lessons, although many teacher candidates point out how Eliza protests that she already possesses the initial skill in a form that Higgins (and society) will not accept. Proper reading ability, then, unlocks high culture and becomes a tool of social mobility. To supply the lower classes such opportunities requires discipline from teachers in identifying the most effective curriculum and tools and from students, who must put forth the concentrated and continuous effort until "By George, she's got it!" By following these values, all lower classes could be successful: It's on them.

Dead Poets Society

Although *Dead Poets Society* (Haft et al., 1989) was released in 1989, most teacher candidates have watched the entire film previously. An alumnus, John Keating, returns to teach English at a New England prep school for boys. His approach to poetry catches the imaginations of many of his adolescent students, who accept and act on Keating's thesis that an intellectual and emotional commitment to poetry is a metaphoric step toward becoming fully human and "thinking for yourself." The film's plot follows the students in their collective and individual pursuit of that curriculum within and against the strictures of 1959 societal norms. We focus on two relatively early scenes. The first is Keating's introduction of his approach and pedagogy surrounding poetry, and the second follows a student-formed group named the Dead Poets Society to a clandestine reading.

Teacher candidates recognize immediately that the definition of reading has changed from *My Fair Lady* (Warner & Cukor, 1964) from one clip: After pretending to follow the advice of a textbook author about how to measure the value of poetry, Keating calls that approach "excrement!" He tells the students to rip the introductory chapter—a skills and single meaning approach—out of their poetry anthologies. Rather than a mastery of skills, reading enables one to find passion, beauty and love symbolized in each poem. Through reading, Keating claims, "In my class, you will learn to think for yourselves again. You will learn that words and ideas can change the world." Although initially reluctant, the glee with which the students take up the task of eliminating the competing definition of reading brings another teacher into the classroom to quell the "rebellion." That Keating repels McAllister with a simple statement—"I am present"—signifies to the teacher candidates that a teacher should have control over his pedagogy.

Huddled in the middle of his classroom with boys sitting on two rows of desks that are bolted to the floor, Keating quotes from Walt Whitman: "The powerful play goes on and you may contribute a verse." He repeats that phrase for emphasis. Typically, this causes disagreement among teacher candidates, who wonder about the word "may" in the second phrase. "May" requires permission, while "can" connotes ability. This difference bothers at least some teacher candidates during each viewing, who suggest that the film title and the reading of Tennyson's "Ulysses" and chanting of Lindsay's "The Congo" (during the second scene) show that these relatively affluent boys will be allowed to think for themselves ("run the country") only after they have internalized the high culture captured in the poems. To quote one preservice teacher, "You can't think for yourself until you learn to think like the teacher." Once articulated, this idea invites others to note that the ultimate role for reading in *Dead Poets Society* (Haft et al., 1989) and *My Fair Lady* (Warner & Cukor, 1964) seems similar, but the pedagogies differ greatly, as do the gender and social class of the students.

A League of Their Own

We watch three scenes from *A League of Their Own* (Abbott et al., 1992), a film about the All-American Girls Professional Baseball League in 1943. The first depicts the tryout at Harvey Field in Chicago, where women from all over the country have gathered to audition for a position on one of four teams from the upper Midwest. The women demonstrate various levels of mastery of fielding, hitting and running before they assemble to learn who has "made the teams." Shirley Baker, an outfielder in bibbed overalls, is left fretting before the team rosters, unable to read her name. A future teammate rescues her by finding her name on the list. The second scene shows a game situation in which the catcher provides winning advice to the team manager and famous former major leaguer, Jimmy Dugan, who uses the strategy successfully but opines, "I still say you're not real ballplayers." In the third scene, Mae Mordabito is sitting next to Shirley, listening and mediating Shirley's reading from a paperback while they travel by bus at night between games.

That Madonna portrays Mae is not lost on the teacher candidates, who comment that she is not a formal teacher, but clearly has Shirley reading at a level well beyond the ability to recognize her name. Two points stand out for the teacher candidates. First, Mae rebuffs a call from the *Dead Poets Society* that the instruction should stem from classical literature when a teammate asks, "Mae, what are you giving her to read?" and Mae replies, "What difference does it make—she's reading okay." Second, they take Shirley's facial expression as a sign that she comprehends when she reads—"ripped her kkk ("kimono" pronounced by Mae) off and grabbed her mmiilllky whiiiite berrrressst." Turning the page, Mae says, "It gets good after that—the delivery man walks in." Reading becomes, then, a means for gaining employment ("read the roster") and pleasure, and while these purposes might serve society, they are first meant to serve the individual. Some preservice teachers contrast Higgins's denial of Eliza's colloquial vowels with the manager's statement that the women are not real ballplayers. In *My Fair Lady* (Warner & Cukor, 1964), Eliza must master Higgins's pronunciation to be accepted, but in *A League of Their Own* (Abbott et al., 1992), Dugan acknowledges eventually the women's abilities and talents by simply watching them play. This connection makes it more difficult for some teacher candidates to forgive the film's heavy-handed symbolism of the overalls for those who should be taught.

The Color Purple

The Color Purple (Guber et al., 1985) is a not entirely satisfying adaptation of Alice Walker's Pulitzer Prize–winning novel; few teacher candidates have watched it previously. Walker takes up the depths of love and family ties, while exploring issues of racism, sexism, sexual orientation, violence and segregation in the South during the 1930s. Spielberg's adaptation highlights the role of literacy in the power struggle between genders and, despite its lack of Walker's complexities, Spielberg's choices make the scenes remarkably useful for my purposes.

We sample seven scenes from this film that create an overview of the novel. Celie is a teenager in an abusive arranged marriage when her sister Nettie arrives to escape their father's sexual advances. Despite her husband Mister's attempt to separate them to control Celie, the sisters pledge that they will remain close through letters. In the short time before Mister forces her to leave, Nettie uses the alphabetic method—pronouncing a word, spelling by its letters and then pronouncing the word—in order to teach Celie to read. The instruction takes place in the kitchen, where labels have been affixed to objects. For fluency and comprehension, Nettie and Celie read from Dickens's *Oliver Twist*. Just before Nettie leaves, the sisters carve their initials on a tree to signify that "now, he'll never break us apart." Spielberg symbolizes the passing of time by showing Celie growing to adulthood, while rocking in a chair, reading *Oliver Twist* more fluently. In order to keep the sisters apart, Mister forbids Celie to touch the mailbox and he intercepts Nettie's letters as they arrive. Celie grows bold enough to confront Mister only after she discovers his stash of a decade's worth of Nettie's letters.

Although all the films deal with oppression at some level, teacher candidates mention power explicitly for the first time after these clips. They report that reading can liberate by encouraging solidarity among those who suffer systematically at the hands of others, exemplified by Spielberg's choice to have Celie read over time the opening sentence from Chapter 2 of *Oliver Twist*: "For the next eight to ten months, Oliver was the victim of a systematic course of treachery and deception." The means of teaching seem to be less important than the powerful caring relationship between teacher and student. Skills must be learned but classics can be read—and the teacher can be a more able peer. Learning requires commitment and persistence, but the payoff is both immediate as well as long-term. Some teacher candidates note that Celie's continual reading of *Oliver Twist* after Nettie has left is a powerful form of solidarity and an intimate connection between sisters. These teacher candidates surmise that, even without the letters, this act contributes eventually to Celie's ability to overcome Mister's dominance.

Who Am I?

With charts completed, the teacher candidates begin to talk about their experiences with each of the competing discourses represented and framed in the films.

Mostly kinder, gentler forms of Henry Higgins are associated with their memories of elementary school; duller John Keatings remind some fondly of secondary school, and often, not so generously about their general education courses; less glamorous Madonnas become their friends who demonstrated how to play League of Legends, introduced them to John Green novels or taught them to post on YouTube. Few have referent experiences for the passionate Nettie's blending of the personal, social and political. We discuss what these associations and absences might mean for the work ahead of them in their course work and in their future classrooms. In a way we are living vicariously, trying on the competing identities of both fictional and remembered teachers.

Invariably within these discussions of possibilities, teacher candidates begin to bridge the materiality and mentalities of the apparatus of governmentality. Some wonder aloud, "We are not free to choose because schools are already organized." And so they are. Such statements open up a need for more discussion of these discourses rather than close our inquiry and determine our choices about reading education. According to the media, government officials, business representatives and the public think schools are in trouble and need to be reformed. How different groups represent and frame the "trouble" and their putative reforms map onto the discourses we've just considered but have yet to name. For example, the No Child Left Behind expectation that all students would be proficient readers by 2014 mimics the bet between Higgins and Pickering that learning is simply a matter of applying the correct technology to any and every student. The Common Core State Standards' emphasis on close reading echoes Mr. Keating's caveat to learn the Dead Poets before permitting Madonna or Shirley to apply personal experiences and make choices about what to read and what it might mean. And where do such education policy moves position Celie and Nettie?

We compare and contrast the values of these metaphoric teachers and their positioning of students in the scenes we've viewed together and debate how these lessons confirm and challenge the public's and our understandings of what reading education is and could be. Rather than come to conclusions, we are left with questions on the blackboard to consider: Is reading a skill or a practice? Should reading for interest count or does reading only the best literature matter? What determines success: mastery or application? What's a good reader? Who's a good teacher? All that seemed so solid about reading education when class began melts within the hot air of our statements and questions. Catchphrases such as "what works," "best practices" and "research-based" become confounded within the values of the discourses and are met with more questions: Works toward what ends? Best for whom? Based on what assumptions? The answers to such questions that make reading education "already organized" become issues as much of the power behind the discourses as they are of rationalities within the discourses.

By harnessing the public pedagogy of these films, teacher candidates are afforded opportunities to engage the advantages and limits of the assigned roles and practices within competing iterations of reading education. Together, we pose questions about the discourses behind their representations and framing of reading education. We compare and contrast our answers to those questions in order to explore the positions they offer to students and teachers. We associate them with our experiences (and lack of) and begin to consider how the discourses have material consequences for reading and lives in and out of schools. While teacher candidates might not be free to choose, they are not free from choices. I like to believe that their agency in making those choices is supported, even furthered, by their collective and individual "readings" of these films that they will use to negotiate the courses, field experiences and careers before them. If we will counter governmentality, we must see that agency lies in "imagining not what is, but what might be" (Davies, 2000, p. 67).

References

Abbott, E., Clemmer, R. D., Greenhut, R., Hartwick, J., Lemish, A., . . . Pace, B. (Producers), & Marshall, P. (Director). (1992). *A league of their own* [Motion picture]. United States: Columbia Pictures.

Bakhtin, M. (1992). *The dialogic imagination: Four essays.* Austin: University of Texas.

Barthes, R. (1975). *The pleasure of the text.* New York, NY: Hill & Wang.

Carnoy, M., & Rothstein, R. (2013, January). *What do international tests really show about U.S. student performance?* Economic Policy Institute. Washington, DC. Retrieved from http://www.epi.org/publication/us-student-performance-testing/

Davies, B. (2000). *A body of writing: 1990–1999.* Lanham, MD: Alta Mira.

Davies, B., & Harre, R. (1990). Positioning: The discursive production of selves. *Journal for the Theory of Social Behavior, 20,* 43–63.

Foucault, M. (1991). Governmentality. In G. Burchell, C. Gordon, & P. Miller (Eds.), *The Foucault effect: Studies in governmentality* (pp. 87–104). Chicago, IL: University of Chicago.

Gee, J. (2001). What is literacy? In P. Shannon (Ed.), *Becoming political, too: New readings and writings on the politics of literacy education* (pp. 1–9). Portsmouth, NH: Heinemann.

Guber, P., Isenberg, C., Jones, Q., Kennedy, K., Marshall, F., . . . Spielberg, S. (Producers) & Spielberg, S. (Director). (1985). *The color purple* [Motion picture]. United States: Warner Bros.

Haft, S., Henderson, D., Witt, P. J., Thomas, T. (Producers) & Weir, P. (Director). (1989). *Dead poets society* [Motion picture]. United States: Buena Vista Pictures.

Hall, S. (1997). The work of representation. In Hall, S. (Ed.), *Representation: Cultural representations and signifying practices* (pp. 13–74). London, UK: SAGE.

Kellner, D., & Share, J. (2007). Critical media literacy, democracy, and the reconstruction of education. In D. Macedo & S. R. Steinberg (Eds.), *Media literacy: A reader* (pp. 3–23). New York, NY: Peter Lang.

Reardon, S. (2011). The widening academic achievement gap between the rich and poor. In G. Duncan & R. Murnane (Eds.), *Whither opportunity? Rising inequality, schools, and children's life chances* (pp. 207–228). New York, NY: Russell Sage.

Sandlin, J., Schultz, M., & Burdick, J. (Eds.). (2009). *Handbook of public pedagogy: Education and learning beyond schooling.* New York, NY: Routledge.

Shannon, P. (2013). An evidence base for the common core. In P. Shannon (Ed.), *Closer readings of the common core* (pp. 1–20). Portsmouth, NH: Heinemann.

Warner, J. L. (Producer), & Cukor, G. (Director). (1964). *My fair lady* [Motion picture]. United States: Warner Bros.

17

WHY *BAD TEACHER* IS A BAD MOVIE AND WHERE THE REAL CRISIS IS

Implications for Teachers and Teacher Education

J. Patrick McGrail
Ewa McGrail

In this chapter, we analyze and critique the film *Bad Teacher* (Dietrich et al., 2011). In our view, it cynically panders to the worst aspects of contemporary pessimism toward educational outcomes in the United States (Beck, 2012; Thomsen, 1993; Vandermeersche, Soetaert & Rutten, 2013). We argue, however, that *Bad Teacher* is actually consonant with Hollywood's well-known narratives of redemption of the fallen (Carter, 2009; Reyes & Rios, 2003). In the past, however, the persons usually occupying the role of the rescuable fallen have been the "unfortunate" students, many of whom have been non-White and who had to be "saved" by a middle-class, often White educator representing traditional authority and American values (Grant, 2002; Matias, 2013). In the film *Bad Teacher*, on the other hand, the redeemed is a stunningly inappropriate, reprobate teacher who is herself inept yet sneers at the professionalism and decorum of her peers and ignores the welfare of her students. At the conclusion of this ostensible comedy, however, she becomes the school's guidance counselor.

In our analysis, we consider the ways in which the representation of teachers, such as the one depicted by Cameron Diaz in *Bad Teacher* (Dietrich et al., 2011), may influence preservice teachers' professional beliefs and attitudes and perceptions of self-efficacy (Grant, 2002; Kaşkaya, Ünlü, Akar & Sağirli, 2011), as well as those held by Americans in general. We suggest opportunities for preservice teachers to examine their own beliefs and conceptions about teachers and the teaching profession, based on *what actual teachers do and are called to do* versus what the public—including preservice teachers—may encounter in movies. We conclude that the film evinces a view of teaching that is at least as misleading as the iconic, heroic portrayals of the near past.

Problems With Hollywood Teacher Depictions

Scholarly examinations of the depictions of teachers have frequently noted the unrealistically heroic nature of teachers in popular American films, such as *Dangerous Minds* (Bruckheimer et al., 1995), *Stand and Deliver* (Labunka, Law, Musca & Menéndez, 1988) and *Dead Poets Society* (Haft, Henderson, Witt, Thomas & Weir, 1989), in which the protagonists valiantly strive to inculcate youth with the all-American values of intellectual curiosity, thrift, sexual moderation and interpersonal courtesy (Carter, 2009; Harris, 2009; Matias, 2013). Some critics argue that while such heroic characteristics may seem to be desirable modeling for a teacher of today, they may also "feed on a collective-anxiety-type drama" by, for example, "subjecting a fresh-faced young teacher to public humiliation at the hands of unruly teens of color" (Gillard, 2012, p. 5). Gillard points to the movie trailer for *Up the Down Staircase* (Pakula & Mulligan, 1967), in which a green teacher walks past groups of African American and Latino students in Spanish Harlem with a concurrent voice-over intoning, "'What's a nice girl doing in a crazy place like this?'" (Gillard, 2012, p. 5).

Even when a film strives to avoid subtle racism in its depictions of teachers, as in, for example, when the teacher is Black (Morgan Freeman in *Lean On Me* [Avildsen, Schiffer, Seelig & Twain, 1989]) or Latino (Edward James Olmos in *Stand and Deliver* [Labunka et al., 1988]), some critics have pointed out that the unrealism of these films lies in an unstated philosophical approach that such teachers seem to take: that schools are inherently corrupt (Krausz, 2003) and only a highly individualistic maverick can rescue students from the uncaring maw of mass education (Beck, 2012; Kelly & Caughlan, 2011). Beck (2012) explains the latter point of view in these words, stressing how this position relieves administrators and policy makers from actually addressing the real problems directly and systematically:

> Problems can be handled only because of the special gifts of the single person, and no social reforms can or need be made. It's a good thing, too, because there seems to be no chance of such reforms being made, not of creating social justice, nor of revising the distribution of wealth or opportunity or normative approval, nor of the introduction of more humane relationships among people. The high expectations and sentimental honor we assign to teachers in popular culture is complementary to the continuation unchanged of the real world outside of school. We need not change because heroic teachers will change our inner predispositions.
>
> *(p. 90)*

However, the problem with most film characterizations of teachers is that they create unrealizable expectations for real-world teachers (Marshall, 2007): "With some exceptions, films that center on teachers tend to show them as almost superhuman, capable of permanently changing lives in a short period of time" (Farhi, 1999, p. 157). Remarkably few day-to-day professional details are depicted, whether teaching activities (e.g., planning, homework support, test preparation) or supplemental matters and events (e.g., hall duty, parent-teacher conferences, calls to students' homes, unit and department meetings). Unsurprisingly, these latter activities often compete with teaching preparation time. Such details are, however, swept away as probable detractors from the cinematic myth of the "superteacher"—and "by forcing them to compete with their cinematic coun-terparts, the superteacher myth places an impossible burden on real teachers" (Farhi, 1999, p. 157).

Analyzing Hollywood Depictions of the Profession and Teacher Education

Research has pointed out the problems in portrayals of teachers in mass media, especially film and television, as sources for teacher identity formation and teacher pedagogy modeling. One critic, Gregory Marshall (2007), has said that popular movies and television series "are not well suited as a medium for accurate pic-tures" (p. 21) because they reproduce "recycled stereotypes" that "mislead, confuse, and impoverish [teachers' and students'] evaluations of and expectations about the nature of genuine education" (p. 7).

Vandermeersche, Soetaert and Rutten (2013) offer a differing perspective. Instead of discrediting movies and television programming as appropriate sources for school and teacher identity representations, they recommend that teacher education programs use them as a "basis for critical discussion in classes for pre-service teachers" (p. 89). The viewpoint of these researchers was inspired by Wayne Booth's (1988) advice that "if the powerful stories we tell each other really matter to us—and even the most skeptical theorists imply by their practice that stories do matter—then a criticism that takes their 'mattering' seriously cannot be ignored" (p. 4). *Bad Teacher* (Dietrich et al., 2011) is therefore prime for such critical analysis and evaluation.

Perhaps as a result of the 15-year "education wars" propagated by recent presi-dential administrations (Kumashiro, 2012; Rochester, 2013), the movie seems to presuppose a reservoir of bad feeling about education in the hearts and minds of the American public (Beck, 2012). Against this presumed backdrop of contempo-rary doubt, cynicism and criticism of the worth of today's teachers (Beck, 2012; Thomsen, 1993; Vandermeersche et al., 2013), *Bad Teacher* (Dietrich et al., 2011) appears to confirm the lay public's worst fears about the profession: that a slovenly, sexually profligate, emotionally shallow woman with substance abuse issues and a complete lack of professionalism might be educating its children.

In this chapter, we take on the semantic and symbolic perspectives of pro-duction and reception in film analysis (Mikos, 2014) to "observe how the structures of film function in the framework of the communication processes they are bound up in" (p. 410). Structures are "the means a film employs to communicate meaning with viewers" and they include "content, acting, dramaturgy, narrative and aesthetics" (p. 410). For this short analysis, we focus primarily on plot, characters and their representation through the art of acting. In our analysis, we are interested in exploring how that which is being communicated by a film about teachers reflects—or does not reflect— real teachers and teaching in the classroom and how such depictions may influence preservice teachers' professional beliefs and attitudes, as well as their perceptions of self-efficacy (Grant, 2002; Kaşkaya et al., 2011). Secondarily, we are concerned with the impact such a distorted and exaggerated portrayal of teachers might have on the public at large.

Characters and Their Representation

The protagonist of *Bad Teacher*, Elizabeth Halsey, is portrayed through a carefully orchestrated series of plot events as being spectacularly ill-suited to the teaching profession. She is an attractive but calculating and foul-mouthed young woman who is "temporarily" a middle school teacher, following her ouster from an engagement to a wealthy man. Teaching is merely a way to support herself while she schemes to marry a fellow teacher who is a wealthy heir. She also attempts to raise enough money for breast implants in order to compete with what she calls the "Barbie Doll types" that she believes are out-competing her for marriage to wealthy men. A chance remark by a fellow teacher lets Halsey know about a contest that awards $5,700 to the teacher with the highest student scores on a high-stakes state test. Because winning would permit the impecunious Halsey to get the breast implants she wants, she blackmails the state test administrator to get a copy of the test answers and preps her students accordingly. Her scheme appears at first to be successful, and she is given the winning check.

However, her colleague Miss Squirrel suspects, and then confirms, that Halsey has cheated and notifies the principal and the school superintendent. The quick-thinking Halsey turns the tables and successfully accuses Miss Squirrel of being a drug user. During the course of all this, the gym teacher, Russell Gettis, takes a liking to Halsey but she scoffs at his attentions because he isn't wealthy. Nevertheless, his persistence pays off and she finally agrees to date him. The final scene shows Halsey leaving the classroom to become the school guidance counselor.

While Halsey is brash and resourceful in a street-smart sort of way, her colleagues are portrayed as timid, doctrinaire, out-of-step social misfits. The rather-too-pointedly named Amy Squirrel is at first presented as an overenergetic friend to all of her students with nonstandard, more "fun" ways of reaching them. She is soon revealed to be mentally unstable, with an unnamed incident in her past marking her professional career in a negative way. When Halsey expresses disbelief at her unusual name, Miss Squirrel does an impression of a squirrel eating a nut, confirming her own acceptance of her unusual moniker. Miss Squirrel is depicted throughout as having a surfeit of energy and a self-professed teaching acumen, which she is only too happy to foist upon other teachers, particularly Halsey, whom she mistakenly views at first as being merely too timid in her approach to educating her students. Part of the plot turns upon her gradual realization that Halsey is merely completely uninterested in educating her students, at least in the beginning of the film.

Bad Teacher and Real Teachers

In studying students' perceptions of quality instruction and quality teacher-student interactions, Läänemets, Kalamees-Ruubel and Sepp (2012) reported the following traits and behaviors students expected of good teachers: "[being] friendly; being understanding and caring; being calm or balanced, and being joyful or positive" (p. 29). In addition, students appreciate when teachers are kind and "are able to listen to students and understand them" (p. 30). In terms of skills and expertise, the students in the study underscored that good teachers are knowledgeable; "make learning interesting, exciting, or diverse; they can explain everything so that you can understand; and they can teach their subject well" (p. 29).

Unfortunately, none of these personal and professional traits and behaviors are evident in the portrayal of Elizabeth Halsey. Instead of being friendly, understanding, caring, calm or balanced, joyful or positive, Halsey frequently scowls at students and writes comments on their papers such as, "Are you fucking kidding me?" Instead of listening to students and understanding them, Halsey declares one "hopeless" and opines that another will not lose his virginity until age 29. Instead of making learning interesting, exciting or diverse, or explaining everything and teaching her subject well, Halsey plays movies in her classroom in lieu of lesson plans, in one scene particularly so that she can surreptitiously avail herself of a stash of hard liquor in her desk.

However, Halsey's *modes d'emploi* change drastically when she realizes that if her class gets the highest scores on a high-stakes test, she will personally receive a check and the breast implants that she believes she needs will be within reach. Even when she realizes her students have to excel for her to win the cash, Halsey's teaching practices remain highly questionable, due to her lack of pedagogical expertise and casual disregard for ethical and professional standards. In a scene probably designed to be comical, Halsey lines her students up in the gymnasium for a Q&A session on the material for the test. If a student responds with the wrong answer, she throws a dodgeball at the student's head (the student is not allowed to duck). If the student gets the right answer, the student is allowed to throw a ball at her. Passing over the fact that such a "learning strategy" is ineffective instruction (Ruan, 2015), such a method could hardly be contemplated by a sane adult, let alone a teacher. Indeed, in light of the Illinois Educator Code of Ethics (2014), Halsey's questionable technique in the gymnasium would have been found to be *per se* unethical conduct, likely calling for disciplinary action or dismissal.

It might be argued at this point that such an over-the-top scene was constructed by the filmmakers for comic or satirical purposes. Nevertheless, comedy—however black—requires an energetic excessiveness for its dart to make contact with the target. Consider the well-known example of Jonathan Swift's *A Modest Proposal* (1729), wherein he proposes that the children of Ireland be served up as food to decrease the surplus population. Few critics, then or now, have entertained the belief that Swift's proposal was to be taken literally. In *Bad Teacher*, however, we are treated to scene after scene, but especially this one, in which the filmmakers seem to suggest that such distasteful events (and teachers!) might likely be real. Even if they do not intend this, the filmmakers make abundantly clear their jaundiced view of teachers through such a scene and, indeed, in many of the other scenes in which Halsey's antics are depicted.

To add insult to injury, Halsey also employs not-so-subtle racist and homophobic language in the film. When her students complain about her "drill and kill" techniques for the upcoming high-stakes test, she opines, "Pathetic. This is why the Japs are overtaking us . . ." At another point, she misunderstands a friendly overture from Amy Squirrel as a sexual come-on and uses an offensive term to describe a sexual practice. Finally, she makes a subtly anti-Semitic remark when she says, "Listen, I could take you day-by-day through my entire syllabus, but that's just not how I do things . . . So that's my spiel, as the Jews say."

Halsey's behavior would not avoid censure in the most permissive of schools, and in the most authoritarian, she would probably be fired, sued or have criminal proceedings brought against her. However, as already stated, all of her behavior is portrayed as being both possible and, in some sense, refreshing, juxtaposed against the ineffective practices of the other teachers. In addition to being unethical, Halsey's antisocial behavior, racist and homophobic language and "put-down" instructional practices are also in direct opposition to what students expect from good teachers and from their interactions with them in the real classroom. We would ordinarily think that to backlight the blanching unprofessionalism of Halsey, the filmmakers might choose to portray her colleagues as more effective, more moderate and more caring. Instead, the filmmakers choose to gleefully lampoon Halsey's colleagues in different ways. We are initially led to believe that Amy Squirrel uses innovative techniques to awake learning in her students, but the screenplay pokes fun at what she does and portrays her as juvenile, naïve and, ultimately, unbalanced. For example, in one class, Miss Squirrel pretends to be an airline pilot, replete with pilot's hat and electronic megaphone, while her students are depicted as bored and empty-eyed.

Realistically—putting aside the wisdom of such overt theatricality in the middle school classroom—teachers in today's challenged classrooms would likely find it more difficult than Miss Squirrel to employ such innovative techniques without some negotiations with their administration and leadership. Negotiation would involve the teacher needing to provide the reasons for using such a tactic and explaining the positive impact it might have on student academic progress. Finding different ways to engage students is nearly always encouraged, but today's emphasis on learning outcomes would likely cause middle school department heads and principals to be skeptical of what Miss Squirrel attempts. The film is mute about the need for such negotiations, however.

In addition, the film represents its more minor characters as personally ineffectual and immature. When Halsey sets her sights on marrying the effete, charming and wealthy teacher Scott Delacorte, Miss Squirrel, who is also smitten with the handsome but unsophisticated teacher, acts in a childish, "middle school" manner. Her hatred of Halsey is made complete when she accidentally discovers that Halsey has rigged the high-stakes test the school gives and has walked away with the winning score and prize money. She reports Halsey to the principal, who tells Miss Squirrel that she has begun to show signs of some kind of mental breakdown, in a scene played strictly for laughs.

Halsey's sidekick at the school, Lynn Davies, is portrayed as so naïve that she believes Halsey to be a "mover and shaker." Davies will seemingly do anything Halsey asks of her, including smoking marijuana and asking strange men to dance. Even the likeable gym teacher Gettis is portrayed as ludicrously flawed, as a pothead who cannot even climb the gym rope that he sets forth for his students. The principal and the other teachers are also portrayed as timid and unimaginative, and their after-hours activities mark them as desperately "uncool," wonkish and dated.

Discussion and Implications

Halsey's teacher character asks us to believe two things: (1) that people like her might well be employed in our secondary education system and (2) that she is somehow an amusing (and effective) foil to the bland and uninspiring "professional" teachers who surround her. If the former is true, then it is clear that, at least to the producers and writers of this film, educators are far from heroic. If the latter is true, the film seems to accept the premise that teaching is the last thing an intelligent, creative person might do with her life. Indeed, at one point in the film, Halsey is actually asked, "What went so wrong that you ended up educating children?"

In this way, the film seems to give filmgoers and preservice teachers a choice. If one chooses the education profession, one is doomed to be either a sad, unhip, fearful rule-follower clinging to a low-esteem job or—in the case of Halsey—a rigger of the system who acts unethically but profitably and who is interested only in improving her economic outlook. As Dalton (2013) asserts, in *Bad Teacher* (Dietrich et al., 2011), "every teacher is revealed to be a bad teacher operating within a corrupt educational system" (p. 79). Hence, just as the public (as well as aspiring teachers) may believe that the heroic traits of Jaime Escalante in *Stand and Deliver* (Labunka et al., 1988) or LouAnne Johnson in *Dangerous Minds* (Bruckheimer et al., 1995) have been exaggerated but are at their kernel true, so it may be that the public and preservice educators might reduce in proportion, but fail to entirely eliminate from the realm of possibility, the existence of an Elizabeth Halsey (or even more than one) in the nation's public schools.

While it may be harmless for the public—or, for that matter, preservice teachers—to imagine that some teachers are nearly or partly as heroic as Escalante or Johnson, the public's assuming that some percentage of teachers regularly indulges in even a small number of the escapades of Diaz's character in *Bad Teacher* (Dietrich et al., 2011) certainly would be a gratuitous error as well as a harmful one. It is deeply unconstructive, in our view, for the film to traffic in naturalistic yet distorted depictions of such unlikely characters in our nation's public schools.

The damage to the reputations of teachers in the public eye is not the sole issue, however. According to the National Center for Education Statistics, there were 3.7 million full-time elementary and secondary teachers in 2012, the last year for which we have reliable figures (U.S. Department of Education, 2013). Of these, 3.3 million are in public schools and each teaches an average of 23 students. Together, they therefore affect the lives of 76 million young people every year. Moving the needle of public and preservice teacher opinion, even if only a small degree, can matter inestimably to the careers and self-esteem of teachers who work in an educational system that the public has viewed as "in crisis" (Kumashiro, 2012) long before *Bad Teacher*.

It is likely that the filmmakers of *Bad Teacher* (Dietrich et al., 2011) intended their film to be a satire of some sort. The smirking, world-weary tropes of cynicism toward educational mores and practices in which the film traffics seek out conspirators in the audience, as if to gleefully suggest, "I'd bet all of you know people like Miss Halsey." The filmmakers, too, have an unlikely ally in the naturalism of their depiction—namely, the relative unfamiliarity of American audiences with the contemporary status of public education. Few adults are personally familiar with what secondary school is like in the second decade of the 21st century, especially if they "haven't been in one since 1975" (Flanagan, 2011 para. 3). Flanagan explains this disconnect in these words:

> I am not convinced that people have good filters for what's true and what's distorted when it comes to the reality of public schooling. I worry, a lot, about discernment—the ability to figure out who's zoomin' who on complex education issues.
>
> *(para. 3)*

Preservice teachers, as shown earlier, seek out and are aware of teacher portrayals in popular culture (Trier, 2001), including those in *Bad Teacher*. Despite the obvious flaws of such portrayals, Ryan and Townsend (2012) observe, "In teacher preparation programs, Hollywood films can help encourage future teachers to examine their beliefs and perceptions of teachers, construct espoused platforms about their own educational philosophies, and enact instructional methods that align with their educational goals" (p. 241). Preservice teachers tend to be media-savvy audiences; indeed, in the collegiate education program at the first author's university, media literacy is a required course for preservice teachers. As Andersen (1992) points out in strongly advocating this literacy for teachers, "Media awareness can help [e]xplode stereotypes and misconceptions so they don't poison attitudes and interpersonal relations" (para. 16). Teacher educators have an opportunity, then, to help them interrogate and question the troubling teacher portrayals depicted in *Bad Teacher*, and in doing so, enable them to develop a counternarrative that they might wish to adopt. Such a counternarrative would involve more truthful and realistic teacher and teaching profession representations for themselves and for their students.

Toward this goal, teacher educators can have preservice teachers conduct mini-ethnography studies of teachers and school cultures, paying attention to the ways in which teachers form and enact professional identities, interact with students and administrators, implement the curriculum and negotiate the day-to-day demands associated with student and teacher accountability. Such work, coupled with discussion, reading and interpretation of educational law and ethics, is central to helping preservice teachers gain a full understanding of teaching and the teaching profession. It is also a reasonable assurance against them falling prey to the many teacher misrepresentations in popular culture and mass media, such as the ones depicted in *Bad Teacher* (Dietrich et al., 2011).

Preservice teachers also have the opportunity to examine in this particular film the portrayal of adolescent students, their developmental needs, attitudes and behaviors and evaluate whether these representations are truthful to this age group. This is important as preservice teachers need to understand adolescence and the physiological, social and emotional problems adolescents typically deal with during this stage of life. This understanding will help preservice teachers know them and their culture and understand their social and academic needs. As a result, they will better be able to design instruction that will succeed with this age group. Gordon (1997) also argues that understanding adolescent culture, which he defines as knowing "adolescents' speech patterns, popular music, styles of dress, favorite movies and preferred places for recreation" (p. 57), is essential to effective classroom management. He urges teacher educators to help preservice teachers acquire such social insight into adolescence. *Bad Teacher* is replete with scenes of adolescent culture that can be critiqued for their opportunity to gain such important insight or discard as unrealistic.

Analyses of films such as this one will also provide preservice teachers with recognition of the specific cinematic and televisual elements needed for them to critically examine mass media portrayals of teachers for realism, ideology, stereotypes, cultural memes, bias and other social constructions and representations. There are lessons to be learned for teacher educators and preservice teachers, even from a bad movie. One is the opportunity to deconstruct and dismantle its profusion of cynically proposed half-truths that constitute what the filmmakers seem to view as the crumbling institution of public education. Those of us who seek fair portrayals of our currently beleaguered American teachers must not avoid the critical analysis of such flawed mass media portrayals of teachers and the teaching profession but should counterpropose realistic and reliable representations of our own instead.

References

Andersen, S. (1992). Making a case for media literacy in the classroom. *Media and Values, 57*. Retrieved from http://www.medialit.org/reading-room/making-case-media-literacy-classroom

Avildsen, J. G., Schiffer, M., Seelig, D., Twain, N. (Producers), & Avilsden, J. G. (Director). (1989). *Lean on me* [Motion picture]. United States: Warner Bros.

Beck, B. (2012). The teacher from the black lagoon: Revenge of the bad teacher. *Multicultural Perspectives, 14*(2), 89–92. DOI: 10.1080/15210960.2012.673316

Booth, W. C. (1988). *The company we keep: An ethics of fiction.* Los Angeles: University of California Press.

Bruckheimer, J., Foster, L., Guinzburg, K., Rabins, S., Simpson, D. (Producers), & Smith, J. N. (Director). (1995). *Dangerous minds* [Motion picture]. United States: Hollywood Pictures.

Carter, C. (2009). Priest, prostitute, or plumber? The construction of teachers as saints. *English Education, 42*(1), 61–90.

Dalton, M. M. (2013). Bad teacher is bad for teachers. *Journal of Popular Film and Television, 41*(2), 78–87. DOI: 10.1080/01956051.2013.787352

Dietrich, C., Eisenbert, L., Householter, D. B., Kacandes, G., Kasdan, J., . . . Stupnitsky, G. (Producers), & Kasdan, J. (Director). (2011). *Bad teacher* [Motion picture]. United States: Columbia Pictures.

Farhi, A. (1999). Hollywood goes to school: Recognizing the superteacher myth in film. *The Clearing House, 72*(3), 157–159.

Flanagan, N. (2011). How people learn about schools. *Education Week, 30*(36), 18–19.

Gillard, C. (2012). Good teachers (the movie you will never see). *The Education Digest, 77*(5), 4–7.

Gordon, R. L. (1997). How novice teachers can succeed with adolescents. *Educational Leadership, 54*(7), 56–58.

Grant, P. A. (2002). Using popular films to challenge preservice teachers' beliefs about teaching in urban schools. *Urban Education, 37*(1), 77–95.

Haft, S., Henderson, D., Witt, P. J., Thomas, T. (Producers) & Weir, P. (Director). (1989). *Dead poets society* [Motion picture]. United States: Buena Vista Pictures.

Harris, A. (2009). The good teacher images of teachers in popular culture. *English Drama Media, 14*, 11–18.

Illinois Educator Code of Ethics. (2014). Retrieved from http://www.isbe.net/prep-eval/pdf/meetings/emag/pdf/educator_COE_0311.pdf

Kaşkaya, A., Ünlü, İ., Akar, M. S., & Sağirli, M. Ö. (2011). The effects of school and teacher themed movies on pre-service teachers' professional attitudes and perceived self-efficacy. *Educational Sciences: Theory & Practice, 11*(4), 1778–1783.

Kelly, S., & Caughlan, S. (2011). The Hollywood teachers' perspective on authority. *Pedagogies: An International Journal, 6*(1), 46–65.

Krausz, P. (2003). Does the cinema represent teachers fairly? *Australian Screen Education, 30*, 62–66.

Kumashiro, K. K. (2012). *Bad teacher: How blaming teachers distorts the bigger picture.* New York, NY: Teachers College Press.

Läänemets, U., Kalamees-Ruubel, K., & and Sepp, A. (2012). What makes a good teacher? Voices of Estonian students. *Delta Kappa Gamma Bulletin, 79*(1), 27–31.

Labunka, I., Law, L., Musca, T. (Producer), & Menéndez, R. (Director). (1988). *Stand and deliver* [Motion picture]. United States: Warner Bros.

Marshall, G. (2007). Real teaching and teal learning vs. narrative myths about education. *Arts and Humanities in Higher Education, 6*(1), 7–27.

Matias, C. E. (2013). On the "Flip" side: A teacher educator of color unveiling the dangerous minds of White teacher candidates. *Teacher Education Quarterly, 40*(2), 53–73.

Mikos, L. (2014). Analysis of film. In U. Flick (Ed.), *The SAGE handbook of qualitative data analysis* (pp. 411–422). Los Angeles, CA: SAGE.

Pakula, A. J. (Producer), & Mulligan, R. (Director). (1967). *Up the down staircase* [Motion picture]. United States: Warner Bros.

Reyes, X. A., & Rios, D. I. (2003). Imaging teachers: In fact and in the mass media. *Journal of Latinos and Education, 2*, 3–11.

Rochester, J. M. (2013). *Class warfare, besieged schools, bewildered parents, betrayed kids and the attack on excellence.* San Francisco, CA: Encounter Books.

Ruan, L. (2015). Language teaching from the view of formative assessment. *Theory and Practice in Language Studies, 5*(1), 92–96.

Ryan, P. A., & Townsend, J. S. (2012). Promoting critical reflection in teacher education through popular media. *Action in Teacher Education, 34*, 239–248.

Swift, J. (1729). *A modest proposal.* Retrieved from Project Gutenberg on October 2, 2015, from http://www.gutenberg.org/files/1080/1080-h/1080-h.htm

Thomsen, S. T. (1993). A worm in the apple: Hollywood's influence on the public's perception of teachers. ERIC document ED359592. Retrieved on from http://eric.ed.gov/?id=ED359592

Trier, J. (2001). Challenging the cinematic construction of "literacy" with preservice teachers. *Teaching Education, 12*(3), 301–314.

U.S. Department of Education, National Center for Education Statistics. (2013). *Digest of education statistics, 2012* (NCES 2014–2015). Retrieved from http://nces.ed.gov/pro grams/digest/d12/index.asp

Vandermeersche, G., Soetaert, R., & Rutten, K. (2013). Shall I tell you what is wrong with Hector as a teacher? The *History Boys* stereotypes of popular and high culture, and teacher education. *Journal of Popular Film & Television, 41*(2), 88–97.

18

PREPARING TEACHERS IN THE TIME OF *SUPERMAN*

The Accountability Narrative of Education Documentaries

Christian Z. Goering
Jen S. Dean
Brandon Flammang

> The constant desire to win is a very American kind of trouble. Less glamorous gains made along the way—learning, wisdom, growth, and confidence, dealing with failure—aren't given the same respect because they can't be given a grade.
> —William Knowlton Zinsser

The current education narrative in America tells of failing public schools, unaccountable teachers, government-sanctioned expansions of "wildly successful" charter schools and increased surveillance and scrutiny vis-à-vis standardized testing. A recent comment by a public school parent, though anecdotal, is perhaps representative of how some citizens view teaching and education writ large: "I just want teachers held accountable." What remains true, and at the heart of the matter, is that the working conditions of teachers are the learning conditions of not only students but also future teachers, conditions we argue are under constant and consistent attack from myriad sources, which include both feature and documentary film genres. For $9.50 per movie ticket, one can learn about a version of teaching faded in and spliced from reality, dystopia and popular mythology.

We collaborated to look more deeply at education documentaries through our connection in Representations of American Education in Film, a course at the University of Arkansas Chris teaches to graduate students in which both Brandon and Jen enrolled. We are teachers and advocates for public education with three distinct backgrounds: Chris taught high school English before entering teacher education; Jen worked for 826 National before beginning her career as a middle school teacher in 2014; Brandon teaches exclusively in alternative education settings. Together, we narrowed our focus to a critical examination of education documentaries produced during 2010–2011 in the considerable wake of *Waiting for Superman's* (Birtel et al., 2010) release in an effort to examine the motivations of these cultural documents and understand this particular context for teaching and learning in America.

Drawing on previous work in cultural studies and critical education, this chapter builds understanding through a lens of critical pedagogy in an effort to explore the context for teaching, learning and preparing teachers while advancing ideas of how preservice teachers and practicing teachers can engage in conversations about these texts. We selected *Waiting for Superman* (Birtel et al., 2010), *The Lottery* (Ashman et al., 2010) and *American Teacher* (Calegari, Davis, Eggers, Roth & McGinn, 2011) for our corpus of education documentaries for three central reasons: (1) The films were produced in the same time frame; (2) the films purportedly represent different perspectives; and (3) the films represent a phenomenon as part of the "new education documentary" (Hermansen, 2014, p. 519) associated with *Waiting for Superman's* release. Creating an understanding of these films in light of current education policy is a model we forward for working with preservice teachers (PSTs), who need to have conversations about the misconceptions widely held about teachers and teaching, the mythology of teachers as saviors and the reality of the responsibility any given teacher has when he/she enters the classroom. Through our analysis, we concluded that modeling analysis patterns for PSTs would serve not only to broaden perspectives on education but also to build PSTs' capacity to take these critical approaches to their own students.

Integrated Framework: Schools Films and Critical Pedagogy

Making meaning from school films is a concept that most comfortably rests in the larger discipline of cultural studies. Scholars such as Stuart Hall, Simon During and bell hooks provide theoretical and practical means of taking apart cultural texts in interests of exploring deeper elements of meaning. Hall's (1997) definition of representation helps guide our work:

> Representation is the process by which members of a culture use language to produce meaning. Already, this definition carries the important premise that things—objects, people, events in the world—do not have in themselves any fixed, final or true meaning. It is us—in society, within human cultures—who make things mean, who signify. Meanings, consequently, will always change, from one cultural period to another.
>
> *(p. 61)*

Dalton's (2010) *The Hollywood Curriculum: Teachers in the Movies* provides an introduction to scholarly approaches taken with school films. She analyzed over 165 films through critical theory, cultural studies and curriculum theory as part of her dissertation study and has followed up with revised editions of her book. What has remained true over the now 20 years since her first analysis (Dalton, 1995) is "that the Hollywood model of the good teacher is still as dominant as ever in motion pictures" (Dalton, 2010, p. ix).

Narrowing our focus by first defining the critical pedagogy lens through which we critically viewed the three selected documentary films creates an antecedent to our understanding of how meaning is made through cultural studies. Following Giroux in *Education and the Crisis of Public Values* (2012), we agree that "culture in this sense becomes the site of the most powerful and persuasive forms of pedagogy precisely because it often denies its pedagogical and normalizing function" (p. 3). In other words, culture becomes reality for the whole of the educational sphere; the narratives of competition, choice and accountability are pervasive and insidious. Our lens pays special attention to the educational depictions of the banking model (Freire, 2000), as it builds on and extends the narratives of privatization: "The more students work at storing the deposits entrusted to them, the less they develop the critical consciousness which would develop from their intervention in the world as transformers of that world" (p. 73). For example, Giroux (2012) explains how *Waiting for Superman* promotes a choice and competition agenda, one that "sits on a faulty premise in that competition begets multiple losers, in addition to the winner" (p. 89). Our lens then is one that views these films anew, examining the group of documentaries for elements of accountability—or, to follow Stuart Hall, we are performing an oppositional reading of the films in an effort to lay bare the inner workings of them. Our pedagogical approach follows those championed by James Trier (2002, 2005, 2007, 2014), who writes extensively on the topic of school films, extending from Dalton's analytical lens to the use of school films in empirical research and specifically engaging PST and in-service teachers in critical pedagogy. Furthering the notion of Debord's "detournement" to encompass the experience, discussion and overall milieu of future teachers examining and discussing school films, Trier (2014) builds pedagogically oriented theory to help future educators' unlock their prejudice, bias and privilege, to enter "mosh-pit pedagogy" (p. 2).

Educational Context

The environment that produced the education documentaries that rest at the heart of this chapter is one difficult to summarize. However lengthy a description is, most will include the 1983 National Commission on Excellence in Education report *A Nation at Risk* (*ANAR*) due to its controversial and incendiary nature, one that continues to draw criticism and simultaneously encode education policy over 30 years after its release. Specifically, as Thomas (2014) states, "While the federal report created fertile ground for state-based school accountability, that proved not to be enough for political leaders, who within 15–20 years began orchestrating national versions of education accountability" (n.p.). No Child Left Behind (NCLB) in 2002 and then the Common Core State Standards (CCSS) in 2010, each advancing high-stakes assessments and "both neatly wrapped in bi-partisan veneer" (Thomas, 2014, n.p.), are the current iteration of *ANAR*.

Further, as Mehta (2013) relates, *ANAR* defined an entirely economic purpose of public education, one that created a need for accountability in the form of standards, assessments and punitive measures for those schools failing in the eyes of the policy makers. Writing in 2009, Berliner shares,

> We live in "outcome-oriented," "bottom line," "accountability" times [. . .] after NCLB has dominated educational discourse [. . .]. This law, reflecting and enhancing the accountability oriented zeitgeist in which we live, focuses almost exclusively on [. . .] reading and mathematics [. . .] test scores.
> *(p. 5)*

NCLB was not enough, and what emanated from the precise context of the documentaries at hand was the coalescence of an economic downturn and the passing of new federal legislation (Race to the Top) that promised millions to states in exchange for their adoption of the CCSS and national assessment consortia. We want to be clear that standards and assessments are not inherently bad but, when coupled with punitive policies like closing schools, they can be:

> Common Core is not some unique and flawed thing, however, but the logical extension of the Reagan imperative to use education accountability to erode public support for public schools so that unpopular political agendas (school choice, for example) become more viable.
> *(Thomas, 2014, n.p.)*

Phrased another way, "accountability built on standards and high-stakes testing (not Common Core *uniquely*) is the problem because it is designed as disaster bureaucracy, not as education reform" (Thomas, 2014, n.p.).

The New Education Documentaries

The three films we selected were each released within 12 months of each other and mark a new age of education reform as exemplified by the early discussions on CCSS launched in 2009 and the release of the U.S. Department of Education's *A Blueprint for Reform* in March 2010. Although we watched many more films than we selected for this chapter, these three exemplified the common theme that emerged: accountability. Additionally, this theme seemed to be constructed within the narrative of the "good teacher."

1. The Lottery *(Ashman et al., 2010)*

The Lottery builds on the premise that a good education is a system of chance in today's educational climate. The documentary focuses on four families who decide that their children will not be victims of a failing education system and, thus, they set out to enroll them in viable alternative charter schools. The film paints a grim picture of today's public schools and attempts to demonstrate that parents and guardians are the only ones holding themselves accountable for the education of children in inner-city neighborhoods. The parental accountability is designed to spur action and demand viewers to ask the question, "Why do parents have to be *this involved* in seeking a good education for their children?" For future teachers, this question may feel condescending as it marginalizes their professional dedication while simultaneously continuing to further the perception that our schools just aren't good enough.

2. Waiting for Superman *(Birtel et al., 2010)*

The premise of this 2010 documentary is centered on Guggenheim's assertion that American schools are leaving children behind at "alarming rates." Building off of the narrative created by *A Nation at Risk* decades ago, Guggenheim criticizes "our buckling public education system, once the best in the world, [that] routinely forsakes the education of millions of children." Guggenheim deftly supports the larger accountability narrative that cries out for someone (anyone, someone, please!) to claim responsibility for our nation's failing schools. Wavering between Michelle Rhee, Geoffrey Canada and a host of other education reformers, Guggenheim's superman is left undefined. Situated within Guggenheim's larger call for accountability is his perpetuation of the myth of the "good teacher." In fact, the film's declaration that "good teachers make good schools" sets the scene for future documentaries that, despite their intentions, extend the accountability narrative to teachers, thereby creating an ideal for preservice teachers that is unattainable.

3. American Teacher *(Calegari et al., 2011)*

The Teacher Salary Project, created by Nínive Calegari, a former educator and cofounder of 826 National, and Dave Eggers, author and cofounder of 826 National, seeks to inform the public of the service teachers do and how they are continuously devalued and underpaid (Teacher Salary Project, n.d.). The organization cites its mission as one that ensures that "teaching becomes the prestigious, desirable, financially viable, and professionally exciting job we all know it needs to be" (Teacher Salary Project, n.d.). They position themselves as advocates for teachers both through their work and their films. While working diligently to promote the ethics and tireless dedication of teachers, *AT* begins to feed the accountability narrative through its exaltation of teachers. Preservice teachers are once again indoctrinated with the message that they must be the "good teacher," which *AT* defines as relentless in her or his pursuit of helping students succeed to the detriment of relationships, pocketbooks and emotional states.

Documentary Film Analysis

We met on consecutive Saturdays to view and analyze films, originally holding ten in our study corpus of both the documentary and feature variety. As the scope of the project began to reveal itself, we narrowed our list by first cutting feature films and then by narrowing documentaries to the related time frame around *Waiting for Superman* (Birtel et al., 2010). While we needed to analyze these films for the purpose of engaging the academic conversation on school films, we also wanted to provide a model that we could adapt and use with classes of middle school, high school and college students, the latter PSTs. In this sense, we approached each film as a researcher might approach a data set and simply viewed the film once. Following a conversation, we created a list of open codes or words and phrases that we felt represented bigger ideas within the film and that might help us further understand its meaning. We next modeled Trier's (2014) "moshpit pedagogy" (p. 2) by engaging in a Google doc conversation while viewing the film a second time, allowing for give-and-take in our analysis. While these approaches taken together led us to ideas other than those featured here, the dominant category or thematic understanding, if you will, revealed that measures of school and teacher accountability were prevalent throughout.

Accountability: Shifting the Blame

The *Oxford English Dictionary* (2015) defines *accountability* as "the quality of being accountable; liability to account for and answer for one's conduct, performance of duties, etc. [. . .]; responsibility (n.p.)." The definition uses the word *accountability* as something an individual is lacking, or "liable to account for." The exaltation of teacher accountability mirrors the connotations of these words and phrases—lacking, accounting for one's actions—reflecting an educational environment that focuses on the negative and the negligent. The implication is that teachers must be held accountable for their actions because their actions are inherently bad.

The accountability movement contradicts the public perception of teachers. For example, in the October 2014 Phi Delta Kappa International/Gallup Poll of the Public's Attitudes Toward the Public Schools, 64% of respondents said they trust teachers in public schools (Phi Delta Kappa International/Gallup, 2014a, 2014b). Furthermore, in the September 2014 poll, respondents identified attracting good teachers as only 8% of the problem in public schools. If the public doesn't believe that attracting and retaining good teachers is a problem and does believe that teachers are trustworthy, then why is there a large-scale movement focused on creating teacher accountability? Ravitch (2013) attributes the movement to an emphasis on test scores, the impetus of No Child Left Behind and a move by some toward attempts at privatizing public education (p. 11). NCLB, passed in 2001, required that all states test and report scores for every student in Grades 3 through 8 in both math and reading. By 2014, all students were supposed to be proficient on state tests. Any school that persistently failed to meet its annual goal for proficiency would be labeled in need of improvement or failing. Student achievement was directly tied to school funds, which subsequently redirected the focus of schools and administration to standardized testing. Furthermore, if students were not demonstrating proficiency, someone had to be blamed.

Individual Accountability: Myth of Teachers as Saviors

Geoffrey Canada, former president of the Harlem Children's Zone in New York, proclaims at the beginning of *Waiting for Superman* (*WFS*) that "No one is coming with the power to save us" (Birtel et al., 2010). Canada tests the waters of accountability, deftly shifting the blame to individuals rather than institutions. Dalton (2010) addresses this concept of rugged individualism in regard to what she calls the "good teacher" (p. 27) model in film. Dalton identifies the good teacher as a portrayed savior positioned against a "backdrop of institutional and societal woe" (p. 23). Canada's statement exemplifies this notion by characterizing teachers as superheroes. Canada's powerful statement on Superman, often shown in the film's trailer, chronicles his own love of the popular superhero. He begins by sharing his obsession with comic books and later reveals the moment when his mother told him that Superman was not real, only a character gifted with the power to save "all the good people" (Birtel et al., 2010). Yet Canada places the onus on teachers to fill the role of Superman by repeatedly touting their power in a school system that is "doing something wrong" (Birtel et al., 2010). Not only must teachers do their job, but they must also save the children who fill the seats in their classrooms in the face of the experiences that each child brings from the world outside the classroom.

In a contrasting vein, *American Teacher* (*AT*) (Calegari et al., 2011) commences with teachers refuting clips from Fox News through the engaging display of passion and commitment to their profession. One teacher declares that she is a teacher "with every fiber of my being" as proof that the hosts at Fox News know little about what it means to be a teacher (Calegari et al., 2011). As the film progresses, the desired results of *AT* become more and more entwined in the mire of education reform and the narrative of individualism. The message, while seemingly unintentional, becomes one of accountability. In the first five minutes, Arne Duncan and President Barack Obama both declare that teachers are the most important factor in schools. This initial indoctrination presents the dichotomy of the teacher as savior message. In subsequent scenes, teachers detail their commitment to the profession—and their students—by revealing that they spend upwards of ten hours per day at school, buy school supplies with their own funds and rarely leave their job behind when they exit the building. These teachers are superheroes—undervalued, underpaid superheroes. They exemplify the good teacher model of Hollywood (Dalton, 2010), they stand out; even the Obama administration positions them as saviors. *AT* further defines teacher accountability by saying that teachers are expected to "be at work" constantly. In order to meet the requirements of a job that doesn't even compensate fairly, one must still go above and beyond.

The Lottery (Ashman et al., 2010), on the other hand, eschews the idea that teachers are saviors and instead positions parents as saviors. While this initially feels like an enlightened perspective, holding parents accountable for the success of their children, it removes all power from teachers and even frames them, as well as schools themselves, as the villains. Eva Moskowitz, founder of Harlem Success Academy, frames this narrative well when she declares that "the overwhelming majority of schools are abysmal academic failures" (Ashman et al., 2010).

Collective Accountability: The Role of Administrators

The rugged individualism of the good teacher is briefly countered in some documentaries through the inclusion of administrator accountability. In *The Lottery*, a key scene with Randi Weingarten (president of the American Federation of Teachers) on Charlie Rose results in Rose asking Weingarten if teachers should be fired for not doing a good job (Ashman et al., 2010). Weingarten stumbles and stammers and Rose repeats the question. The question and inability of Weingarten to provide a satisfactory response communicate that teachers should be held accountable; moreover, the notion that bad teachers should not be fired is difficult to refute by a leader of teachers.

WFS continues this thread of the accountability narrative in its exposition of the "dance of the lemons," the shuffling of bad teachers within districts (Birtel et al., 2010). The documentary reveals the dance that principals play at the end of each school year, pushing off bad teachers onto other principals in exchange for teachers that principals hope will be better than the ones they have relinquished to those other schools. Here the principals and administration are also portrayed as lacking and irresponsible.

The collective accountability proselytized in *AT* extends to administration. *AT*, in its most redeeming, asks the question, if we expect our teachers to be saviors, how can we better support them? Although the messages of the film are counterintuitively subversive at times, it is the only film that asks its audience to consider what it really means to be a teacher in an educational climate that devalues teachers through the accountability narrative. Although asking how we—the public, school administrators, teachers, parents—can support outstanding teachers, it neglects to ask the questions about what they represent. How sustainable and realistic is teaching this way? Does a teaching force willing to sacrifice all else in their lives serve the best interests of all Americans?

Discussion

What then is the most interesting and perhaps troubling aspect of the three education documentaries is the ever present balance of accountability and rugged individualism: how the American meritocracy meets *ANAR*, NCLB, an economic downturn and Race to the Top to create a dystopian narrative that we channeled in the first line of this chapter. Working harder than everyone else may, in fact, not get you ahead, though watching any three of the documentaries leads one to believe that if we only had better teachers who worked harder (or if we ourselves become those hardworking teachers), the nation would be saved from mediocrity and the aggressions or advances of other countries. Peeling back the onion another layer suggests there are deeper problems at hand.

While the documentaries take negative and positive views of teachers, the thesis of the combined films might be *Good, smart, accountable, hardworking teachers are all we need*. As Thomas (2012) relates,

> Reformers are trapped within and depend on American ideology that is contradicted by the weight of evidence about socioeconomic equity, the American meritocracy, social mobility, and the ability of schools and teachers to raise children in poverty out of that destiny.
>
> *(n.p.)*

By focusing on teachers, policy makers are able to continue to ignore America's international standing in terms of childhood poverty: 27th in the world (UNICEF Office of Research, 2014). "On the surface, we see urgency, altruism, and political purity parading in a messianic language of educational reform and a politics of generosity. Underneath this discourse lie the same old and discredited neoliberal policies that cheerfully serve corporate interests" (Giroux, 2012, p. 17).

We found it interesting that this sleight-of-hand approach to education policy is paralleled in the films themselves. For example, in *WFS*, Canada describes the moment his mother told him that Superman wasn't real and claims that was when he realized that no one was coming to save him and he'd have to do it himself. Canada's argument promotes the faulty premise that any problem can be solved with intrinsic motivation and hard work. Yet, if that is the case, why does Mr. Canada claim just moments later in the same film that, if he had gone to his neighborhood school, Morris High, "I would not be sitting with you here today" (Birtel et al., 2010)? If we accept Canada's argument, we must ask the question, could he not have saved himself through hard work and dedication while at Morris?

What does this mean for the PSTs entering colleges and universities to become teachers in these contested times? What will or won't be possible for them and their students? In Arkansas, policies made at the state level recently will directly impact the kind of teacher who may want to join the profession. For example, the state has limited the number of students any teacher can have to 150. Charters in Arkansas are frequently granted waivers to exceed the number of students; recent charter school legislation has granted public schools these same waivers if even one public school student in a district attends a charter school. As a result, many public schools across the state could increase the number of students for any one teacher beyond 150—yet the recommended maximum student load for English teachers is 100 (NCTE, 2014). In these ways, accountability, in one of its forms, is a key to the intensification to which American free market capitalism has resorted to further its mode, method and means (Nealon, 2012). We realize this analysis paints a dark picture for education and those who may be entering the profession, but we are enlivened by the potential of helping to raise a generation of teachers ready to face and overcome these challenges.

Putting It Into Practice

We offer three practices that we employed in our analysis as ways to engage PSTs in these and other important conversations: make popular culture texts central to coursework, develop and share processes to analyze texts, and raise students' voices by demanding their connections through "mosh-pit pedagogy" (Trier, 2014, p. 2). First, we argue it is imperative to create time and space in teacher education programs to take up popular culture and the potential uses of it in K-12 school classrooms as well as rhetorically charged and shifty texts, such as the documentaries examined here. The ability to read against texts of all types is a skill set all future teachers need to have at their fingertips (Freire, 2000; Giroux, 2012; Hall, 1997). In these terms, teachers who enter the profession with a healthy dose of awareness of the forces battling for pieces of their chosen profession will have a greater opportunity to address them.

Providing time and space for this sort of activity is key, but we assert that it's important to help PSTs and teacher educators feel comfortable analyzing pieces of popular culture. Viewing a film following a process of qualitative coding can help put these stakeholders on common ground; in this way, PSTs have the opportunity to create meaning in a purposeful and organized way, marking down ideas and codes and then discussing what they might mean. We also suggest viewing films in light of Trier's (2014) concept of "mosh-pit pedagogy" (p. 2), where students take on the proverbial role of participants in an actual mosh pit at a music concert. Creating with students what "seems to be a whirl of seemingly chaotic yet spontaneously patterned movement in which people are basically moving into one another, [. . .] brushing, [. . .] slamming, [. . .] stumbling, and falling" (Trier, 2014, p. 2) with texts can only deepen and expand the conversations. Our mosh pit occurred synchronously on Google Drive while we watched the films, but it just as easily could have happened in class discussions or on electronic interfaces, such as Blackboard or Twitter.

In spite of the inherent and unavoidable negative narrative created by the accountability charge of the reformers, PSTs must live in the wisdom that "teachers remain the most important component in the learning process for students" (Giroux, 2012, p. 1). They must know that they guide, enhance and empower their students toward an understanding of themselves and their world—that they add a tool to the belt or, at the least, help sharpen one for each student each day. PSTs must know that they are "both caretakers and engaged intellectuals" (Giroux, 2012, p. 3) and be prepared for such a vision that is anything but commonplace.

In closing, the answers aren't easy and new teachers are entering the profession at arguably the most difficult time in the history of American education. To offer an anecdote, Chris has worked to prepare teachers who admitted in their entrance interviews that they were joining the profession following the viewing of *WFS* and other school films, most notably *Freedom Writers* (DeVito et al., 2007). And why not? The social justice notions present in each are laudable; for some of the same reasons, candidates who finish a traditional graduate-level teacher education program are signing up for Teach for America, which happens to feature in all three films. Hollywood notions of what it means to teach are clearly pervasive, returning to Dalton's (2010) point:

> Time and time again as we watch individual teachers do battle with the hierarchy, we have the satisfaction (as an audience) of an implied win on some small front while the collective organizations remain largely intact. Thus, the individual figure Hollywood loves to glorify, the "little man," remains alone without the force of a collective to take truly transformative action, and the institutions remain unchanged.
>
> *(pp. 19–20)*

PSTs enter the profession with idealism and hope for being able to make changes. And let us be clear: We want nothing short of that very thing, but it may also behoove teacher educators to prepare teachers with eyes wide open to the swirling undercurrents of the profession, especially those set out to "hold accountable" and then make a profit on the education of children. It seems that Thomas Jefferson's words are more appropriate today than ever: "The tax which will be paid for this purpose is not more than the thousandth part of what will be paid to kings, priests and nobles who will rise up among us if we leave the people in ignorance" (Jefferson, 1900, p. 278). For those of us, like Jefferson, who believe in the virtues and promise of public education, we wonder if there's someone coming with enough power to save *us*.

References

Accountability. (2015). In *Oxford English Dictionary online* (3rd ed.). Retrieved from http://www.oed.com/view/Entry/1197?redirectedFrom=accountability

Ashman, B., Bartels, T. Lanuti, E., Lawler, J., Sakler, M., Schellpfeffer, B. (Producers), & Sackler, M. (Director). (2010). *The lottery* [Motion picture]. United States: Breaking Glass Pictures.

Berliner, D. C. (2009). *Poverty and potential: Out-of-school factors and school success.* Boulder, CO: Education and the Public Interest Center & Education Policy Research Unit. Retrieved from http://epicpolicy.org/publication/poverty-and-potential

Birtel, M., Chilcott, L., Hindmarch, E., Katz, M., Skoll, J., . . . Weyermann, D. (Producers), & Guggenheim, D. (2010). *Waiting for Superman* [Motion picture]. United States: Paramount Vantage.

Calegari, N., Davis, E., Eggers, D., Roth, V. (Producers), & Roth, V., & McGinn, B. (Directors). (2011). *American teacher* [Motion picture]. United States: First Run Features.

Dalton, M. M. (1995). The Hollywood curriculum: Who is the "good" teacher? *Curriculum Studies, 3*(1), 23–44.

Dalton, M. M. (2010). *The Hollywood curriculum, revised* (2nd ed.). New York, NY: Peter Lang.

DeVito, D., Durning, T., Glick-Franzheim, J., Levine, D., Morales, N., . . . Swank, H. (Producers), & LaGravenese, R. (Director). (2007). *Freedom writers* [Motion picture]. United States: Paramount Pictures.

Freire, P. (2000). *Pedagogy of the oppressed, 30th anniversary edition.* New York, NY: Bloomsbury Academic.

Giroux, H. (2012). *Education and the crisis of public values.* New York, NY: Peter Lang.

Hall, S. (Ed.). (1997). *Representation: Cultural representations and signifying practices.* Thousand Oaks, CA: SAGE.

Hermansen, P. M. (2014). There was no one coming with enough power to save us: Waiting for "Superman" and the rhetoric of the new education documentary. *Rhetoric & Public Affairs, 17*(3), 511–539.

Jefferson, T. (1900). *The Jeffersonian cyclopedia: A comprehensive collection of the views of Thomas Jefferson.* New York, NY: Funk & Wagnalls. Retrieved from http://books.google.com/books?id=icGh3NxREIIC

Mehta, J. (2013). How paradigms create politics: The transformation of American educational policy, 1980–2001. *American Educational Research Journal, 50*(2), 285–324.

National Commission on Excellence in Education. (1983). *A nation at risk: The imperative for educational reform.* Washington, DC: US Government Printing Office.

National Council of Teachers of English (NCTE). (2014). Why class size matters today. Retrieved from http://www.ncte.org/positions/statements/why-class-size-matters

Nealon, J. (2012). *Post-postmodernism: Or the cultural logic of just in time capitalism.* Stanford, CA: Stanford Press.

Phi Delta Kappa International/Gallup. (2014a). Poll of the public's attitudes toward the public schools. Retrieved from http://pdkpoll.pdkintl.org/october/#2

Phi Delta Kappa International/Gallup. (2014b). Poll of the public's attitudes toward the public schools. Retrieved from http://pdkpoll.pdkintl.org/#1

Ravitch, D. (2013). *Reign of error: The hoax of the privatization movement and the danger to America's public schools.* New York, NY: Alfred A. Knopf.

The Teacher Salary Project. (n.d.). About the project. Retrieved from http://www.theteachersalaryproject.org/

Thomas, P. L. (2012). Is poverty destiny?: Ideology v. evidence in education reform. *Daily Kos.* Retrieved from http://www.dailykos.com/story/2012/09/16/1132156/-Is-Poverty-Destiny-Ideology-v-Evidence-in-Education-Reform#

Thomas, P. L. (2014). Thirty years of accountability deserve an F. *The Becoming Radical.* Retrieved from https://radicalscholarship.wordpress.com/2014/12/05/2014-ncuea-fall-conference-thirty-years-of-accountability-deserves-an-f/

Trier, J. (2002). Exploring the concept of "habitus" with preservice teachers through the use of popular school films. *Interchange, 33*(3), 237–260.

Trier, J. (2005). "Sordid Fantasies": Reading popular "inner city" school films as racialized texts with pre-service teachers. *Race Ethnicity and Education, 8*(2), 171–189.

Trier, J. (2007). Guy Debord's the society of the spectacle. *Journal of Adolescent & Adult Literacy, 51*(1), 68–73.

Trier, J. (Ed.). (2014). Introduction: *Detournement as pedagogical praxis*. Boston, MA: Sense.

UNICEF Office of Research. (2014). Children of the recession: The impact of the economic crisis on child well-being in rich countries, *Innocenti Report Card 12*, UNICEF Office of Research, Florence.

Zinsser, W. K. (1989). *Writing to learn*. New York, NY: Harper & Row.

19

NO HUMAN LEFT BEHIND

Falling Skies and the Role of the Pedagogue
in the Postapocalypse

Jeff Spanke

There were nine of us in my student teaching cohort, each one young and powerful and sure and proud. Our college had trained us well, and we felt ready to provide exactly what students *really* needed. In short, we all had an earnest and realistic desire to change the world. Of the nine of us, eight were eventually licensed to teach secondary English language arts. In as many years, six of us left the classroom.

The year I was hired to teach high school English, my school also employed four other first-year teachers: two in math, one in Spanish and one in English. By sheer coincidence, all five of our classrooms shared the same hallway, a narrow corridor whose eastern windows overlooked a sprawling Midwestern cornfield and the railroad track that pierced it. It took less than four years for all five of us to leave the building. The faculty page of the yearbook looks different now and students don't know our names.

I often think back to that time—those nights when my fellow student teachers and I would toast to the lives we would surely change or those faculty meetings when our rookie cohort would annoy the veterans with phrases like, "Yeah, but what if," or "Wouldn't it be cool?" I want to tell myself to stop. To calm down. To humbly accept that perhaps despite their faded classroom posters, stale lifesavers and tired hands weathered by chalk dust, those veterans probably knew more about teaching than the cocky yet untested postadolescents retweeting stories of teacher walkouts and union strikes. I want to tell myself that I had more to learn about teaching. I want to stop myself.

Because we didn't last. We didn't survive. And, like so many teachers in this country, our shortsighted aspirations of impacting student lives *today* overshadowed our capacity to ration our efforts for tomorrow. We were so focused on changing the world that we forgot to consider the realities of our worlds. We were too busy seizing the day.

And so I offer this chapter as a means to express what I wish I could've told myself before I left the trenches: that tales of teacher saviors offer great escapes, but in subscribing to them wholeheartedly, we often abandon our firm grasp on reality. Teachers can and should seek to change the world. But doing so necessitates functioning *within* the world. We cannot impact students if we have no students. Our pictures should stay in the yearbook.

Part I: Mutiny Aboard the T.S. Welton

It seems like our teachers let us watch it every year in school: the library's weathered VHS copy of a deeply seductive and misleading film (Dettmar, 2014). As a student, I remember sitting in my desk, watching our teacher wheel in the department's TV cart, anticipating the saccharine cinematic jaunt to follow. Some of us slept during the boring parts. Others pretended to know about Thoreau or enjoy Emerson. We all thought it was creepy when they stared at the pictures of dead basketball players while a stranger whispered "carpe diem" in their ears. But it was a movie, so we enjoyed it. It made us feel better about ourselves. It made learning seem not only fun but also accessible. Something anyone could do, as if the concepts and ideas foreign to us in other classrooms didn't lie beyond our grasp. If *these* kids could learn poetry from the voice of a genie, then so could we. For children of the late 1980s, *Dead Poets Society* (Haft, Henderson, Witt & Weir, 1989) emblematized what teachers could accomplish if only granted the autonomy we all so desperately wished for ourselves. And the iconic conclusion to the story of Mr. Keating's sailors never failed to make our teachers cry. For some reason.

Baby-faced Ethan Hawke gets on his desk. With tears in his eyes, he weeps the Whitman cry, "Oh Captain! My Captain!" Our Lincoln pivots. His lone soldier stands courageously atop his deck, perched above his peers with the pale complexion of Youth in Revolt. Others follow suit, marching to the beat of their former drummer. The music swells, beginning with the strings. The Man threatens to expel anyone who continues the shenanigans. He wags his finger and blushes; his voice intensifies. No one listens. Heartbeats racing, veins popping. Convictions mount. More shoes on desks, more tears, more smiles of sacrifice, reckless abandon, caution compromised and the unceasing loyalty to the beauty of Then. *Sit down, Mr. Anderson*—no one moves—*Do you hear me?*—no one speaks—*I'm warning you!* But no one cares.

"Thank you, boys," Keating professes finally. "Thank you."

Cut to Hawke, Fade to Black. And the Credits Roll.

Now rewind and pause. Of the 18 desks filling the room, several now sit empty, their former occupants having staked their shaky claims atop these desks' fragile supports. But not everybody's standing. Despite what our youthful nostalgia might otherwise dictate, in the end, ten students defied their supervisor and pledged allegiance to Mr. Keating, while eight refused to do so. Their captain, oh captain, took his final curtain call with roughly a 55% approval rating. He didn't get everybody. Not by a long shot. Instead, he left barely half his students standing nervously on their desks, the integrity of which the weight of their actions would eventually compromise. Regardless of whether they ever chose to descend from their lofty ideals, the school would go on. It must. They still had class, after all. Our tears shield us from two unnerving realities. The first is that Mr. Keating's true legacy has rendered the entirety of his former Welton vessel sinking in a sea of chaos. The other, and perhaps more disturbing, is that despite our better judgment, we remain captivated by the film. We champion Keating even as he leaves all of his children behind.

The Credit/s Came Too Soon.

Despite its flaws, *Dead Poets Society* (Haft et al., 1989) remains one of America's most iconic cinematic representations of inspirational teachers. Since its release in 1989, the compelling nuances of Williams's performance and the lyrical resonance of Hawke's "Oh Captain" have woven their way into the fabric of our educational lore. Still, while navigating the competing but linked tropes of savior and scapegoat, the character of John Keating typifies the unnerving notion that to engage is to enrage and that inspiration leads to termination. Other cinematic teachers followed in *Poets* wake, each highlighting similar classroom departures while leaving audiences wondering just what happens to these student disciples once their saviors have been sacrificed.

As a young teacher, I began to consider how reconceptualizing these narratives could've impacted my teacher preparation. During my first year in the classroom, I felt that these saccharine portrayals of teachers did more to impair my practice than empower it. But what if we framed films like *Dead Poets Society* (Haft et al., 1989) as pedagogical tragedies instead of ideological axioms: as warnings, not beacons? Rather than focusing on Keating's methods, why not discuss the day *after* he left the classroom? Who will he use as a reference? How would he answer an interview question about that kid he once had who killed himself? Turning dangerous minds into freedom writers is indeed a good and noble calling, but why leave students with nothing more than an ellipsis? Why allow burned bridges and terminated contracts to punctuate tenure instead of promotions and pensions? Why do these teacher stories seem to always insist on valuing brilliant brevity over teachers who actually stick around long enough to enjoy a couple of homecoming games or spring musicals? What good's a ship without its captain?

So how can teacher educators frame these narratives in terms of the kids who aren't standing? What about their stories? After all, the cultural praise allotted to tales of teacher subversion oftentimes overshadows the unnerving proposition that perhaps there's as much courage in caution as there is in standing on your desk. As students, we saw ourselves in Ethan Hawke. As preservice teachers, we idolized John Keating. Or at least thought we should. Yet we never considered the students still seated. What would they do in school tomorrow, asked nobody ever. Didn't they deserve a teacher who stuck around? Who would help them cope with whatever it was they might have lost over the course of their broken year?

I stopped asking myself these questions when I sat down to watch a show about aliens.

Part II: What I Learned During the Summer Invasion

Falling Skies premiered on the TNT network in June 2011. Produced by Stephen Spielberg, the postapocalyptic sci-fi series stars Noah Wiley as Dr. Tom Mason: a former Boston University history professor-turned-leader of a fledgling rebellion known as The Resistance. The enemy: an intricate and advanced mass network of alien invaders who, since their arrival on Earth six months prior to the events of the first episode, have reduced the planet's population by 90%. While their intentions remain somewhat ambiguous, we quickly learn of their desire to control children—ages 8 to18—through the use of biomechanical submission devices aptly dubbed harnesses. Any attempt to remove the harness often results in the child's death.

And so the story goes. Aliens attack, people die, cool explosions, we fight back. And repeat. Humans preserving humanity. Their faces are dirty, their weapons primitive and their clothes unapologetically bland. The show's general aesthetic looks like a Gap ad with rifles. The aliens understand English but can't speak it. They fly across galaxies and destroy entire nations with laser beams but somehow struggle against teenagers with shotguns and pipe bombs. The people have no toothpaste but their teeth shine whiteness. Genre clichés abound. The men's beards grow more rugged with each passing episode, illustrating the stubbled means by which they face their oppressors. The women's hair glistens beneath layers of soot, ash and filth that seem to make up their present circumstance. Gray tableaus of dust-covered rubble and decay. Deserted cars heaved into broken telephone poles and massive slabs of concrete inexplicably clogging the street. The sky had indeed fallen on TNT, and I, for one, was hooked. After two years of fighting to stay afloat amidst my own sea of state standards, mission statements, assessment rubrics and salary cuts, at the time, the show seemed like a nice way to spend the summer: a welcome respite from the plaguing confines of Keating, Welton and other childhood myths.

As with many of its doomsday contemporaries, the central themes of *Falling Skies* (Frank et al., 2011–2015) consist of family, resourcefulness and survival. Of the latter, Spielberg describes his initial interest in producing the show by recalling, "I've always been interested in how we survive and how resourceful we are as Americans. How would the survivors feed the children? How do they resupply themselves militarily in order to defend and even take back what they have lost?" (quoted in Rudolph, 2011). Indeed, as I look past the excessive special effects, the contrived dialogue, the elaborate escapes and the constant suspension of logical reality, I argue that the show offers teachers a refreshing perspective on an otherwise trite and predictable narrative.

Tom Mason is an engaging leader who's emerged on a broken scene as an unlikely hero. He's guided by an almost transcendent moral authority, which has allowed him to gain a fellowship and gather a following. He manages to make change within the destructive and suffocating paradigm to which the alien forces beyond his control have assigned him. In fact, all of his actions, choices and consequences seem to mirror the trajectory of the traditional teacher-as-savior narrative. Except, of course, for the fact that after four seasons, he's still fighting. His survival has trumped his sacrifice. Tom Mason remains captain of the Good Ship Human. As a student, I always wanted a teacher like John Keating. As a teacher, though, Tom Mason seems more aligned to my experiences in the high school classroom.

Through equipping his followers with the skills necessary to survive their world, Tom Mason serves as a teacher *and* a teacher educator. He infuses his worldly classroom with lessons accumulated through years of study (in this case, American military history), as well as the material he's creatively and resourcefully gathered along the way. As a soldier very much in the business of training future soldiers, Tom Mason is teacher both in title and in function. Insofar as they will use his training to combat the alien forces that threaten their world, his people likewise operate as both students and teachers in their own right.

Part III: From Renegade Scholars to Resourceful Survivalists

I concede that at first glance, *Falling Skies* (Frank et al., 2011–2015) has little, if anything, to do with teachers and schools. It certainly is a far cry from *Dead Poets Society* (Haft et al., 1989). One features a ragtag band of relatively homogenous civilians, united under a common mission, struggling to navigate the complexities of their internal and external worlds while simultaneously combating an oppressive, systematic regime hell-bent on beating them into submission. The other is about aliens.

But inasmuch as *Falling Skies* (Frank et al., 2011–2015) may fail to translate directly into a preapproved account of American schools, perhaps this abstraction makes it one of the more appropriate analogues to the present state of our educational system. At times postcolonial, at others posthuman (Gough, 2004), *Falling Skies* troubles perceptions of our world as stable, logical or coherent. It weakens our stranglehold on tradition and forces us to reexamine our most precious yet naïve notions of progress, potential and pride. Most teachers never have to worry about extraterrestrials invading their classrooms, but few would dispute the impact that outside forces have on their daily classroom lives. Whether it's a new assessment model, a modified set of state standards, assorted community partners, principals, parents, pep rallies or prom committees, surviving teaching requires much more than content knowledge, a positive attitude and the ability to write a lesson plan.

And Teachers, of Course, Know This.

The profession itself cannot be translated, despite politicians, producers and pundits who insist otherwise. Rubrics can't confine teachers, and teaching can't be reduced to reading Whitman in caves or finding ourselves through the lyrics of Bob Dylan. It's ignorant to believe that it can and even more dangerous to practice. While these activities may certainly contribute to liberating education, in themselves they serve as shallow and potentially offensive representations of Cool Teachers Changing Lives. Standing on desks may give students a different perspective on the world but it probably won't help them pass their biology test. Even dogs can rip pages from books. Teaching demands the sophisticated negotiation of humility and confidence: the embrace of discomfort, coupled with the stamina to transcend it. A rich, natural ambiguity predicates the job that so few outsiders recognize but all teachers accept. At least the ones who survive. Sadly, too often those outsiders—those alien to the profession—have the unfortunate luxury—and power—of dictating educational policy. And in the wake of these various invasions, some teachers resist, others submit and others simply serve as casualties of a war they never wanted but somehow always saw coming from above.

The Sky Sometimes Really Is the Limit. It May Also Be Falling.

Because *Falling Skies* (Frank et al., 2011–2015) doesn't take place in any semblance of a traditional classroom nor feature a teacher operating in a conventional pedagogical capacity, the show seeks to forge linkages through the "unstable elements of literature and life"—what Bhabha (1994) calls "the dangerous tryst with the untranslatable" (p. 227)—rather than adhering to the accepted teacher paradigm. Through rejecting his Keating-esque predecessors, Tom Mason's character translates his pedagogical role as one of survivor—or, as Derrida (1979) argues, one who personifies the act of "living on borderlines." Clandinin and Connelly's (2000) topographic metaphors of borderlands and knowledge landscapes further highlight Tom Mason's relational transactions with the conflicting narrative planes his people and his oppressors respectively occupy. As a character, Tom Mason lives in the liminal space between existence and extinction. As a show, *Falling Skies* lands somewhere on the border between Welton and reality.

If *Falling Skies* (Frank et al., 2011–2015) highlights anything about the educational system, it's this: No classroom exists independently of its surrounding world/s, and the borderlines between the sanctity of the school and the monstrous unknown of Out There will forever remain fragile at one end and blurred beyond recognition at the other (Wallin, 2008). There will always be aliens in schools. And while these external tensions may manifest in/as/through a variety of fashions, resisting their pressure to submit while still preserving professional selfhood remains perhaps one of the greatest challenges of contemporary American educators.

As one such educator, Tom Mason approaches the challenges of his new circumstances with an acute creativity and refined resourcefulness that have thus far allowed him to survive in a world at risk. He doesn't quit. He doesn't complain. And he doesn't pretend that the world around him doesn't exist. Instead, he accepts the reality of the world with which he's been presented, despite the temptation to abandon it. Tom Mason doesn't read poetry in caves just because caves are sexy; there *is no* sexy in Tom Mason's world. And caves are for shelter. He doesn't care if his soldiers like him, and he knows that hubris kills. He teaches people to hide under desks—not stand on them—and that they should rip pages out of books only when they need a fire. He feeds the hungry and mends the sick, rests when they need it and runs when they need to. He listens to the cries of the masses, offers his silence and shoulders their burden. Tom Mason has the pulse of his people. In the interest of survival, he accepts that the worst mistake he can make is caring if these people think he's nice or fun or cool or exciting.

And His People Survive. Some Even With Honors.

Tom Mason knows not to overuse the phrase "crisis" because his world, quite literally, is in one. And, especially given the aliens' vested interest in youth, he strives throughout the series to protect the children. When I first encountered the show as a secondary English teacher, I found it interesting that the manners by which the aliens harness and control the human children bear an eerie similarity to the rhetoric surrounding the industrialization of American schools. Similar to how Frederick Taylor once conceived of schools as parallel to the efficiency model he espoused for America's factories, *Falling Skies* often depicts harnessed children laboring on alien assembly lines and performing various linear, mechanized tasks (Tyler, 1949). Why aliens would need kids to build stuff the show never explains, but the scenes of these kids slaving away in alien sweatshops echo the gritty black-and-white images of 19th-century factory workers that Tom Mason would have undoubtedly once found in his U.S. history textbooks.

From an educational perspective, perhaps what *Falling Skies* does so effectively is open up spaces for discursive contestation. As a tangential comment on American schools, *Falling Skies* queers the cultural representations of teachers—the saviors, scapegoats or schoolmarms that typically underscore the dominant narrative—as well as the prevailing perceptions of schools as the only place where learning occurs (Dewey, 1938; Freire, 1970; Pinar, 2012). Tom Mason's survivalist impulse severs the ties to the singular teacher-as-savior-as-martyr narrative, thus highlighting the Bakhtinian (1981) struggle between the centripetal forces that perpetuate the closure of language and the centrifugal forces that strive to liberate it. Both Keating and Mason view their "students" as captives in their own right. Yet whereas Mason's soldiers seek to create an entirely new life for themselves, free of alien obstruction and tyranny, Keating's sailors will forever operate within the conventions of an artificial world prescribed for them. Their "liberation" serves more to perpetuate the dominant narrative rather than forging a new one; though expelled, those standing will likely just move to another version of the same corrosive paradigm. Yet in *Falling Skies* (Frank et al., 2011–2015), we uncover new ways of talking about teachers, schools and students, as well as the various means by which all three participate in the organic and fluid exchange of knowledge and skills.

Bakhtin approaches language, and in particular stories, as a medium through which "one participates in a historical flow of social relationships, struggles, and meanings" (Bailey, 2012, p. 501). This conceptualization of language-as-medium necessitates a dynamic in which people are always resisting, renegotiating, rejecting, reaffirming and reifying their respective relationships with otherness. *Falling Skies* seems to perpetuate this dynamic: an innovative, albeit alien, discursive realm in which we speak of teachers as survivors instead of sacrificial lambs and schools as more conceptual places of learning as opposed to brick facades with lockers and detention centers. Above anything else, Tom Mason always strives to resist, renegotiate, reject, reaffirm and reify his people's relationship with the invaders. In doing so, he literally functions as the mason charged with crafting his people's alternate narrative.

Rather than maintaining stories of teacher self-sacrifice, *Falling Skies* orients us to the perspective of alterity, of difference. In the process, the contained, isolated world of Welton Academy morphs from functioning as what Bakhtin (1981) would call "a dead, thing-like shell," in which language serves as simply a descriptive mechanism, to more of an "alien territory," in which the role of the teacher seeks the introduction of new and unfamiliar elements. This is the story of Tom Mason and *Falling Skies*: the story of how people survive uncertainty and cope with confusion. It's no less the story of an alien apocalypse than it is of the characters in our own classrooms. Clandinin (2013) echoes this awareness of narrative's "struggle for coherence" (p. 49) amidst a sea of chaos, inconsistencies and flashes of experience by noting that "we begin in the midst, and end in the midst, of experience" (p. 43). Once again, *Falling Skies* achieves just that: grounding the series in an invasion already in progress, one that threatens the extinction of mankind.

Four seasons later, mankind fights on as guerillas in the midst.

Part IV: Once More Unto the Breech

Beneath John Keating's charismatic charm lurks a man whose philosophical inflexibility and professional myopia ironically match that of the very institution he so fatally sought to dismantle. He and Welton are the same: both unflinchingly stubborn and equally convinced of the unquestionable viability of their respective methods. Sure, it's easier to rally behind Keating because standing on desks is more fun than sitting in chairs and because reading in caves makes us feel like a Mark Twain character. But Keating was a novelty and novelties tend to be plastic and cheap. Still, Keating's campiness didn't seem to bother his students. But did these apostles ever *really* have a choice? What if the students didn't *want* to seize the day? What if they *liked* Welton and the promise it offered of a better tomorrow? What if they spent a lot of money on their books and didn't really appreciate being told to rip out the introduction? What if they didn't agree with Keating? What if they thought *he* was an alien?

It behooves the entire teacher education paradigm—teacher educators, pre-service teachers and active teachers—to approach the Keating narrative with a certain degree of caution, lest we fall victim to its alluring guise. We cannot allow the hope embedded within Keating's message to overshadow the reality of his methods, for in doing so we risk equipping future generations of educators with the false and dangerous assumption that Weltons exist and that gluttonous egos bear no weight. Certainly one can find Weltonesque imitations on any teacher job forum: homogenous, wealthy, privileged institutions shrouded in tradition and nestled safely beneath the canopies of century-old legacies and endowments. The facades of Welton exist in our world. But within their halls labor teachers stripped of Keating's luxury of renegade teaching and moonlit forest frolics. And if these teachers ever get fired from their jobs, there's no shortage of applications pouring into the valley. There's a reason they never made a sequel.

Keating didn't last a year. Granted, 55% of his students sank their futures alongside him, but his professional demise leaves teachers with very little gauge of his effectiveness. He just couldn't hack it. Despite our romantic childhood longing for liberating education, the Keating narrative should no longer function as our guiding light. Instead, teachers could benefit from a narrative that encourages professional survival and perseverance that derives from working *within* a system—however near it may venture toward chaos—rather than fleeting impact and surfaced encounters. Students and schools could certainly benefit from teachers who stick around long enough to fight the good fight instead of falling victim to alien encounters that just get a little too close. Tom Mason's classroom may have burned to the ground but he's never stopped teaching. And like him, his people survive.

Mason's world has no pretense: only narratives that live and die in the contact zones between borders. Tom Mason occupies the same space as our students, where boundaries can serve more to unite than divide. John Keating denied these borders and fled to the caves; Tom Mason thrives in them. Of the two distinct narratives, his offers the most conducive means to train future educators because it relies on the assumption that homogenous, privileged niceties of Welton Academy can never exist outside its protected walls, and that the educational world will always find itself mired in oftentimes combative negotiations with other, more alien, narrative planes. How teachers reconcile their various presences on these planes will determine their characters and careers as professional educators. *Falling Skies* (Frank et al., 2011–2015) and the Mason narrative frame education as an untamed, alien landscape, an endless series of terrains rife with potential snares and ripe with poignant successes. Safely navigating this wilderness in order to fight another day remains the goal of characters like Tom Mason. Training to survive the classroom and its surrounding worlds remains the duty of future teachers and their educators. Some kids will always choose to sit; a good teacher, though, may convince them to stand. But only if they stick around long enough.

References

Bailey, B. (2012). Heterglossia. In M. Martin-Jones, A. Blackledge, & A. Creese (Eds.), *The Routledge handbook of multilingualism*. New York, NY: Routledge.

Bakhtin, M. M. (1981). *The dialogic imagination: Four essays*. Austin: University of Texas Press.

Bhabha, H. K. (1994). *The location of culture*. New York, NY: Routledge.

Clandinin, D. J. (2013). *Engaging in narrative inquiry*. Walnut Creek, CA: Left Coast Press.

Clandinin, D. J., & Connelly, M. (2000). *Narrative inquiry; Experience and story in qualitative research*. San Francisco, CA: Jossey-Bass.

Derrida, J. (1979). Living on: Border lines. In H. Bloom, P. De Man, J. Derrida, G. H. Hartman & J. H. Miller (Eds.), *Deconstructivism and criticism* (pp. 62–142). New York, NY: Seabury Press.

Dettmar, K. J. H. (2014). *Dead Poets Society* is a terrible defense of the humanities. *The Atlantic*. Retrieved February 19, 2014, from http://www.theatlantic.com/education/archive/2014/02/-em-dead-poets-society-em-is-a-terrible-defense-of-the-humanities/283853/

Dewey, J. (1938). *Education and experience*. New York, NY: Free Press; Reprint edition (1997).

Frank, D., Schofield, S., Spielberg, S., Dube, M., Beeman, G., . . . Falvey, J. (Producers), & Beeman, G. (Director) (2011–2015). *Falling skies* [Television series]. United States: Turner Network Television.

Freire, P. (1970). *Pedagogy of the oppressed*. New York, NY: Bloomsbury Academic; 30th Anniversary Edition (2000).

Gough, N. (2004). RhizomANTically becoming-cyborg: Performing posthuman pedagogies. *Educational Philosophy and Theory*, *36*(3), 253–265.

Haft, S., Henderson, D., Witt, P. J., Thomas, T. (Producers), & Weir, P. (Director). (1989). *Dead poets society* [Motion picture]. United States: Buena Vista Pictures.

Pinar, W. F. (2012). *What is curriculum theory* (2nd ed.). New York, NY: Routledge.

Rudolph, L. (2011, June 28). Steven Spielberg talks *Falling Skies* and upcoming TV projects. *TV Guide*. Retrieved from http://www.tvguide.com/news/steven-spielberg-talks-1034672/

Tyler, R. W. (1949). *Basic principles of curriculum and instruction*. Chicago, IL: University of Chicago Press.

Wallin, J. (2008). Living with monsters: An inquiry parable. *Teaching Education*, *19*(4), 311–323.

CONTRIBUTORS

Carey Applegate is an assistant professor at the University of Wisconsin–Eau Claire, where she teaches English education, popular culture/texts and composition. Her primary scholarship focuses on education narratives in popular culture, the rhetoric of education reform and grassroots education activism in digital spaces.

Benjamin Boche is an assistant professor of literacy and middle-level education at Concordia University Chicago. His research interests include children's and young adult literature, literacy and technology and preservice teacher education.

Ashley Boyd is an assistant professor of English at Washington State University, where she teaches graduate courses in critical theory and undergraduate courses in English methods and young adult literature. Her research interests include cultural studies, adolescent literature and social justice pedagogies.

Dawan Coombs is a former high school English and reading teacher. She currently works as an assistant professor of English at Brigham Young University in the English teaching program.

Jen S. Dean is an 8th grade English teacher in Leander, Texas. She formerly worked for 826 National in San Francisco, a nonprofit organization dedicated to helping students with expository and creative writing. Her research interests and scholarship include teaching English in the secondary classroom, arts integration and educational policy.

Sarah Fischer is a former elementary school teacher. She currently serves as an assistant professor of literacy education at Messiah College, where she teaches courses in literacy education and children's literature. Her research focuses primarily on the intersections of children's reading experiences and theories of place.

Brandon Flammang taught public school in Austin and Dallas, Texas. He currently teaches in the largest district in Arkansas. He works solely in alternative or nontraditional learning environments. He is currently obsessed with reading and writing contemporary poetry and short fiction.

Christian Z. Goering serves as an associate professor of English education and director of the Northwest Arkansas Writing Project at the University of Arkansas. He is current coeditor of the "Speaking Truth to Power" column in *English Journal* and blogs at www.edusanity.com. His research interests and scholarship coalesce around popular culture, teaching English and educational policy.

Charles Hohensee is an assistant professor in the School of Education at the University of Delaware. He also prepares future elementary teachers, teaching mathematics content courses for future teachers. He is a former high school mathematics teacher and studied filmmaking before becoming a teacher.

Amanda Jansen is an associate professor in the School of Education at the University of Delaware. As a mathematics educator, she prepares future elementary and middle grades teachers. She teaches courses such as mathematics pedagogy and mathematics content courses for future teachers. Prior to entering academia, Mandy was a junior high mathematics teacher.

Mark A. Lewis is an assistant professor of literacy education at Loyola University Maryland, where he teaches courses in children's and young adult literature, content area literacy and English methods. His research examines literary competence, conceptions of youth and young adult literature.

Sheryl Long is the director of Teacher Education and Graduate Studies at Salem College in Winston-Salem, North Carolina. Her research interests include 21st-century literacies, the use of film in teacher education and professional development for literacy educators.

Ewa McGrail is an associate professor of language and literacy at Georgia State University. In her research, she examines digital writing and new media composition, copyright and media literacy, technology in teaching and learning, and multimodal assessment. She is also an ardent supporter of students and educators from outgroups or those who are otherwise not in the mainstream.

J. Patrick McGrail is an associate professor of communication at Jacksonville State University, where he teaches media literacy, broadcast news and video production.

His research interests include copyright and media law and policy, and objectivity and narratives in journalism. Prior to his career in academia, he worked in television and radio as an actor and director.

Jonathan Ostenson taught junior high and high school English for 11 years before joining the faculty at Brigham Young University as an assistant professor, where he now teaches in the English Education program. His research interests include digital literacies and new media, teacher development and young adult literature.

Chea Parton is a doctoral student at Purdue University. She taught English in a rural high school in the Midwest for three years before returning to graduate school. Her research interests include teachers and students as cultural constructs, the use of art in English classrooms and literacy in the content areas.

Carol A. Pope is a professor of literacy and language arts education as well as middle grades education in the Curriculum, Instruction & Counselor Education (CICE) Department at North Carolina State University. She focuses her research efforts on middle grades education, middle school students and teachers as coteacher educators, technology and ELA teacher preparation, and teachers as leaders.

Ian Parker Renga is an assistant professor of education at Western State Colorado University. A former middle school teacher, he holds an MEd from Harvard University and a PhD in teacher education from the University of Colorado at Boulder. His current scholarly work investigates the role of desire in teacher preparation.

Rodrigo Joseph Rodríguez is an assistant professor of literacy and English education at the University of Texas at El Paso. His scholarship focuses on classroom and social contexts that inform students' learning gains through culturally sustaining pedagogy and socially responsible literacies, including the teaching of children's and young adult literatures.

Patrick Shannon is a distinguished professor of education at Penn State University and a member of the Reading Hall of Fame. His most recent books are *Closer Reading of the Common Core* (Heinemann, 2013), *Reading Poverty in America* (Routledge, 2014) and *The Struggle to Continue* (Garn, 2016). He is the director of the Integrated Undergraduate/Graduate Program for the Departments of Special Education and Curriculum and Instruction.

Melanie Shoffner is an associate professor of English education at Purdue University in West Lafayette, Indiana, where she holds a joint appointment in the

Departments of English and Curriculum & Instruction. Focusing on secondary English teacher preparation, her research explores issues of reflective practice, dispositional development and meaningful integration of technology. Dr. Shoffner is currently chair of the Conference on English Education (CEE) and editor of *Contemporary Issues in Technology and Teacher Education (CITE): English.*

Carol A. Smith has taught at Elon University in the Department of Health & Human Performance since August 1999. She has served as president of the North Carolina Alliance of Athletics, Health, Physical Education, Recreation & Dance and vice president of Sport & Leisure of the Southern District of SHAPE America.

Jeff Spanke earned a PhD in English education from Purdue University. Prior to returning to graduate school, he taught high school English for three years in the rural Midwest. Currently, he teaches composition courses and education methods courses as a limited-term lecturer at Purdue. His research interests include adolescent writing instruction, teacher recruitment and retention, and alternative sites of learning. He lives in West Lafayette, Indiana.

Walter E. Squire is an assistant professor of English and director of the Film Studies Program at Marshall University. He has published articles and book chapters on Disney adaptations, the relationship between Nathaniel Hawthorne and American mad scientist films, *The Wonderful Wizard of Oz*, and labor activism by women.

Nalova Westbrook is an assistant professor of literacy at Calvin College, where she teaches introductory reading courses and content area literacy courses. Her past teaching experience, as well as current research, is in media literacy education.

Jason Whitney is an instructor of education at Penn State in secondary English education. Before that, he taught high school English and worked as a script reader in Hollywood.

Shelbie Witte is an associate professor of adolescent literacy at Oklahoma State University, where she serves as the Kim and Chuck Watson Endowed Chair and the director of the Oklahoma State University Writing Project. Her research interests center on 21st-century literacies and the intersections of popular culture and pedagogy in literacy learning.

INDEX